Ethics as Foreign Policy

Ethical foreign policy has often been considered utopian, unrealistic and potentially very dangerous. Dan Bulley argues for a reconceptualisation of ethics *as* foreign policy, as both look to how we can, and ought to, relate to others.

Inspired by the deconstructive thought of Jacques Derrida, Bulley studies the ethical claims of British (1997–2007) and EU (1999–2004) foreign policy. These claims are read against themselves to illustrate their deep ambiguity. A textual analysis of speeches, statements and interviews given by foreign policy makers shows that a responsibility to save 'Africa', to protect Iraqis and to hospitably welcome the Balkans into the EU is also irresponsible, inhospitable and unethical.

The author contends that foreign policies making a claim to morality are ethical *and* unethical, in their own terms, suggesting that while a truly ethical foreign policy remains ultimately unachievable, it does not justify abandoning a responsible relation to others. Rather, a negotiation of ethics as foreign policy suggests potential individual, context-bound decisions which remain open to contestation and permanent critique. Bulley argues that the goal of ethical foreign policy must be maintained as a productive hope of what is neither completely impossible nor entirely possible.

Dan Bulley is a Lecturer in International Relations in the School of Politics, International Studies and Philosophy at Queen's University, Belfast. His research focuses on international political theory and the possibility of international ethics. He has contributed articles to the *Review of International Studies* and the *British Journal of Politics and International Relations*.

Interventions
Edited by Jenny Edkins and Nick Vaughan-Williams
University of Aberystwyth and University of Exeter

This series provides a forum for innovative and interdisciplinary work that engages with alternative critical, post-structural, postcolonial, psychoanalytic and cultural approaches to international relations and global politics.

The series aims to advance understanding of the key areas in which scholars working within broad critical post-structural traditions have chosen to make their interventions and to present innovative analyses of important topics. The titles in the series engage with critical thinkers in philosophy, sociology, politics and other disciplines and provide situated historical, empirical and textual studies in international politics.

Critical Theorists and International Relations
Edited by Jenny Edkins and Nick Vaughan-Williams

Ethics as Foreign Policy: Britain, the EU and the Other
Dan Bulley

Ethics as Foreign Policy

Britain, the EU and the Other

Dan Bulley

Routledge
Taylor & Francis Group

LONDON AND NEW YORK

First published 2009
by Routledge
2 Park Square, Milton Park, Abingdon, Oxon, OX14 4RN

Simultaneously published in the United States and Canada
by Routledge
711 Third Avenue, New York, NY 10017

Routledge is an imprint of the Taylor & Francis Group, an Informa business

First issued in paperback 2011

Typeset in Times New Roman by Cadmus

British Library Cataloguing in Publication Data
A catalogue record for this book is available from the British Library

Library of Congress Cataloging in Publication Data

Bulley, Dan.

Ethics as foreign policy : Britain, the EU and the other / Dan Bulley.

p. cm.—(Interventions)

Includes bibliographical references.

ISBN 978-0-415-48361-2—ISBN 978-0-203-87885-9 1. Great Britain—Foreign relations—1997-
—Moral and ethical aspects. 2. European Union countries—Foreign relations—Moral and ethical
aspects. I. Title.

JZ1572.B85 2009

172'.4—dc22

2008044880

ISBN 10: 0-415-48361-1 (hbk)
ISBN 10: 0-415-66511-6 (pbk)
ISBN 10: 0-203-87885-X (ebk)

ISBN 13: 978-0-415-48361-2 (hbk)
ISBN 13: 978-0-415-66511-7 (pbk)
ISBN 13: 978-0-203-87885-9 (ebk)

For Bali

Table of Contents

Acknowledgements

Many thanks are due, both to those involved with this book and for those who helped in the way it began life as my PhD thesis. The first must go to my wife, Bal Sokhi-Bulley, who faultlessly proof-read the original work. She also put up with my incessant ranting about many of the issues involved, not least in my sleep. Similarly, to my mother, Carol Shergold, who listened to many crucial monologues on Derrida while walking her dogs, and to my father, Colin Bulley, who challenged my ability to convey ideas with clarity. Fiona Pollard and Cathy Bulley offered great emotional support throughout; Cathy with her own past research experience, Fiona with constant and priceless friendship. I owe Nathan Bulley for having given me the original idea of looking at ethical foreign policy. Charis Joyce was a great encouragement, and Peter Turnill maintained an infectious enthusiasm for my work even when my own lapsed. Thanks to Rani Sokhi for perpetual belief and samosas; Allison and Ian Pollard for providing a refuge. The support of the late Frank and Joyce Shergold made everything achievable.

An enormous debt is owed to Maja Zehfuss and Philippa Sherrington, my tutors from my undergraduate years, who became amazing PhD supervisors and good friends. Maja's comments on all my work, as well as continual advice and support, have been of incalculable value. For comments and advice, thanks also to Ben Rosamond, David Campbell and Stuart Elden. Helping me through some tough times at Warwick, a special thanks is due to James Brassett, who provided constant friendly (pub-based) academic criticism and has been a great friend. Also, for friendship, support and comments on papers at Warwick, thanks to Andres Moles, Anil Awesti, Ted Svensson and Owen Parker. This research at Warwick would not have been possible without the 1+3 award from the ESRC.

In terms of turning this work into a book, many thanks to Craig Fowlie, Jenny Edkins and Nick Vaughan-Williams, who showed great confidence in it as the first in this promising and exciting new Routledge Series. Jenny Edkins' comments on two drafts were extremely valuable and have made this a *much* better book. I have greatly benefited from Peter Lawler's interest in the book and comments on sample chapters (especially when a non-security studies based book seemed a forlorn hope). Martin Coward offered timely advice on publication and asked challenging questions of my conference papers which produced this volume.

Finally, writing the last drafts of this book has been achieved in part because of the warm, friendly environment provided by all at the School of Politics, International Studies and Philosophy at Queen's University Belfast. In making myself and Bal welcome and familiar with Belfast and its ways have been the symbols of hospitality: Debbie Lisle and Andrew Pepper. Debbie also provided many extremely challenging comments on the original book proposal, all of which have benefited it greatly. Big thanks for their hospitality and comments are also due to Andrew Baker, Mike Bourne, Keith Breen, Susan McManus, John Garry and Tarik Kochi.

Abbreviations

AKP	*Adalet ve Kalkinma Partisi* (Justice and Development Party)
AU	African Union
BiH	Bosnia and Herzegovina
CFSP	Common Foreign and Security Policy
DRC	Democratic Republic of Congo
ECOMOG	Economic Community of West African States Monitoring Group
ENP	European Neighbourhood Policy
ESDP	European Security and Defence Policy
EU	European Union
FCO	Foreign and Commonwealth Office
FP	*Fazilet Partisi* (Virtue Party)
FPA	Foreign Policy Analysis
FYROM	Former Yugoslav Republic of Macedonia
G8	Group of Eight
HR	High Representative
ICISS	International Commission on Intervention and State Sovereignty
IMF	International Monetary Fund
IR	International Relations
MNC	Multinational Corporation
NATO	North Atlantic Treaty Organisation
NEPAD	New Partnership for Africa's Development
NGO	Non-Governmental Organisation
QUANGO	Quasi-Autonomous Non-Governmental Organisation
RP	*Refa Partisi* (Welfare Party)
UN	United Nations
WMD	Weapons of Mass Destruction
WTO	World Trade Organisation

1 Introduction

On 12 May 1997, an ethical foreign policy suddenly appeared possible. British Foreign Secretary, Robin Cook, announced that British foreign policy was to have an 'ethical dimension' under his leadership.[1] The new Labour government had promised many things since being elected with an enormous parliamentary majority just 11 days earlier, but few were as energising or unexpected as Cook's announcement. This was what prompted my early interest in the possibility of ethical foreign policy. Was that all it took? Did one need to only declare that an 'ethical dimension' to foreign policy was now possible? If so, why did it seem that no one, including the previous Conservative government, had done it before?

The idea of an ethical foreign policy had precursors in the form of Jimmy Carter's ultimately doomed promotion of human rights in the 1970s and the Australian foreign policy in the late 1980s and early 1990s under Bob Hawk and Paul Keating.[2] Talk of ethics, morality and values in foreign policy increased exponentially in world politics after the cold war. Whatever the particular policy area, from the arms trade to debt relief, from humanitarian intervention to supranational cooperation and trade sanctions, morality appeared to be playing a role. For some, an ethical foreign policy simply became 'more affordable'[3] from the 1990s onwards. Freed from the strictures of superpower rivalry, Western states were suddenly capable of flexing their principles, which generally revolved around the promotion of democracy, human rights and liberal economics.

Labour's declaration nevertheless struck a chord with many, as, despite the fall of the Berlin Wall, the 1990s had not seen the new ethical order that had initially seemed achievable. The United States had been slow to respond to ethnic cleansing as Yugoslavia fell apart from 1993 onwards. Meanwhile, Britain and France actively obstructed attempts to save Bosnian victims.[4] There was similar inaction and obfuscation when, in 1994, genocide in Rwanda led to the deaths of around 800,000 Tutsis at the hands of rival Hutus. Was a traditionally narrow focus on the 'national interest' really acceptable in such an international context? Were there not more ethical ways to react to such extreme and unnecessary violence, suffering and death? To those, such as myself, who felt that *something more* was necessary (without necessarily knowing what), the 'ethical dimension' was a sign of great hope.

Although disagreement will remain as to the nature of Cook's announcement, and many doubted its motives[5] and wisdom,[6] the temptations of ethical foreign policy are unlikely to disappear, especially in the two examples I explore in this book. Although the initial high tide of moralism may have passed in British foreign policy following Prime Minister Tony Blair's departure from government, the first post-Blair foreign secretary, David Miliband, signalled that the 'moral impulse' was still motivating Britain's external relations.[7] In fact, following the loud proclamations of ethical commitments since 1997, it is difficult to see any future British government escaping the scrutiny of its international morals.[8]

Similarly, moralism is going nowhere in the European Union (EU). After Romano Prodi's presidency of the EU Commission (1999–2004), in which he stressed the 'ethical dimension to politics' upon which the EU and its foreign policy was built,[9] greater attention has been focused on the values that the EU promotes through its foreign policy.[10] Despite the EU's failed attempts to further formalise its foreign policy in the Constitutional (2004) and Lisbon (2007) Treaties, morality, values and norms are ever present in the speeches and interviews of key EU foreign-policy makers such as Jose Manuel Barroso and Javier Solana.[11]

Given the rise of ethical foreign policy and the controversy that still surrounds it, the inevitable query emerges: is a genuinely ethical foreign policy really possible? This is the central question I explore in this book. Concentrating on the worst consequences of the so-called 'War on Terror', we might be tempted to respond negatively to this question. Especially since 2001, though also beforehand, Blair's foreign policy took on a Manichean moralism, with the world divided into good and evil, right and wrong, humane and inhumane. It has resulted in the military invasions of territories in Europe (Kosovo), Africa (Sierra Leone) and the Middle East (Afghanistan and Iraq). Similarly, after eight years of morally charged US foreign policy under George W. Bush, with the atrocities of Abu Ghraib, detention of suspects in Guantanamo Bay and the spectre of rendition flights and torture, a genuinely ethical foreign policy may look further away than ever. At best, Bush's moralism is seen by many as a public cover for more base intentions. This is reflected in Peter Singer's story that, when he told friends he was writing a book about 'Bush's ethics', two responses were common: either the phrase was an oxymoron or his book would be very short indeed.[12]

For others, in contrast, Blair and Bush's actions demonstrate that ethical foreign policy is not only possible but becoming normal. After all, values and principles had perhaps never been so clearly articulated in foreign policy. These principles seemed more ethical than those that went before: the human rights of those suffering had long been sacrificed to the pre-eminence of state sovereignty; the invasion of Iraq demonstrated that sovereignty no longer held such a moral sway.[13] Responsibility for the rights and well-being of our fellow humans no longer stopped at the borders of a state. This duty to promote human rights now appeared genuinely universal, even if it involved the violation of a potentially dangerous state's sovereignty. The invasion of Iraq was, therefore, presented by Fernando Tesón as an ethically unifying force, a legitimate moral action demonstrating that, whether '[c]onservative, liberal, or progressive, we should not protect tyrants under the guise of defending peace'.[14]

Both these positions oversimplify and are ultimately unsatisfactory. Part of the problem responding to the question posed is the apparent necessity of doing so within the dichotomy it implies: ethical foreign policy is *either* possible *or* impossible. After all, it is not as if we could decide that our foreign policy would no longer contain ethics. Moral values can neither be left out from the beginning nor expunged once a policy has been initiated. Rather, as Mervyn Frost argues, foreign policy 'necessarily has an ethical dimension.... *We are ethically constrained in everything we do*'.[15] Through participating in the practices of foreign policy (such as diplomacy, treaties, international summits and so on), the state or organisation is constructed as an international actor. Part of this social constitution means that the actor accepts the principles and values fundamental to the process: the necessary ethical dimension of foreign policy.

I would argue, however, that the link between ethics and foreign policy goes even deeper than this. Questions of ethics and morality[16] are essentially about how we ought to conduct ourselves in relation to others, to strangers, to those who are different and to otherness in general. Such an ethics will depend entirely upon a context. As I will show throughout this book, morality emerges from who the 'we', as a collective subject, considers itself to be; who or what we construct as other, as different, to this 'self'; and how we conceive of our duty to such an other. Therefore, there cannot be a singular, general other, definable outside of a context. Otherness, and ethical action towards it, is constructed within a specific situation, along with the subject. To speak of ethics then is to speak of how a subject should act in relation to an other, when the self and the other are both produced within a particular context.

In his reading of foreign policy as a politics of identity, David Campbell draws a distinction between two understandings of foreign policy: what he calls 'foreign policy' and Foreign Policy.[17] The broader practice of 'foreign policy' refers to discursive 'practices of differentiation or modes of exclusion (possibly figured as relationships of otherness) that constitute their object as "foreign" in the process of dealing with them'.[18] This is foreign policy seen as a general practice of constituting 'sameness' and 'otherness' through their representation – of differentiating and excluding the 'foreign' from the 'domestic', the 'inside' from the 'outside', the 'other' from the 'self'. Foreign Policy, on the other hand, is how the disciplines of international relations (IR)[19] and foreign policy analysis (FPA) generally conceive foreign policy: as a state-based practice towards that which is beyond the state's borders,[20] that which is 'foreign' and not 'domestic' or part of the collective 'self'. The capitalised Foreign Policy is, therefore, a particular and highly circumscribed instance of the 'foreign policy'[21] that everyone takes part in, both individually and collectively, from moment to moment.

This refiguration of foreign policy means that not only does it have a necessary ethical dimension but the two are in fact concerned with precisely the same matter. Both ethics and foreign policy consider how we constitute and relate to otherness. This flies in the face of traditional assumptions. FPA as a discipline was founded on the complete marginalisation of ethical issues from the study of foreign policy. James Rosenau, in trying to produce a rigorous academic study of foreign policy, condemned the 'bewildered simplicity and moral fervor' marking much early commentary.[22] The discussion of foreign policy 'seems to invite the abandonment of scholarly inclinations', and this led him to plead for a 'scientific' consciousness without moral debate.[23]

Any attempt to fully and finally separate the fields of ethics and foreign policy is futile, however, as both tackle identical issues. The subject of ethics *is* foreign policy: it examines how we *ought* to relate to otherness. And if foreign policy is a practice of constructing otherness and relating to it, *the* question of foreign policy must be how we *ought* to do this: a question of ethics.[24] Indeed, far from disconnected areas joined by an 'and' or an 'of',[25] it is much better to see ethics *as* foreign policy. Even if questions of 'ought' are not posed in foreign policy, assumptions are made that presuppose a certain production of and relation to otherness, a certain 'self' and a certain 'other' and the way they ought to relate. Thus, even in the 'scientific' early works of FPA, ethics is folded into theories of foreign policy without ever being acknowledged.

An excellent example of this is Rosenau's hugely influential essay, 'Pre-Theories and Theories of Foreign Policy'.[26] Here, Rosenau notes several theoretical shortcomings with FPA, one of which is the outdated tendency to maintain a firm separation of national and international political systems.[27] To tackle this, he offers the concept of a *'penetrated political system'*.[28] Such a system is marked not only by 'the presence of non-members who participate directly in a society's politics' but also 'by a shortage of capabilities on the part of the penetrated society'.[29] The non-members try to compensate for or take advantage of this shortage. Some penetration is 'thoroughgoing', whereas others, such as that of Britain, are limited to certain issue areas, such as defence.[30]

Penetrated systems are thereby constituted by a lack, a deficiency that somehow makes them not a 'whole' or full 'national system'. The examples he gives are nations defeated in war (Japan and Germany post–Second World War), communist countries run, to an extent, from Moscow (Cuba and Vietnam), hopelessly poor states (Congo) or former great empires (Britain).[31] Although it is acknowledged that the United States is penetrated, this is a very different matter. The United States is penetrated by those seeking aid and support; it is penetrated for the *opposite* reason – a 'relative abundance' of capabilities.[32]

What results then is an apparently innocent separation of penetrated systems and national systems that works to impose a hierarchy on the world: at the top is the United States, marked by 'abundance', then come 'normal' national systems and finally 'deficient' penetrated systems, marked by 'lack'. Such separations are treated as existent in the material world, hence they remain unquestioned, but, being *constructed*, this seemingly objective hierarchy conceals an ethics, a way of relating to otherness, and has major ethical implications. It can justify any type of intervention (after all, a penetrated system's 'lack' leads to non-member participation anyway) from sanctions and blockades to counterinsurgency and regime change. In this way, while 'purging' all moral reasoning from FPA, Rosenau conceals a profound notion of how relations with others ought to be conducted. He is discussing ethics *as* foreign policy without recognising it.

If we consider ethics as foreign policy, this means we can no longer answer within the dichotomy imposed by the question: is a genuinely ethical foreign policy possible? Every foreign policy contains an ethics, a conception of otherness and how a 'we' ought to act in relation to it. In this sense, every foreign policy is an ethical foreign policy. My aim in this book, therefore, is to draw out the conception of ethics as foreign policy in a British and EU context and then examine whether it works in its own terms. Extracting the logic contained in the British and EU discourse, I will read this logic against itself: how it deconstructs, undermines and undoes itself when studied closely. What this analysis reveals is that these constructions of ethics as foreign policy do not work in an ethical manner when judged against their own conception of ethics. Both British and EU understandings of a responsible relation toward the other are also irresponsible; their idea of ethics is also unethical.

The deconstruction of British and EU foreign policy discourses will reveal that far from an ethical foreign policy being simply possible *or* impossible, it is both and neither. It is possible because a foreign policy cannot help but be ethical, and these examples make explicit their conception of ethics. However, it is impossible because these claims to morality cannot help but undermine themselves, deconstructing under their own logic and revealing their immorality. Therefore, any ethical, responsible relation to otherness is also always an unethical irresponsible relation. The possibility of a genuine ethical foreign policy is, therefore, *undecidable*: neither fully possible nor impossible.

This undecidability is, however, far from negative; undecidability is not the same as impossibility, and it calls for the opposite of an abandonment of ethical foreign policy. The aim of deconstruction is to reveal the complexity and the contradictions within what one strives to enact and make possible. While there is what Jacques Derrida calls a 'Necessity' compelling a deconstruction, everything that he seems to oppose through it 'is exactly what I'm after in life. I love the voice, I love presence'.[33] Equally, my noting the decon-struction of ethical foreign policy is not opposed to its possibility but is inspired by a desire for an ethical, responsible relation to the other. Yet, to be dedicated to such a goal means to also obey the 'necessity' of interrupting this desire and showing that its achievement is never possible, if not neces-sarily *impossible*.

Thus, the attraction and appeal of a deconstructive approach also lies in its resistance to the apparent paralysis of undecidability. Far from justifying a rejection of any prospect of an ethical foreign policy, deconstruction calls for a testing and 'negotiation' of its promise. It allows that there continues to be that in the concept of ethics as it arises in foreign policy texts – the aspiration of a responsible relation towards the other and otherness – which remains valuable and worth struggling for. While exposing the fundamental im-possibility of *achieving* this promise, deconstruction gives no excuse or justification for its abandonment.

Deconstruction: foreign policy as text

As mentioned earlier, foreign policy in IR and FPA is broadly conceived as a state-based practice towards that which is beyond the state's borders.[34] Such a general definition, however, hides a great deal of disagreement about pre-cisely what such a 'practice' involves. There is no consensus on what exactly foreign policy is. For example, in a groundbreaking early study, foreign pol-icy was characterised as a series of decisions,[35] but more recently, foreign policies have been defined as 'events',[36] an 'activity',[37] a bureaucratic product,[38] 'actions',[39] 'spoken utterances'[40] or the sum of 'official external relations'.[41]

A deconstructive reading essentially undercuts all these claims. Inspired by the thought of Jacques Derrida, I treat foreign policy as a text that can be read. Any attempt to define what foreign policy is will always be insufficient because whatever we understand by 'foreign policy' must be interpreted, relayed and described through discourse. We can never grasp a foreign pol-icy action or activity in itself but can only have access to the way it is repre-sented. It is because we cannot present foreign policy as such that we must 'go through the detour of the sign',[42] *re*-presenting it through language using other signifiers (events, bureaucratic product and so on). In this way, foreign policy can only be understood as an interweaving of these references, repre-sentations and chains of signifiers; it is this interweaving that Derrida calls a text.[43]

This does not mean that deconstructive readings simply suspend reference to a 'reality'. Rather, reality 'functions inside the text to indicate that which exceeds the text *but can be given no fixed form outside some sort of textualisation*'.[44] 'Reality' can only ever be textually constituted. This is what Derrida means when he says, '[t]here is nothing outside of the text [there is no outside-text; *il n'y a pas de hors-texte]*'.[45] What is rarely quoted beyond this sentence is revealing. He observes that what is 'behind' the text, the 'real life of these existences "of flesh and bone"', is simply 'substitutive significations which could come forth in a chain of differential references, the "real" supervening, and being added only while taking on meaning from a trace'.[46] Thus, there being nothing outside the text means nothing other than 'there is nothing outside context', and context means 'the entire "real-history-of-the-world"'.[47]

By treating foreign policy as text we do not suspend reference to 'reality,' world, history and so on, as to speak of these things is only ever done 'in a movement of interpretation which contextualizes them according to a network of differences'.[48] Rather than suspending reference, it actually *increases* references, it opens up every context and it shows that context/text can never be totalised or totally comprehended. Every text refers to other texts, to other experiences and to cultural and historical interpretations within a 'general text' that is 'everywhere'.[49] Thus, what is called deconstruction can be seen as 'the effort to take this limitless context into account, to pay the sharpest and broadest attention to context, and thus to an incessant movement of recontextualisation'.[50]

This expansion of reference means that 'foreign policy' is no longer strictly circumscribed to governmental, or intergovernmental, activity at all. The foreign policy text cannot be exhaustively ring-fenced, and thus we can never say that a certain aspect of life, history or culture is irrelevant to a foreign policy decision. All text, all experience refers to and is constituted by other texts; they are *intertexts*, spaces where representations overlap, blend and clash.[51] This means that we are no longer able to say that foreign policy is simply made by 'foreign policy makers'. Rather, as everyone works to constitute and reconstitute the societal context, everyone makes foreign policy; after all, Foreign Policy is merely a particular manifestation of 'foreign policy'.[52]

This means that there can be no ultimate justification for limiting my reading to the speeches and speech makers on which the next three chapters concentrate. The speeches and public statements of the Prime Minister and British foreign ministers from 1997 to 2007,[53] and those of the High Representative (HR) for the EU's Common Foreign and Security Policy (CFSP), the Commissioner for External Relations and the President of the Commission in EU foreign policy from 1999 to 2004, do not exhaust, or fully constitute, their foreign policy texts. The context is inexhaustible. However, it is suggested that the posts mentioned are uniquely suited to communicating 'Britain' and the 'EU' to the world. They both speak and *are spoken by* the texts of British and EU foreign policy in a way that, for example, a Minister for Finance, a journalist or an 'ordinary' citizen are not.

Although everyone to some extent 'makes' foreign policy then, this does not mean that the terms 'foreign policy' and 'foreign policy maker' cease to function. As Derrida makes clear, just because a sign refers to no transcendental signified, no 'reality' we can access outside of text/context does stop the sign's operation, and it can remain indispensable within limits.[54] As will become clear throughout the discussion of subjectivity in Chapter 2, and subsequently in Chapters 3 and 4, the myth of the responsible subject will continue to function and produces effects even while its mythical status is explicated.

Perhaps most importantly, however, the absence of anything called 'foreign policy' outside of text allows me to take at face value the logic asserted by British and EU foreign policy when they make a claim to ethics. Much extant literature rules out this approach by arguing, for example, that such claims actually serve as rhetorical devices to hide a conventional power politics,[55] or as a cynical attempt to evade domestic political accountability by appealing to a universal morality.[56] These criticisms of an ethical foreign policy appeal to a *real* driving force behind foreign policy, which is never ethics. Those who support the opposite view tend to argue that moral norms really do influence foreign policy decision making.[57]

In contrast, this book does not have to take a position on whether policy makers actually were, in reality, trying to act ethically in British or EU foreign policy. Simply put, it does not matter and for at least two reasons. First, we cannot know such a 'reality' – all we can know is its representation in discourse. Thus, we are perfectly justified in examining how this textualised reality is presented. Second, it does not matter because my aim is not to make claims as to whether foreign policy was, or is, based on an ethical dimension. Rather, the goal is to show how these claims to the ethical deconstruct (how their logic undermines its own basis) and ask where we can go from there.

If a foreign policy is textually constituted, how do we read it, and how does it deconstruct? Deconstruction is not a form of analysis or a method that can be applied to a text;[58] indeed, it cannot be formalised[59] or defined outside of a context.[60] Although it cannot be made into a technical procedure, there 'are also some general rules' that can be 'transposed by analogy'.[61] These rules are always different as they depend upon the specific text. Meaning in any text is created through a system of differences, or binary oppositions. Traditionally, key binaries in Western thought have been, for example, presence/absence, subject/object, good/evil, speech/writing, reason/passion, nature/ culture and sensible/intelligible. Such oppositions, however, are not two terms equally confronting each other but, rather, violent hierarchies where the second term is subordinate to the first.[62] The first term is primary and the second merely derivative; as Jonathan Culler has it, the second is a complication, negation or disruption of the first term.[63] The concept of foreign policy is built upon such an opposition, the domestic/foreign or inside/ outside dichotomy.[64] Any individual deconstruction will differ according to the specific differences, meanings and references contained in the text.

Deconstruction operates by subverting these binaries through a double gesture: it 'puts into practice a *reversal* of the classical opposition *and* a general *displacement* of the system'.[65] Such a double gesture regarding the subject/object, responsible/irresponsible and hospitality/hostility binaries will be illustrated throughout the following three chapters. The 'first' gesture (and Derrida makes clear, they can only be separated artificially and 'for the sake of clarity')[66] looks to reverse or overturn the violent hierarchies imposed by Western thought, making the first term a derivation or complication of the second. Perhaps most famously, Derrida reveals that the classic opposition between speech and writing, where speech has been traditionally privileged over writing as closer to the meaning of thought itself, is misplaced. In fact, because we can never have access to meaning itself, speech becomes a generalised form of writing, or text, where the meaning can only be represented.[67] Thus, '[t]o deconstruct the opposition, first of all, is to overturn the hierarchy at a given moment'. This phase of deconstruction is absolutely essential, if sometimes brushed over. Ignoring it, however, reduces the influence a deconstruction has in a particular field.[68]

Stopping at this overturning phase would still remain within the dichotomies of modern thought: although the dichotomy would be inverted, the hierarchical binary remains. The other gesture of deconstruction displaces this system by moving toward the 'irruptive emergence of a new "concept", a concept that can no longer be, never could be, included in the previous regime'.[69] Such a movement beyond Western metaphysics is, however, impossible. Thus, the displacement envisaged by deconstruction is a 'marking of the interval' between a remaining *within* and a complete *transgression* of this system of thought. To 'better mark' this interval, Derrida allows certain words, or marks, within the history of philosophy and the literary text that, by analogy, he calls 'undecidables'.[70]

Undecidables are points of weakness within a given text, entry points at which an intervention is possible that disrupts a system of thought and its binary oppositions. They are fault lines in an apparently impregnable text, points at which the text disrupts itself. Such undecidables cannot be reduced to an opposition (they are neither, for instance, fully present nor absent) but reside within it, 'resisting and disorganising it, *without ever* constituting a third term', and thus without ever becoming dialectical.[71] Undecidables are terms that exist neither simply inside nor outside of traditional discourse and its constitutive binaries but rather work on their margins and limits, disrupting and displacing them. As such, their status is inherently *undecidable*. A deconstructive reading seeks out the undecidability operating at the margins to subvert and disorder the text being read. It seeks to 'make use of insurrectional textuality':[72] that within the text which threatens its own logic.

Outline of the book

To explore the possibilities of an ethical foreign policy, I look to two examples where foreign policy is explicitly portrayed with an 'ethical dimension'. Given the fact that such open discussion of ethics is rare, it is crucial to see how an ethical foreign policy is described as possible in these cases and whether their logic stands up to scrutiny. In the terms just outlined, my aim in the next three chapters (2, 3 and 4), in particular, is to read these foreign policy texts, looking for points of weakness where deconstruction operates to overturn and displace the binary hierarchies that govern them. This is a search for undecidability that works within a discourse of ethical foreign policy to reveal how that discourse breaks down and indeed how it was always broken even when we imagined it to be solid.

The specific texts examined are British foreign policy[73] from 1997 to 2007 and EU foreign policy from 1999 to 2004. Another interesting example would have been US foreign policy from 2001 to 2009. This period was marked by a proclivity, led by President George W. Bush, to divide the world into 'good' and 'evil', a tendency that was not confined only to foreign policy.[74] However, unlike British and EU foreign policy, the discourse of ethics in US foreign policy was primarily confined to the War on Terror, the main reference being the Just War tradition. The likes of Cian O'Driscoll and Tarik Kochi have analysed US foreign policy and the War on Terror in precisely these terms.[75] Although of undoubted importance, it is clearly beyond the limits of the present volume to give sufficient attention to both US foreign policy and the Just War tradition.

The foreign policies of Britain and the EU are interesting cases primarily because of the prominence both give to the ethical. This could not have been clearer in the case of British foreign policy: within two weeks of the new Labour Government's election to office, the new foreign secretary claimed that, '[o]ur foreign policy must have an ethical dimension and must support the demands of other peoples for the democratic rights on which we insist for ourselves'.[76] Subsequently, Cook distanced himself from specific use of the term 'ethical dimension', and the term 'ethical foreign policy' was denied, as it was 'too easily capable of being misunderstood as grandstanding'.[77] Paul Williams and Mark Curtis even suggest that this meant the 'ethical dimension' had been officially 'ditched'.[78]

However, far from fading with Cook's disquiet, the language of ethics and morality came to play a *greater* role in the British foreign policy discourse. John Kampfner, for instance, notes that Prime Minister Tony Blair's language in particular increasingly invoked morality, drawing instant comparisons with Cook's 'Mission Statement'. Blair 'had [by 1999] belatedly found an ethical dimension of his own. The detail was different in places, but the idea was not'.[79] Similarly, Tim Dunne and Nick Wheeler note that, while the ethical 'volume control' may have been turned down by 2001, after September 11, Blair's 'view of foreign policy became wedded to an even deeper attachment to ethical principles'.[80] Chapters 2 and 3 indicate the ways in which this ethical dimension was understood, how it was developed and sustained over 10 years in the public statements of Blair and his foreign ministers. Crucially, these chapters also explicate the way this ethical dimension falls apart under the weight of its own internal contradictions.

Academic debate surrounding EU foreign policy has rarely focused on ethics, instead concerning itself with whether the EU can be seen as having a foreign policy at all.[81] Federicha Bicchi claims that this has changed in recent years, as the days of asking such questions 'finally recede into the past'.[82] In line with this, by rethinking foreign policy as text, as a representation of the means by which otherness is constituted and related to, we can see that questioning whether the EU is capable of foreign policy *per se* is no longer pertinent. Whatever be its institutional and conceptual dissimilarity to a nation-state (its lack of an executive, foreign policy bureaucracy and resources),[83] the EU actively works to both construct and interact with a 'foreign' otherness through representational practices.

Bicchi points out that academic discussion of EU foreign policy now often surrounds Europe conceived as a 'normative power'.[84] In Ian Manners' original formulation, the idea of 'normative power Europe' was about the EU's 'ability to shape conceptions of "normal" in international relations'.[85] This notion has come under attack from not only familiar Realist sources[86] but also those who question whether the EU can legitimately extend its own norms.[87] Manners himself has queried whether the rising military capability of the EU weakens its normative claims.[88]

The precise link between this debate and the ethics of EU foreign policy is not always clear. Manners originally argued that 'normative power' meant the EU could be conceptualised as a changer of norms, that the EU in fact does act to change norms and 'that the EU *should* act to extend its norms in the international system'.[89] In other words, the debate for Manners seems to contain an ethical argument. More recently, Manners has clarified that '"normative" does not mean the same as "ethical" but is part of being honest about why and how foreign policy is conducted'.[90] Yet, he claims that speaking normatively is about affirming how things should be, judging and directing human conduct.[91] If 'normative' is about how things *should* be, then it is implicitly about ethics. Despite this, the debate has pushed the issue of the 'values' of the EU to the front of the debate,[92] a particularly ambiguous term that is acceptable to most and clearly defined by few.

The academic literature has not been alone in thinking the EU in normative, or ethical, terms. Like the British text, EU foreign policy has also apportioned great significance to the ethical; indeed, Hazel Smith even claims that the EU 'seems to view itself as an intrinsically ethical foreign policy actor'.[93] Although Smith offers no evidence for this, textual support abounds. Prodi, for instance, declares that, as Europeans, 'our distinguishing feature is our sense of responsibility',[94] while Solana emphasises that this responsibility extends to those beyond the EU's borders.[95] It would be 'morally untenable, sometimes unthinkable, to sit idle, without reacting to... human misery and distress. Therefore, we are compelled to act'.[96]

The period between 1999 and 2004 in EU foreign policy provides a useful contrast to British foreign policy. The British text gives a long-term and comparatively clear line in ethics, whereas the EU text provides a concise, yet more ambiguous, understanding of the possibility of enacting ethical foreign policy. This period also encapsulates the dates of the Prodi Commission, which saw the coming together of three key figures (Prodi, Patten and Solana, who took up his position as HR for the CFSP in 1999) joined by a belief in what Prodi calls 'an ethical dimension to politics'.[97] The nature and understanding of EU foreign policy's ethical dimension, as well as its deconstruction, is examined in detail in Chapters 2 and 4.

What emerges from the empirical research into British and EU foreign policy is that, in both cases, ethics is understood as a matter of *responsibility*. An ethical foreign policy is constructed as a responsible relation to otherness. Although there is more to the 'ongoing historical practice'[98] of ethics than 'responsibility', its centrality here arises from the texts of the two foreign policies examined. As observed earlier, deconstruction occurs at points of undecidability in apparently coherent and cohesive texts. With this in mind, Chapters 2, 3 and 4 are structured around such undecidable moments in the British and EU texts, points where Britain and the EU's construction of their relation to otherness unravel. These are, first, their claims to subjectivity or rather their construction of the subject of ethical foreign policy as a subject capable of being responsible for others; second, the account of a responsibility to protect and save in British foreign policy; and third, the exercise of responsibility as an offering of hospitality to others in EU foreign policy.

These foreign policy texts rely on the possibility of a collective subject of ethical foreign policy; they require a 'we', an 'our', an 'us' which *can* act ethically. This subjectivity is conceived differently in the British and EU texts. As Chapter 3 shows, 'Britain' constructs itself as able to enact an ethics globally, whereas the 'EU' is far more circumspect in this regard, preferring to restrict itself to a regional role. Nonetheless, Chapter 2 illustrates the way both foreign policies understand subjectivity as the capacity of *taking responsibility* for others in world politics through foreign policy. It is this 'ability to take responsibility' around which British and EU representations of their own and others' subjectivity undermines itself. A parallel reading of Britain's 'failing state' discourse alongside Derrida's portrayal of democracy as autoimmune reveals that a 'successful' subject of responsibility is also always already a 'failing' object. Similarly, a close reading reveals that the 'we' affirmed as subject is constantly shifting within the text, never allowing a stable representation of that which is capable of responsibility (subject) and that which is not (object). The subject of ethical foreign policy is, thus, undecidably affirmed and denied as both possible and impossible, yet neither simply one nor the other.

As suggested earlier, British and EU foreign policy differ substantially in their representations of how responsibility is enacted. The British text focuses on the relatively straightforward responsibility to protect human life from tyrannical regimes in other countries and the responsibility to save human life from poverty and disease by also saving failing (mainly African) states. Chapter 3 outlines the way in which both descriptions of enacting responsibility are also necessarily *irresponsible*. The responsibility to protect works both for and against the ethics of a 'humanitarian intervention' to protect life. This can be demonstrated through the centrality of an apparently marginal case: the 2003 invasion of Iraq. Equally, the responsibility to save is irrevocably tied to both a responsible compassion for the other *as other* and an irresponsible contempt for the other until it becomes the *same*. The possibility of ethical and responsible foreign policy is irrevocably and undecidably tied to an unethical irresponsibility.

In contrast to the comparatively conventional line taken in the British text, EU foreign policy enacts responsibility by offering hospitality to the countries and regions surrounding it. This hospitality, analysed in Chapter 4, is offered through three policies: the policy of enlargement, the policy towards the Balkan countries and the European Neighbourhood Policy (ENP). The different degrees of conditionality and entry into the European 'home' attached to these policies, however, help illustrate what Derrida calls the two laws of hospitality. The *law* of hospitality demands an unconditional openness towards otherness, whereas the laws place conditions upon this hospitality. The fact that the latter needs the former (and vice versa) means that the hostility of conditions and questions is necessarily installed in hospitality; ethical and responsible hospitality is always already an unethical, irresponsible hostility. This undecidability is equally constitutive of unconditional hospitality; allowing anyone and anything into one's home means that it is no longer one's home but rather a place of hostility where one is held hostage.

If my argument in this book was merely that an ethical foreign policy is neither possible nor impossible, but undecidably both and neither, this is where the analysis could rest. Both British and EU texts reveal this constitutive im-possibility and ir-responsibility. However, the implications of such undecidability could be taken as an excuse to further marginalise discussion of the ethical in foreign policy. Undecidability potentially provides a new means, a new rationale, for this marginalisation. Such a position is directly opposed to the inspiration of my argument: that the goal of an ethical foreign policy as a responsible relation towards otherness is worth preserving in the perfectibility of its promise. Thus, the opportunity of a movement through, or a living with, undecidability is proposed in Chapter 5, a movement that seeks to maintain the openness of undecidability as the condition of politics and ethics, while negotiating the closure of a decision.

Negotiation is outlined as a potential for individual, context-bound, ethico-political foreign policy decisions. It can perhaps best be conceived as an oscillating movement between equally imperative injunctions: an undetermined and a fully determined subjectivity; a responsibility to all others and one other; an unconditional hospitality and its conditional form. In this vein, Chapter 5 goes on to offer illustrative suggestions of what negotiation may, perhaps, look like in the context of British and EU foreign policy. It is in the nature of negotiation that these cannot be prescriptive or concrete, being outside the immediacy of a context, but rather they have the character of tentative proposals. In relation to British foreign policy, the perhaps radical notion is that negotiation could bring the end of British foreign policy. It is suggested that, in negotiating a greater openness to otherness, 'Britain' may simply be too closed a subjectivity to allow for an invention of the ethical. Regarding EU foreign policy, it is argued that negotiating a policy of hospitably welcoming otherness may produce an argument for accelerating Turkish accession. However, unlike conventional arguments for Turkish accession, a negotiating of hospitality may demand that far from Turkey becoming more like the EU, it in fact remains as non-European as possible.

It is important to stress that these policies are not to be argued for as policies. They are not recommendations for what should be the case. Rather, they are indications of what could be possible as inventions of an ethico-political foreign policy. As I conclude in Chapter 6, such risky, unsatisfactory negotiations of foreign policy decisions cannot make an ethical foreign policy possible, or decidable. However, this negotiated movement through undecidability is, *perhaps,* the best way to preserve the promise of an ethical foreign policy 'to come'.

2 The Subject of Ethical Foreign Policy
Britain, the EU and others

The subject is central to any discussion of the ethical. Indeed, it allows the possibility for the representation of 'something' or 'someone', acting responsibly, hospitably or *ethically*. In this vein, Maja Zehfuss notes that we cannot judge the ethics of the 2003 invasion of Iraq without first questioning the prior existence, independence and invulnerability of the 'we', separate from a 'them', that claimed the right to invade.[1] The possibility of ethics is necessarily premised upon the existence of a coherent subject. Importantly, however, foreign policy has become 'an arena of practice in which some subjects emerge with the status of actors' and others do not.[2]

This observation hints at an important point about the modern subject. Although it has long been of 'ontological centrality' to international relations, just as with all modes of social enquiry,[3] the status of the subject is never assured.[4] Rather, subjectivity is always a constructed basis for knowledge and action; it is always a representation of something that is never present in and of itself. Nonetheless, the possibility of subjectivity is still of great importance to the possibility of ethics. Derrida observes that, even after the 'postmodern' displacements of the subject, we must still ask 'who or what "answers" to the question "who"?'[5] For Caroline Williams, it remains crucial 'to consider the position from which the subject may speak and act', as what is 'still required by classical and deconstructive positions alike is a certain responsibility'.[6] The possibility of ethics demands a subject that can speak and act.

British and European Union (EU) foreign policy is replete with assertions of such subjectivity. Indeed, Cook launched the 'ethical dimension' with immediate claims to a collective British ethical subject:

> *We* are instant witness in *our* sitting rooms through the medium of television to human tragedy in distant lands, and are therefore obliged to accept moral responsibility for *our* response... *Our* foreign policy must have an ethical dimension and must support the demands of other peoples for the democratic rights on which *we* insist for *ourselves*.[7]

The claims to subjectivity, the 'we', the 'our' and the 'ourselves' are the basis for the ethical dimension. There would be no possibility of an ethical dimension without a 'we' to accept or enact it.

Such declarations are also a refrain of EU foreign policy from the beginning of the period I focus on. Javier Solana, in one of his first speeches as the new HR for the EU's Common Foreign and Security Policy (CFSP), asserted that the EU could not ignore others' conflicts. '*Our* survival is not always at stake, but *our* moral standing is'. Europe, he claims, is 'above all a community built on a set of principles and a set of values. And *we* must be intransigent when these fundamental values and principles are under threat'.[8] Again, 'we' must safeguard 'our' moral standing and principles, and this subjectivity makes the claim to an ethical foreign policy possible.

I argue that a fully present subject, which is simply assumed as the sure foundation for an ethical foreign policy, is ultimately impossible. However, policy makers cannot be blamed for this inevitable failure. and EU foreign policy construct subjectivity, both their own and that of others in international politics, as the ability, or capacity, to take responsibility for the prevention of human suffering. Here we begin to see how responsibility becomes the dominant signifier for their representations of ethics. Rather than subjectivity, responsibility and hospitality being strictly separate concepts in the foreign policy text, they all refer to a responsible relation to otherness, the 'foreign'. However, moments of undecidability appear in this construction of the subject, especially regarding the successful or failing state dichotomy, and the use of several signifiers for the subject. This undecidability undoes the possibility of ethical foreign policy while not fully demonstrating its impossibility.

Constructing subjectivity

How do Britain and the EU constitute a coherent picture of themselves as subjects of ethical foreign policy? And how do they understand others' subjectivity? The British and EU foreign policy texts have significant overlap and yet are very different in this regard; therefore, each will be tackled in turn. The conception of subjectivity affirmed for both Britain and other actors in the British text is highly assured. To be a subject is to be a member of the 'international community', which gives the subject both rights and responsibilities. It is the capacity to accept and fulfil these responsibilities, which defines the subject in Britain's foreign policy. Britain in this case, considers itself a leading member of the international community.

In contrast, the EU discourse is differentiated and insecure. In terms of a general structure of subjectivity, it largely adheres to the British construction as that which is capable of taking responsibility. However, the EU represents its own status as a subject as highly circumspect. It describes itself as *maturing* toward the ability to take responsibilities globally. The greatest responsibility claimed is towards those nearest to it: a responsibility of proximity or a territorialized responsibility.

The subject in British foreign policy

The connection between the 'we' and the taking of responsibility is immediately apparent in Cook's inaugural foreign policy speech of the new Labour Government. 'We' are imagined as 'witnesses' to suffering and as such are 'obliged to accept moral responsibility for our response'.[9] The construction of this subjectivity around responsibility and community begins to emerge later, when Cook declares the starting point of British foreign policy to be that 'in the modern world all nations belong to the same international community'; as such 'it is reasonable to require every government to abide by the rules of membership. They are set out in the Universal Declaration of Human Rights'.[10]

From 1999 onwards, this framing idea of the international community develops, and a conception of subjectivity is at its heart: the subject of international politics as that which is capable of taking responsibilities and accepting rights. Thus, in fleshing out the international dimension of his domestic 'Third Way', Blair emphasises over and again that its basis is an international community 'defined by common rights and shared responsibilities'[11] for its members. In his speech to the Global Ethics Foundation in June 2000, Blair stressed that community, whether national or international, is 'based on the equal worth of all, on the foundation of mutual rights and mutual responsibilities'.[12] This idea was still being emphasised in British foreign policy by March 2004.[13]

Jack Straw adds steel to the argument, observing that '[t]he rights of members of the global community depend exclusively on their readiness to meet their global responsibilities'.[14] In this way, the British foreign policy text constructs its concept of the subject as a member of the international community, with rights and responsibilities. However, Straw clarifies that the subject's rights depend 'exclusively' on the 'readiness to meet their global responsibilities'.[15] In other words, responsibilities come first. Essential, and of primary importance to the definition of the subject in the British foreign policy text is this capacity to take responsibility.

Nonetheless, despite the emphasis on responsibilities, subjects do have rights as members of the international community. They have the right to receive development aid and relief from their debt burden, to experience an unpolluted environment and to trade in free markets.[16] Subjects have the right to enter into international treaties and organisations, such as the North Atlantic Treaty Organisation (NATO), the World Trade Organisation (WTO), and even the EU. For example, Cook emphasised to the Bosnian government (in language that would become rife in EU foreign policy) that if they fulfilled their responsibilities, '[w]e can then welcome you back into the family of European nations'.[17] Blair went further, saying that if responsibilities were accepted, there is a 'moral duty' to offer accession to the EU.[18]

The central right of a subject is, however, 'the right to live free from the threat of force'.[19] As a member of the international community, one's sovereignty and territorial integrity is respected. If you are not part of the international community, this right is relinquished. Thus British foreign policy's construction of subjectivity makes freedom from force conditional. Initially this is played down: the 'principle of non-interference' remains valid, but it 'must be qualified in certain respects'.[20] For Mark Wickham-Jones, this demonstrated the 'quiet burial of the doctrine of non-intervention'.[21] Later, the burial is emphasised. The new doctrine is represented as breaking from the 'traditional' philosophy of international relations, which has 'held sway since the Treaty of Westphalia in 1648'.[22] It is no longer the case that 'a country's internal affairs are for it and you don't intervene unless it threatens you, or breaches a treaty, or triggers an obligation of alliance'.[23] Denis MacShane thus declared in 2002 that '[t]he West-phalian era of inter-state relations is over. The days when what happened inside a state was of no interest to other nations is over'.[24]

However, it is the fulfilment of one's responsibilities that allows an actor to be considered a subject with rights in British foreign policy. There is no definitive list of these responsibilities, but human rights are crucial. Cook even stated that respect for human rights formed the 'rules of membership' of the international community.[25] Bill Rammell, a Junior Minister at the Foreign Office under Jack Straw, observes that '[t]he core role of any state is to guarantee basic human rights: life, security, the rule of law. But some fail in this responsibility'.[26] Thus, the primary responsibility of a subject of ethics as foreign policy is to respect and protect the human rights of one's population. Another general responsibility is not threatening international peace and security, either by committing acts of genocide and producing refugees,[27] or by threatening its neighbours.[28] Subsequent to the terrorist attacks of September 11, 2001, two others grew in importance: a responsibility not to support terrorism;[29] and a responsibility neither to develop weapons of mass destruction (WMD) nor to proliferate them to other countries.[30]

If others fail to meet these responsibilities, the international community itself has a responsibility to act.[31] Thus, by 2004, the principle of non-interference was dug up and loudly reburied by Jack Straw:

> States have the right to non-interference in their internal affairs; but they also have responsibilities, towards their own people, and towards the international community and their international engagements. Where those responsibilities are manifestly ignored, neglected or abused, the international community may need to intervene: the cost of failing to do so in Rwanda or in Bosnia still haunts us today.[32]

The construction of subjectivity in British foreign policy then comes down to this: if one does not fulfil one's (normally a state's) responsibilities, one ceases to be a member of the international community, and therefore ceases to be considered a subject of international politics. In this case, one can be treated as an *object*, something incapable of knowing and acting (taking responsibility), and thus only capable of being known and being acted upon. That which does not have the capacity to take responsibility thus becomes the *object* of a subject's responsibility.

There are also a range of responsibilities which link directly to some of the rights that were mentioned first. These responsibilities, however, are generally used in reference to African nations, or 'Africa' more generally. For example, the right to development aid depends upon the responsibility to use the aid productively and not corruptly.[33] The same goes for debt relief. To gain the benefits of free trade, access to markets and IMF or World Bank assistance, there is the responsibility to comply with internationally agreed rules on trade and market regulation.[34] 'Africa' is seen and spoken differently to other subjects. It has a specific responsibility, as I will discuss further in Chapter 3, as what Blair calls a 'scar on the conscience of the world'.[35]

Nonetheless, in summing up the help Britain and the G8 gave African nations in 2002, Blair still speaks of the rights and responsibilities of both sides; such responsibilities are just different. A massive increase in aid is granted, but only 'provided the Africans keep their side of the bargain',[36] their responsibility to make progress on education, infrastructure and governance. These responsibilities are later outlined as 'a whole series of initiatives on the rule of law, on proper commercial and legal systems, on rooting out corruption, on respect for democratic rights, and the process of democracy'.[37] More or less specifically for Africans then, we can add to the list of responsibilities one must be capable of fulfilling to be considered a subject: the maintenance of the rule of law, ending corruption and preserving democratic processes (or putting them in place).

Now, what is the specificity of the British subject; what identity does the 'we' take on as a 'we' in international politics? Cook's 'mission statement' aimed to 'make Britain a leading partner in a world community of nations', and as such, 'a force for good in the world'.[38] At times, Britain declares itself to be a global leader, such as when welcoming others back into the international community,[39] and on debt relief.[40] Britain apparently takes on more responsibility than other members of the international community. For example, Blair claims that Britain has a 'special responsibility' for Africa.[41] When human rights have been threatened in Africa 'we' are said to be always at the forefront, taking responsibility.[42] Thus, in Sierra Leone, Britain did what it could to 'save African nations from barbarism and dictatorship and be proud of it'.[43] Yet British leadership is not just evident in Africa: when the values of the international community – described as freedom, democracy and the rule of law – are threatened in Iraq, 'Britain will defend them with courage and certainty'.[44]

The subject in EU foreign policy

This general construction of subjectivity as the capacity to accept responsibility is also in evidence from an early stage in the EU foreign policy discourse. However, in contrast to British foreign policy, the EU text focuses on affirming, justifying and describing its own status as a subject, its own capacity to accept responsibility. This is unsurprising when one considers the evident insecurity the EU demonstrates in claiming to be an independent, autonomous international actor. Chris Patten, EU Commissioner for External Relations (1999–2004) illustrates this on a visit to New Delhi:

> The last time I came here, it was in my capacity as the British Development Minister. In those days, I never needed to explain what Britain was, or how it fitted into the world. My French or German counterparts – indeed representatives of any EU member state – were similarly never called upon to do so. But today I am here to represent the European Union. An entity, a construction, that is far from clear to many outsiders. And frequently opaque to some of those inside as well.[45]

Unlike 'Britain', the 'EU' is a problematic subject. Britain simply *is*, one does not even need to explain *what* or *that* it is, but the EU's subjectivity needs to be proven, publicised and performed. Although Patten is right regarding the EU, precisely such a performance of subjectivity is also being made in every statement of British foreign policy.

Patten continues by stating that 'Europe wants to live up to its international responsibilities… Europe's Common Foreign and Security Policy now has operational teeth'.[46] The EU's problem living up to its international responsibilities means it rarely considers itself fully present as a subject of foreign policy. This is reflected in the academic literature, where Roy H. Ginsberg notes that scholars agree the EU 'has an international "presence"' in that it is 'visible in regional and global fora' (thus present only to the extent that it is visible), but that it only 'exhibits some elements of "actorness"'.[47]

Many EU foreign policy speeches appear as justifications for this lack of full presence. In 2003, Javier Solana recalls what he claims is sometimes forgotten: it was only in 1993 that the EU began to build a CFSP.[48] While he admits that much 'remains to be done', he intriguingly suggests that in foreign policy 'we are moving from a phase of theory to a phase of practice. We therefore stand on solid ground'. Crucially, Solana claims the EU now has significant responsibilities, '[b]ut I am convinced that the same reasons that give us responsibilities – our size and interests, our history and values – also equip us to take responsibilities'.[49] The movement from theory to practice, to the EU becoming a subject of international politics and proving its presence practically, is a movement towards taking on responsibilities.

Foremost in demonstrating the EU's practical presence on the world stage (as responsible subject) is the European Security and Defence Policy (ESDP), which comes under the remit of the CFSP. For some, this represents the possibility of the EU moving from 'weakness to power'.[50] Others see its operation as finally demonstrating the EU's 'claim to have become a fully-fledged actor in its own right'.[51] This is demonstrated by the examples of ESDP peace-keeping actions in Bosnia, the Former Yugoslav Republic of Macedonia (FYROM), and the Democratic Republic of Congo (DRC).[52] 'Actorness' is clearly being equated with what I am calling 'subjectivity'.

Solana proposes that the ESDP is a sign that 'the Union is not prepared to stand idly by in the face of crises. Nor always to let others shoulder responsibility'. Thus, as an instrument allowing the EU to 'shoulder' responsibility, '[i]t will be a sign that the European integration dreamed by Europe's founding fathers has come of age'.[53] The ESDP signifies the maturation of the EU as an international subject, its becoming capable of taking responsibility. A few months later, Solana claims that '[w]e need effective common foreign and security policies, with sufficient means and sufficient capabilities... The time has come for us to take our responsibilities seriously'.[54] Even by 2003, the EU appeared not to have fully achieved foreign policy subjectivity. Thus, Solana says, 'the EU has achieved a degree of maturity in this area – without yet having entirely grown up'.[55]

Romano Prodi, president of the EU Commission (1999–2004), suggests that the events of 11 September 2001 had a big impact on the development of the EU as a subject. The terrorist attacks on New York and Washington, DC,

> ...have forced Europe to face up to its own responsibilities in a new way. Until not very long ago, it was possible to conceive of Europe playing a part on the international stage as a 'civil power', an actor promoting specific principles and values without any autonomous capacity for political action. Today we cannot allow ourselves the luxury of that kind of Europe.[56]

In fact, this is similar to what Patten and Solana were saying pre-September 11 about the ESDP – the EU is being forced to accept responsibilities and thus become a subject of international affairs. As Ann Deighton suggests, the ESDP ended 'the age of "innocence" of *civilian power* Europe'.[57] For Prodi, however, this is not a neutral ending but a decisive rejection of the EU as 'civilian power'. It is important to consider why this is rejected: a civilian power, for Prodi, has no 'autonomous capacity for political action' in the international sphere.[58] In other words, it cannot fulfil its responsibilities and so cannot be considered a subject – autonomous, with control and capability of action. As Solana confirms, '[h]aving the capacity to use force when all other means fail is an *essential* component of a credible foreign policy'.[59]

Crucially, during 1999–2004, the foreign policy discourse of the EU never stabilized around an assured conception of its own subjectivity in global affairs. Nation states' capacities appear static and given, whereas the EU's capacities are represented as constantly developing and maturing. Considering the EU's concentration on its own subjectivity, it is perhaps unsurprising that it has little to say about subjectivity in general. The rare times that subjectivity, as the capacity to accept responsibility, is attributed to another entity is in relation to the Balkans. This is dealt with in more detail in Chapter 4, but a brief introduction is necessary here.

The EU accepts significant responsibility for the plight of the Balkans.[60] However, as the reconstruction process gets underway, it is increasingly emphasised by Prodi,[61] Patten[62] and Solana[63] that the Balkan nations themselves are responsible for their own recovery. For example, in a speech to the Kosovar Assembly in Pristina, Patten emphasises the role of the Assembly in a successful dialogue with Belgrade. This, he says, would

> ...send a very positive message to the international community, as it would show that your leaders are capable of assuming their responsibilities in a constructive manner. It would clearly show that when we say that Kosovo is on the path towards Europe it is not solely because geographically and politically you are part of the old continent but because you are mature enough to talk to those with whom you have extremely strong disagreements.[64]

In other words, EU foreign policy encourages Kosovo to do exactly what the EU is telling itself to do: grow up, mature and show itself capable of assuming its responsibilities; show itself capable of subjectivity. In this way, the EU replicates the discourse of British foreign policy, which constructs a more general subject of international affairs within an international community. The EU's representation of Kosovo's problem is essentially that of Kosovo showing itself to the international community as capable of responsibility. They are being told, and helped, to become a subject.

The EU has significant doubts regarding its own subjectivity and its presence on the global stage. The area in which it is most confident, its status as a regional 'home', capable of taking responsibility for those closest to it, will be examined in Chapter 4. However, as a subject of *world* politics, the EU emphasises its own insecurity throughout the period. It does not represent itself as ever fully present. Thus, the deconstructions that follow will primarily focus on subjectivity in British foreign policy though they will resonate with the EU text because of the overlap in their constructions of subjectivity.

Failing subjectivity

Especially in British foreign policy, other bodies were conceived to be subjects if they have the capacity of accepting the responsibilities required of them. Throughout this section, I argue that the most important signification for entities deemed incapable was the 'failing state'. State failure is what Roxanne Lynn Doty, invoking Laclau and Mouffe, calls a 'nodal point' – a privileged discursive point, or master signifier, that establishes the oppositions that make meaning possible and fix it there.[65] In this sense, the text of British foreign policy is built upon an oppositional structure of succeeding (subjects) and failing (objects), a structure that is deeply problematic when read opposite the terrorist attacks on London in July 2005.

The concept of the 'failing state' plays no great role in EU foreign policy. Nonetheless, it developed as a line of representation after 11 September 2001. The failing state is never particularly well defined here, but in October 2001, Solana began to see economic and political failure of states as the key source of conflict in the world.[66] Patten uses them as an example of the inefficacy of unilateralism. Afghanistan, he says, should have taught us that we cannot ignore 'these festering parts of an anarchically dangerous world. The international community has *no choice* but to work together to manage and resolve the problems caused by state failure'.[67] In 2003, Patten connects state failure to a failure of good government, poverty, AIDS, terrorism and international crime. As such it can neither be risked nor be tolerated.[68]

The discourse on failing states is far more developed in British foreign policy. The biggest responsibility of any entity wishing to be considered a subject of international politics (and member of the international community) is the responsibility to be successful. This is the nodal point, the master signifier that all other responsibilities refer back to. In 1999, then Foreign Office minister, Peter Hain, argued that Britain's policy in Africa was 'clear, transparent and unequivocal. We will back success'.[69] The successful, he claimed, are 'those who stand up for democracy and human rights', who 'want to reform their economies' and who commit to 'freeing their people from poverty'. Yet, but 'the reverse is true as well. We will not support corrupt governments... economic mismanagements... repression or bankroll dictatorship' because such 'evils have failed Africa. And we will not back failure'.[70] This is an early dichotomisation of international politics into successful and failing states. Success means democratic, protecting human rights, reformed, poverty-free economies; failure means corruption, mismanagement, repression, dictatorship and evil.

State failure only became central to the discourse after Straw was made the foreign secretary in 2001. States such as Somalia, Liberia and the DRC, Straw observed in 2002, are failing to such an extent that they resemble Thomas Hobbes' state of nature. 'As members of an international community', Straw argues, we must be worried for the human rights and freedoms of those caught in this chaos,[71] and this chaos may spread, as it did in Afghanistan. A failing state cannot be a subject, as it is incapable of accepting its responsibilities. Failing states can no longer be seen as *subjects*, capable of taking action and responsibility; they can only be seen as *objects* of international politics, capable only of being acted upon and taken responsibility for. Success and failure is a variation upon the classic opposition between subject and object.

There is another example of state failure, however, which matches neither Hobbesian 'chaos' nor the category of an object. The best example of this type of failing state is the pre-intervention Iraq.

> ...in Iraq it is an all too powerful state – a totalitarian regime – which has terrorised its population in order to establish control. From one perspective, totalitarian regimes and failed or failing states are at opposite ends of the spectrum. But there are similarities: one is unable to avoid subverting international law; the other is only too willing to flout it. And in failing to secure widespread popular support, both have within them the seeds of their own destruction.[72]

The 'seeds of destruction' metaphor is important and will be called upon later. However, Straw's point is clear: failing states do not live up to the responsibilities required of subjects; for some this is because they cannot (e.g. Somalia); for others this is because they refuse to (e.g. Iraq). This is a significant distinction. Although Iraq may not be an object, as 'it' is certainly represented as capable of taking responsibility, but it chooses not to. It deliberately flouts its responsibilities and thus is a subject which can be treated as an object. It places itself outside the international community by refusing to accept its responsibilities.

Effectively this has produced a division within the 'failing state' concept. On the one hand, there are those regimes, like Milosevic's Serbia in 1999, the Taliban's Afghan in 2001 and Saddam Hussein's Iraq in 2003, who are all failing in not accepting their responsibilities. Arguably, these regimes do act as subjects and do accept responsibility but crucially not in the way that British foreign policy defines as 'good', 'right' or indeed 'ethical'. This means that they can be treated with discursive violence, called evil, cruel and barbarous dictators (Milosevic);[73] described as the 'sworn enemies of everything the civilised world stands for' (the Taliban);[74] or brutal, dictatorial,[75] barbarous,[76] evil,[77] depraved, cruel beyond comprehension and 'without an ounce of humanity' (Saddam Hussein).[78] These are still subjects, but subjects that choose not to act as such and thus have all their rights removed. Their rights, including that of non-interference, are removed because, as we heard earlier from Straw, '[t]he rights of members of the global community depend exclusively on their readiness to meet their global responsibilities'.[79]

On the other hand, there are the *genuine objects* of ethics and foreign policy, those that cannot do, but can only be done to, those incapable of any responsibility. Blair describes these in his 2001 Labour Party Conference speech as 'the starving, the wretched, the dispossessed, the ignorant, those living in want and squalor from the deserts of North Africa to the slums of Gaza, to the mountain ranges of Afghanistan'.[80] This gives us a clear distinction between 'Milosevic' (and his regime) on the one hand and 'Serbians' on the other, between 'the Taliban' and 'Afghans', between 'Saddam' and 'Iraqis'. Blair clarifies this distinction, saying 'we' have no argument with the 'Afghans' as '[t]hey are *victims* of the Taliban regime. They live in poverty, repressed viciously, women denied even the most basic human rights and subject to a crude form of theocratic dictatorship that is as cruel as it is arbitrary'.[81] Thus, 'the people' ('Afghans', 'Serbians' and 'Iraqis') of these countries are seen as a hapless object, powerless victims unable to assume any responsibility for their barbarous leaders.

Generalising failure: The autoimmune subject

The British foreign policy text carefully divides the world into subjects (successful) and objects (failing), though the latter hides a division between genuine objects and subjects who act as objects. Subjectivity is constructed in this manner first by dichotomy but subsequently by the use of analogy. Straw's keynote speech 'Failed and Failing States' includes an important section sub-headed 'Diagnosing State Failure'.[82] This section explicitly treats state failure as a *disease* or medical condition to be *treated*. After 11 September, Straw says that he asked officials at the Foreign Office to 'look more closely at the underlying causes of state failure and identify a broad "at risk" category'.[83] Those at risk could easily slide towards failure 'causing significant problems for the international community'. Straw compares this to risk assessments made by corporations before investing in certain markets. Governments 'now need to put similar calculations at the heart of their foreign policy'. This leads to a medicinal metaphor:

> In medicine, doctors look at a wide range of indicators to spot patients who are at high risk of certain medical conditions – high cholesterol, bad diet, heavy smoking for example. This does not mean they ignore everyone else nor that some of those exhibiting such characteristics are not able to enjoy long and healthy lives, against our expectations. But this approach does enable the medical profession to narrow down the field and focus their efforts accordingly. We should do the same with countries.[84]

Straw recommends that with sharpened criteria and weighting, we can and should be able to intervene before states fail. 'Returning to my medical analogy, prevention is better than cure. It is easier, cheaper and less painful for all concerned.'[85]

The fundamental test of the onset of such disease and failure is the health of human rights. Straw notes that 'the key measure of a state's success is the extent to which it guarantees the human rights of its population'.[86] Thus, human rights and the rule of law should be used as an 'early warning system' of future crises and state failure.[87] To extend Straw's analogy, we could say that human rights are the immune system of the international community. They reveal signs of disease and can be used to fight against this disease both by those within the state and, if need be, by the international community. Thus, the first line of Straw's definition is that a state fails when it is unable to 'control its territory and guarantee the security of its citizens; to maintain the rule of law, promote human rights and provide effective government'.[88] To establish failure, one must ask whether there are areas of its territory the state cannot control, significant terrorist activity or ethnic or religious tension.[89] Fundamentally, a state's success depends on whether it is strong enough to control this conflict and maintain the safety, security and human rights of its citizens.

Derrida used a similar medical metaphor, that of 'autoimmunity', to explain the contradictory, even suicidal, nature of democracy. Democratic states essentially work against their own 'success', against their own subjectivity in the terms used here. 'Autoimmunity' is a 'strange illogical logic by which a living being can destroy, in an autonomous fashion, the very thing that is supposed to protect it against the other'.[90] It describes a biological process in which an organism's immune system turns on itself, on its own cells, thus destroying its own immunity. Hence it is 'quasi-*suicidal*' as it 'works to destroy its own protection, to immunize itself *against* its "own" immunity'.[91]

Democracy is not just a system of government confined to the state according to Derrida. Following Plato's portrait of the democrat in the *Republic,* Derrida associates democracy with freedom or liberty (*eleutheria*) and license (*exousia*), which is also whim, free will, ease, freedom of choice and the right to do as one pleases. Thus, from ancient Greece onwards, 'democracy' is conceived on the basis of this freedom.[92] This freedom and license associates itself with the concept of human rights, the rights that protect one's democratic freedoms. As such, both Britain and the EU can be seen to define their own subjectivity (as those with a responsibility to protect such rights and freedoms) as successful – and successful as democratic. Yet, the point of autoimmunity is to show that such democratic subjectivity attacks its own defences from within.

This happens for at least two reasons. First, the very openness of democracy – the free speech, the right to stand for election to public office, and so on – can allow a party intent on ending democracy to triumph legitimately by election. An example used by Derrida is Algeria in 1992, where an extremist Islamic party was expected by many to triumph, to 'lead democratically to the end of democracy'.[93] In this situation, the Algerian government decided 'to suspend, at least provisionally, democracy *for its own good*, so as to take care of it, so as to immunize it against a much worse and very likely assault'.[94] Democracy always has this quasi-suicidal possibility within itself – it may commit suicide (impose authoritarian rule and end democracy) to prevent its murder (the democratic end to democracy).

The second autoimmune reaction is far more applicable to our current deconstruction, as it comes through terrorism. The attacks in the United States during September 2001, in Madrid during March 2004 and in London during July 2005 all attest to how the openness and freedom of a successful, democratic subject can literally be seen as 'contain[ing] the seeds of its own destruction' (as Straw says of failing states).[95] Those who flew planes into the World Trade Center in New York were armed and trained to fly in the United States;[96] similarly, it would appear that the Madrid train bombings were perpetrated by mainly resident Moroccans, but also some Spaniards.[97]

In London, three of the four bombers were born in Britain as second-generation British citizens, raised and educated locally in West Yorkshire.[98] The fourth bomber, Germain Lindsay, although born in Jamaica, moved to Britain when he was five months old. The radicalisation of these men, while largely unaccounted for, appears to have taken place almost entirely in Britain.[99] The bombers were allowed to attend meetings where terrorism was praised and were encouraged to acts of murder all the time in Britain. On 7 July 2005, these British nationals were allowed to travel to, and through, a capital city carrying deadly bombs without let or hindrance.

The successful democratic subject is here caught in a double bind. On the one hand, the very openness of Britain and the EU's democratic culture of freedom and rights, which signify precisely success and subjectivity, are in fact the very source of their own failure as subjects. Britain and the EU can no longer claim to protect the human rights, freedoms and security of their own citizens (the definition of a successful state/subject), and specifically because of the human rights they seek to protect. On the other hand, however, what is represented as the necessary solution to this suicidal openness is a strengthening of the invasive powers of the state and a basic suspension of human rights and democratic freedoms.

This was revealed in the starkest terms on 22 July 2005, when the Metropolitan Police implemented a 'shoot to kill' policy against suspected suicide bombers for the first time. A Brazilian electrician, Jean Charles de Menezes, was shot seven times in the head and once in the shoulder as he boarded a train at Stockwell underground station. Britain, as a state, was not only incapable of protecting human rights on 7 July; two weeks later it was actively attacking them, attacking its own immune system. The immune system continued to be attacked with proposals instituted by the Labour Government, presented precisely as necessary curbs on human rights. Primary among these was the ability to detain suspects without charge for up to 28 days (contravening Article 5 of the European Convention on Human Rights) and the attempt to increase this period further to 90 days. Those who opposed and eventually defeated this measure where branded 'irresponsible' by Blair for their defence of human rights.[100]

In June 2006, a further high-profile instance saw the police raid two houses in Forest Gate, London, and arrest two men, shooting one of them.

The lawyer for one family involved highlighted the state's failure, declaring that they were 'assaulted and unlawfully detained', that this action 'was as lawless as the wild west'.[101] One could easily dispute the severity of these failures. Yet, whatever the severity, the point remains that failure is inherent. Framing these issues as marginal, as operational 'mistakes' specifically avoids their necessity brought about by the logic of autoimmunity, meaning a state's success can only ever also be a failure.[102] Democratic rights are suspended in order to preserve them. The double bind of the successful, *healthy* state subject is that it necessarily attacks itself, its 'early warning system', making itself *diseased* – whether by terrorists attacking it due to its very openness or by its own closure through suspension of democratic rights. Successful state subjects, those that are capable of taking responsibility for their own and others' citizens' security, rights and freedoms, cannot help but always be inhabited and defined by failure.

To some extent, this structural failure is acknowledged within the foreign policy text. In an interview afterwards, Straw was asked what reassurances could be given that this would not happen again. He replied that the only reassurance is to 'level with people... We cannot provide a reassurance that nothing like this will happen in the future... We have been successful in many ways, *but you can never provide 100 per cent security*'.[103] It may seem harsh to expect the state to provide such total security. Yet this has been the standard that British foreign policy has held other states to: states must '*guarantee* basic human rights: life, security, the rule of law';[104] a state fails when it is unable to 'control its territory and *guarantee* the security of its citizens'.[105] If no assurance can be given and insecurity is inherent, then there can be no successful state or subject.

However, as Derrida makes plain, the most unsettling element of autoimmunity is that it is always a matter of the self revealing the impossibility of the self. Because the self cannot help acting against its self, the self cannot be singular but must be split and divided. Autoimmunity 'consists not only in committing suicide but in compromising *sui*- or *self*-referentiality, the *self* or *sui*- of suicide itself'.[106] Placing the *sui* in doubt threatens to 'rob suicide itself of its meaning and supposed integrity'.[107] The very fact that this endangering of the state subject is done by the self and to the self is the most terrifying thing about terrorism, revealing that there is no self-same self in the first place. The self is fragmented, constituted by difference as well as identity or sameness, a difference that *attacks* the coherent self-sameness of the subject. The terrorists who committed the London bombings were British nationals operating domestically. No matter how much the government tried to construct the bombers and their ideology as *foreign*, as exterior, as coming from outside Britain,[108] it always recalls that terrorism is more or less *interior*, it 'has something "domestic", if not national, about it'.[109]

The London bombings therefore disturb the simple inside/outside, self/other, domestic/international boundaries upon which Britain's subjectivity is built (as a successful state, which has the capacity to responsibly protect 'its' citizens both within 'its' territorially drawn state and in others' territorially drawn states). Shortly after the bombings, Blair asserted that their origins were 'in an ideology born thousands of miles from our shores'.[110] He would later restate this claim as to the foreignness of the bombings' ideology in keynote foreign policy speeches in 2006.[111] These peculiar stipulations attempt to make Britain as a subject appear less autoimmune (as the attack came from the *other* not from the *self*), less unstable, less incapable, less fragmented and less failing. Efforts to portray the bombings as an attack of a foreign ideology will always fail because it merely recalls that Sadiq Khan and the other bombers were British, that their 'ideology' was taught in Britain, that the attack was a 'British' attack on 'Britain'.

Now we are in a position to appreciate the aptness of Straw's medical analogy. What Straw describes is the structure of all subjectivity. If failing subjects are diseased, then they are far from abnormal. The successful/failing dichotomy is reversed and displaced by the generalisation of failure. The double bind of autoimmunitary subjectivity means that Britain and the EU can never be anything but failing subjects/objects – and by their own description – attacking themselves and putting their very 'selves' in doubt. Either their openness allows their subjectivity to be attacked from within or they commit suicide by attacking this very openness, which makes them what they claim to be. Their inherent autoimmunity means that they undo their own understanding of their subjectivity; they 'themselves' are incapable of accepting responsibility, and this reveals the instability of the 'themselves'. 'Britain' and the 'EU' are always already both subject and object, yet fully neither at the same time. Their autoimmune subjectivity is inherently undecidable.

Supplementing the subject(s)

Subjectivity, especially in the British foreign policy text, relies upon an internally contradictory notion of success over failure. When failure is shown to be general, (that all subjects must fail by their own definition), we can see that the subject of an attempt at ethical foreign policy is always inhabited by its object. Another approach to the deconstruction of subjectivity would be to ask what precisely is affirmed as subject of ethics when Blair, Straw, Cook and so on say 'we' or 'our'. Is it the same entity every time? If not, what implications does this have for the presence of the subject itself? This section argues that the affirmation of a 'we' is that of a different 'subject' at different times. Rather than demonstrating several subjects, this merely confirms that the 'we', the subject, that which can take responsibility, never fully achieves this ability at any point.

Who, or what, answers to the question 'who' in British and EU foreign policy? Who or what is it that takes responsibility? At times, although very rarely in both cases, 'Tony Blair' and 'Javier Solana' are affirmed as the subject of their 'ethical' foreign policies. While it is the 'we' that has been drawing attention, the 'I' is also used when taking responsibility. Asked in an interview if he felt responsible for what happened in Abu Ghraib, Blair responded that 'I feel a responsibility for everything that happens in Iraq'.[112] Questioned on why the EU failed to speak with one voice over Iraq, Javier Solana agrees that '[t]here we failed'. It was the 'we' of the 'EU' that failed. Yet Solana goes on to take personal responsibility, observing that 'this is most bitter for me, as I saw this as my task'.[113] Straw manages to further diffuse the concepts of responsibility and subjectivity. Speaking of the decision to invade Iraq, Straw claims, 'I believe that I and we and the British Government and above all the British Parliament made the right decision'.[114] Hence, which is the subject taking responsibility for the decision here? Is it the 'I', the 'we', the 'British Government' or the 'British Parliament'?

Even when a 'we' is affirmed, it is very rare that this 'we' is simply 'Britain' or the 'EU'. For the EU, this is often due to the aforementioned insecurity about its own subjectivity beyond its region. We can see this in operation when Solana, having claimed a few months earlier that the EU failed as a subject of foreign policy over Iraq, now says that it was not the EU's responsibility.

> I think it would have been better to have a common position on Iraq... [but] it was not a possibility for those four members of the Security Council that belong to the European Union to have a common position. But it is a problem for them, not a problem for the European Union. It's at this point, it's a subject which is beyond the European Union.[115]

It is no longer a problem that the EU is incoherent as a subject of ethics as foreign policy. It is simply stated that the EU cannot take responsibility in this matter – essentially Solana affirms the EU as an object, or failed subject, in this discourse – and the problem is now one for individual member states. Thus subjectivity passes from the EU towards its members, and this does not seem to trouble Solana in the way it did so bitterly a few months earlier.

There is a similar, though less predictable, problem with the subjectivity of 'Britain'. When the 'we' is affirmed, it is sometimes simply 'Britain', though more rarely than would be expected. For instance, Blair stressed on September 11 that '[w]e... here in Britain stand shoulder to shoulder with our American friends in this hour of tragedy, and we, like them, will not rest until this evil is driven from our world'.[116] Here, the 'we' of Britain is clearly separated from the 'them' of the United States, as well as the evil to be driven from the world. Similarly, in summarising the security response to September 11, Blair observed that '[h]ere in Britain, we have instituted certain precautionary measures of security'.[117] However, later in the speech, a shift is marked toward a different subject: '*as a world we* have not been effective at dealing with them'.[118] The 'we' is now the 'world', though this generality is narrowed as Blair continues, '[w]e are democratic. They are not. We have respect for human life. They do not. We hold essentially liberal values. They do not... These beliefs are the foundation of *our civilised world*.[119]

This is a shift to a more inclusive subject (whether as 'world' or as 'civilised world'), a shift that is not peculiar to this period of British foreign policy. In fact, from the end of 1998 onwards, Blair begins to imply that the subject of British foreign policy is no longer 'Britain'; often the 'we' is the 'international community', which is then charged with taking responsibility. For example, speaking in September 1998 regarding Kosovo, Blair notes that the *international community*, rather than Britain, has 'clear responsibilities'.[120] These affirmations increase in 1999 around the time Blair formalised the importance of 'community': if countries do not live up to their responsibilities, Blair argues, 'the international community has a responsibility to act'[121] – not Britain. Similarly, Cook observes that, faced with overwhelming humanitarian violence, the international community must intervene.[122]

This probably reached its zenith when Blair answered *as* and *for* the international community rather than for Britain. At Prime Minister's Question Time in 2006, Sir Menzies Campbell asked, with hundreds of thousands dead and two million people displaced, 'have we not failed the people of Darfur?'[123] One can perhaps assume that when Campbell asks about a 'we' in the British Parliament, to the British Prime Minister, he is asking about 'Britain' and *its* failure to take responsibility. Blair's response was revealing, beginning with '[t]he international community is failing the people of Darfur...'.[124] In one sense, this response demonstrates that the international community is failing to accept its responsibility, and thus showing its failure as a subject. However in another, it shows that Blair is now answering for the international community, rather than Britain. The subject, the 'we' and 'our' affirmed by British foreign policy since late 1998, has often been the 'international community'.

Questioning the subject of ethics and foreign policy in the British text becomes even more complicated in the period after September 11. Here we see the appearance of an entity called the 'international coalition'. By the end of October 2001, the 'international community' has been replaced in Blair's representations of British foreign policy, by the 'international coalition' that 'remains strong'.[125] Making a tour of the Middle East, apparently gathering support for this new subject, Blair stops in Riyadh and thanks Crown Prince Abdullah and Saudi Arabia for their assistance; '[t]hey are very much part of the international coalition against terrorism'.[126] A clear separation is made between the 'international coalition' and the 'international community' when Blair thanks the Austrian Chancellor, who has been 'immensely important in sustaining this international coalition against terrorism, and the fact that that coalition is so broad has, I think, been something of an enormous comfort to the international community'.[127]

Despite its initial importance, the 'international coalition' falls into disuse as a subject of British foreign policy after the invasion of Afghanistan. In the escalation towards conflict in Iraq, it is the subjectivity of the United Nations (UN) which is both affirmed and questioned. For example, in November 2002, the passing of UN Security Council Resolution 1441 (demanding that Iraq allow the re-entry of, and comply with, UN weapons inspectors) was represented by Straw as showing that the 'UN has declared itself ready to accept its responsibilities'.[128] The UN now appears to be the privileged signifier for the subjectivity of the international community itself. It is further endowed with subjectivity in 2003, when Blair claimed that by 'going down the UN route we gave the UN an extraordinary opportunity and a heavy responsibility'.[129] The opportunity is to 'meet the menace' of Iraq 'collectively and as a united international community... The responsibility, however, is to deal with it'.[130]

The UN appears to have subjectivity bestowed upon it by the British foreign policy text and is then put on trial as a subject: it has the right to be considered the forum for action by the international community, but only if it can accept the responsibility to deal with this. This representation builds such that it is not only the UN that is questioned as a subject, but the international community itself. Twice in one day, Blair declared Iraq to be a 'test' for the international community.[131] Nonetheless, despite the UN and the international community's failure to accept its responsibility over Iraq, this failure is short lived; as observed earlier, by 2006, Blair is again answering on behalf of the international community as the subject of British foreign policy.

Chain of supplements

There is no clear answer as to who answers to the question 'who' in British or EU foreign policy. For the EU, subjectivity is variously invested in 'Solana', the 'EU' and, when the latter fails by being incapable, the individual member states. In the British text, the subject could be seen as 'Blair', 'Britain', the 'international community', the 'international coalition' and the 'UN'. What does this show us? What is the relationship between these various bodies that are endowed with subjectivity? Why is there a need for so many, especially in British foreign policy?

One characterisation of the relation between these entities is that they are supplementary. Each supplements the other. When British foreign policy no longer speaks for 'Britain', but also for the 'international community', the 'international community' is being used as a supplement to the subjectivity of 'Britain'. A supplementation is not, however, an apolitical or uncontroversial move. Derrida notes that Rousseau describes the relationship between speech and writing as one of supplementation. For Rousseau, speech is more highly prized than writing, as it is closer to the self-presence of thought; writing is a technical ploy that merely represents thought in the absence of speech.[132] As such, Rousseau sees writing as a 'dangerous supplement' to speech, making thought function *as if* it were present.[133]

Derrida points out that there are at least two meanings in this use of the word *supplement*. First, it is an insignificant and inessential extra, a surplus to what was already complete in and of itself.[134] Speech does not need writing, and thus writing is merely an addition. Similarly, the addition of the 'international community' and 'international coalition' merely adds to the responsibility already accepted by Britain as subject. It is inessential, though helpful, to have the international community's support for the invasion of Iraq. Likewise, it is pleasant, if not compulsory, that the international community should be widened by the additional support of the international coalition when attacking Afghanistan.

Second, the very possibility of this surplus supplement suggests that what is supplemented is incomplete. Why else would the supplement be added? As Culler describes it, when a supplement is added to a dictionary, it is an extra section which is added on, 'but the possibility of adding a supplement indicates that the dictionary itself is incomplete'.[135] Thus the second term 'adds only to replace' the first,[136] and this is why Rousseau describes the supplement of writing as 'dangerous', because it adds to replace. In the same way, if 'Britain' is a subject, fully capable of accepting responsibility, why should it be nice to have the support of the 'international community'? It would be entirely unnecessary. Equally, why should it be, as Blair claimed, that the breadth of the 'international coalition' should comfort the 'international community'?[137] Surely, if 'Britain' or the 'international community' were capable of accepting responsibility on their own, the breadth of the 'international coalition' would be wholly irrelevant. Rather, the supplementation of each (of 'Britain' by the 'international community', and subsequently of the 'international community' by the 'international coalition') reveals that the initial subject was insufficiently capable: insufficiently a subject. It required an addition that inevitably replaces the first term.

Yet, as we have seen, there is a perpetual movement of supplementation, especially in British foreign policy. Each 'subject' is found to be insufficiently endowed with subjectivity: inadequately capable of taking responsibility. We have seen how the 'UN' is criticised for failing the test of subjectivity set up for it,[138] and equally 'we', the 'international community', Blair says, is failing in Darfur.[139] Therefore each needs supplementation, producing a whole series of signifiers. Derrida clarifies the significance of this in *Of Grammatology*:

> Through this sequence of supplements a necessity is announced: that of an infinite chain, ineluctably multiplying the supplementary mediations that produce the sense of the very thing they defer: the mirage of the thing itself, of immediate presence.[140]

The chain of supplements reveals that the discourse never rests on a subject, an entity that will answer to the question 'who', that will accept responsibility.

It shows that the discourse is made up of a chain of substitutive and supplementary signifiers with no signified where it can settle as presence. And it does not rest because it cannot. There is no subjectivity ever simply present in British or EU foreign policy. Rather, both are marked by an absence of subjectivity, which requires constant supplementation.

At the 'origin' of an ethical foreign policy then is not the presence of a subject, a 'we', a 'Britain' or an 'EU' that is capable of accepting responsibility. Rather, '[t]he concept of origin or nature is nothing but the myth of addition', the constant supplementation of an 'originary *différance*'.[141] The word *différance* is a neologism that Derrida formed from the two meanings of the French verb *différer*: to defer, or 'the action of putting off until later... a detour, a delay'; and, the more common usage, to differ, or 'to be not identical, to be other'.[142] When I say that the origin of ethical foreign policy is *différance* then, I am referring to both these significations: differing and deferring. First, that its origin is a system of differences: between a present subject and an absent object, between state success and state failure. Such differences are simply 'effects of *différance*'.[143] Second, that its origin is a *deferral*: that each difference, each supplementary addition of a new signifier ('Blair', 'Britain', 'international community' and so on) constitutes a moment of *deferral*, a delay in the presence of the subject itself. Thus, the subject is both present in these differences and absent as the full presence of a truly responsible subject is constantly deferred.

This is not, however, to suggest that the hierarchy of subject/object, a hierarchy that goes back as least as far as Kant,[144] has simply been inverted and that deconstruction merely elucidates the absence of the subject. Christina Howells criticises Derrida precisely for this, suggesting that his 'conception of the subject seems uncannily stuck in what he himself might call the "reversal phase"'. Thus, it 'appears closer to the *non*-subject of structuralist discourse than to a radically deconstructed subject'.[145] Yet the subject, as an effect of *différance*, can never be simply absent, just as it cannot be simply present either. Rather, as Williams says, 'différance envelops the subject before itself, forever preventing and unsettling its attempts to *become* a subject', and thus the moment of full presence or constitution 'never quite arrives'.[146] The subject is neither object nor non-subject; rather, it never fully *is*. It is never fully either present or absent, subject or object, capable or incapable of taking responsibility; yet it is both at the same time. It is always a becoming object of the subject and a becoming subject of the object, or, as Williams more elegantly puts it, '[s]ubjectivity undergoes a perpetual play of (de)constitution or "constitutive loss of self."'[147]

Subjectivity, both in EU and British foreign policy, has only ever made itself present as a chain of supplements. 'Britain' was supplemented by the 'international community', the latter with the 'international coalition', and so on. Never was any signification of subjectivity able to fully demonstrate its capacity to accept responsibility. This chain of signifiers revealed the lack of a signified, the lack of a subject capable of making itself present. Rather,

presence is always deferred and subjectivity becomes explicable as a supplementary *différance*. Each body invested with subjectivity by the British and
EU foreign policy text is at once capable and incapable of accepting their
responsibility, but never fully realisable as either. The subject of ethical foreign policy is necessarily undecidable.

These deconstructions then do not mean that the subject no longer exists,
that it has been in some sense liquidated or destroyed. As Derrida affirms,
'[t]here are subjects, "operations" or "effects" of subjectivity', but this does
not mean that we have to believe 'the subject is what it *says* it is'.[148] Rather,
we need to 'resituate' the subject, thinking it differently, as a constantly failing, always deferred presence. This leaves us in the position of examining
the effects of a resituated subjectivity for ethical foreign policy. The effects,
I will argue, are primarily a matter of *enacting* responsibility in British and
EU foreign policy.

3 Responsibility

Protecting and saving the other in British foreign policy

What does it mean to act responsibly in international affairs? How does an international actor go about enacting responsibility? With the shift in language from a 'right' to humanitarian intervention to a 'responsibility to protect' individuals proposed by the International Commission on Intervention and State Sovereignty (ICISS),[1] much more attention has been given to this topic.[2] However, very little of this increased interest focuses on precisely what we mean by 'responsibility'. More consideration seems to be centred upon who, or what, has responsibility for protecting people in a given situation, such as the apparent genocide in Darfur.[3] Too often, it is simply assumed that we know, even if intuitively, what the responsible thing to do is; all we need is to set out who should do it. In fact, this is rarely the case. Responsible action is always a political and ethical *question*, rather than a known fact.

Both British and European Union (EU) foreign policy texts place the capacity for responsibility centrally in their construction of the subject. Within this representation, 'Britain' is described as leading the way. This chapter moves from the *taking* of responsibility to the *being* responsible or, rather, the *enactment* of responsibility. These two aspects of responsibility are not wholly separable, but the division can be maintained for heuristic reasons. Because of the structure of the international community set up in its text, British ethical foreign policy engages a global sense of responsibility. This ostensibly deterritorialised ethics and responsibility can be organised around two notions: a responsibility to protect and a responsibility to save. Particularly from 1999 to 2004, the responsibility to protect was the primary way responsibility was represented in British foreign policy; to protect human life, regardless of location. However, from 2004, but stretching back much earlier, the issue of a responsibility to save in 'Africa' is given primacy.

The distinction between the two responsibilities is essentially one of human agency. People need protecting from others' agency (e.g. Milosevic's); people and states need saving from others' negligence (e.g. corrupt African government's). Britain's ethical responsibility does not extend to disasters that involve no agency: 'acts of God' such as the Asian tsunami of December

2004. In Blair's first press conference after the tsunami, he makes it quite clear that it will not take his attention away from Africa, '[t]he tsunami is not a political issue... Africa is a political issue, that is an issue of real political leadership'.[4]

Despite this stress on agency, the responsibility Britain seeks to enact can only be thought as a question, as an undecidable, the possibility of which can never be assumed. The textual analysis of both the responsibility to protect and the responsibility to save reveal deeply problematic ir-responsibility, attesting to both the possibility and impossibility of ethical foreign policy. First, however, it is necessary to explore the construction of responsibility in British foreign policy, the way it answers the question 'why act responsibly?'

Why act responsibly?

If ethical foreign policies speak of responsibility, it is essential to ask where such a sense of obligation comes from. In this case, we must ask how 'Britain' represents itself as being obliged to act ethically. What is the ethical foundation of the foreign policy, its guiding principle? Britain's responsibility appears to come from two sources, one of which emerges as the basis for the other. First, though this is often taken for granted, it is the prevention of human suffering that forms the ethical foundation of British foreign policy. Cook's May 1997 'Mission Statement' declared that '[w]e are instant witness in our sitting rooms through the medium of television to human tragedy in distant lands, and are therefore obliged to accept moral responsibility for our response'.[5] It is the human tragedy (and the 'witnessing' of it) that provides the motivating force for British moral responsibility.

In his 2001 party conference speech, which Michael White described as the most powerful of his career,[6] Blair defended Britain's intervention in Kosovo in similar terms. He continued by arguing that 'if Rwanda happened again today as it did in 1993, when a million people were slaughtered in cold blood, we would have a moral duty to act there also'.[7] Jack Straw similarly argued that it was the 'humanitarian catastrophe' in Kosovo that made 'the British Prime Minister's moral case for a military response unanswerable'.[8] Again, it is human suffering motivating British ethical concern.

This is gradually refined, especially in relation to Africa. Blair claims in 2005, 'it barely needs saying, but it cannot be morally right that so many people die when their deaths could be prevented'.[9] It is not simply death and humanitarian disasters that demand responsible, ethical foreign policies, it is *preventable* suffering and death. Kim Howells, a junior minister at the Foreign Office, makes a slightly different, if more traditional, point in justifying the concentration on Africa,

> There is of course a clear moral reason for us to do so. How could there not be? In the decade beginning in 1994 it is estimated that in Africa

alone, more than nine million people died as a result of conflict. That's more than the number killed on all the horrific battlefields of the first world war. Moreover, the vast majority of the deaths in Africa were non-combatants – women and children struck down by disease and malnutrition.[10]

Both Blair and Howells emphasise the perfectly evident nature of this moral basis (it 'barely needs saying', the moral reason is 'clear'). However, for Howells, it seems to be that, by definition, the death of 'non-combatants' is *outrageous*, presumably because of their innocence. The implicit assumption is that only certain death and suffering 'counts' as a moral issue. Some death and suffering appears as *unavoidable* and so does not 'count'. But the intrinsic value of human life means that preventable and outrageous misery is morally repugnant. The prevention of preventable and outrageous loss of human life then is the seemingly unproblematic basis for a responsible, ethical foreign policy.

The second reason Britain acts responsibly has already been mentioned and is clearly built on this underlying foundation: that of the doctrine of international community. Community, whether domestic or international, Blair tells us in his Global Ethics Foundation speech of 2000, is based on the 'equal worth of all'.[11] If human life has intrinsic moral value, responsibility can have no territorial boundaries. Here we see a key difference as compared with the explicitly territorial and proximity based ethics of EU foreign policy.[12] As a member of an international community, a subject is responsible for protecting and saving life regardless of that life's location. This is further emphasised in the party conference speech of 2001, where Blair stresses, 'our cause' is those people suffering 'from the deserts of Northern Africa to the slums of Gaza, to the mountain ranges of Afghanistan'.[13]

Therefore, setting out proposed guidelines for humanitarian intervention, Cook states that, in the face of a humanitarian catastrophe that a state is failing to prevent (or even seeks to promote, as in Kosovo), 'the international community should intervene'.[14] Straw further stresses this in 2004, arguing that where a state's responsibilities are 'manifestly ignored, neglected or abused, the international community may need to intervene: the cost of failing to do so in Rwanda or in Bosnia still haunts us today'.[15]

These two principles are the basis of how the ethics of responsibility are represented in British foreign policy. First, human life is intrinsically morally valuable, and it is, therefore, ethical to seek the prevention of preventable and outrageous death and suffering. This value is equal no matter where the life happens to be. Such equality gives the basis for the second principle: a logic of international community. International community means that where human life is being ill treated, the rest of the community is morally obliged to prevent the ill treatment.

If these are the reasons why British foreign policy describes itself as ethically obligated, this responsibility has taken two forms. The first case explored is the responsibility to protect human life from aggressive forces within a state. In other words, this is a direct intervention in a state's affairs by military force to protect the lives of the state's citizens.[16] In terms of subjectivity, this means the responsibility to protect is enacted towards two types of international entities, both presented as failing state-subjects. This could be, first, states conceived as objects, with no central control, security or guarantee of human rights over a territory. There are surprisingly few examples of an intervention represented in this way in post-1997 British foreign policy – only Sierra Leone and perhaps, at times, Afghanistan. The responsibility to protect is more commonly represented under the second category, as enacted towards the helpless objectified citizens of states as subjects-treated-as-objects. These are subjects that, though capable of taking responsibility, act as objects in refusing to do so:[17] Kosovo, Afghanistan (though this has elements of both) and Iraq.

The second responsibility I will look at is generally enacted, by consent, in the affairs of other state-subjects. As subjects, these states are capable of responsibility and thus capable of giving consent. This responsibility to save human life is invariably invoked in relation to 'Africa' in British foreign policy. Such a responsibility to save has very much come to the fore since late 2004, with Britain holding the G8 chair and the EU Presidency, and is far less controversial than the stark interventions by force in Afghanistan and Iraq. However, both these representations of an ethical, responsible foreign policy deconstruct, destabilizing their own claims to ethicality and responsibility.

Responsibility to protect

Cook's 'Mission Statement' reveals how Britain's post-1997 'ethical dimension' was represented early on as being concerned with human suffering. However, beyond this, there was remarkably little initial detail, or focal point, to the 'ethical dimension'.[18] This is reflected in the literature: in *New Labour's Foreign Policy: A New Moral Crusade?*, examining the first two years of Labour's foreign policy, Richard Little and Mark Wickham-Jones collected chapters on a diverse range of subjects with little or no focal point – arms sales, human rights, Iran, the 'Third Way', Kashmir, internal Labour party politics and so on.[19] Only in 1999 did elements of a 'responsibility to protect' begin to emerge. From then on, it became much more difficult to claim that the ethical foundations of British foreign policy were 'usually vague and unarticulated'.[20]

With civil war and ethnic cleansing once more breaking out in the Balkans, Blair took up the concept of 'international community' as the structure for a much more focused moral vision. In his now famous speech in Chicago on the 'doctrine of international community', Blair argued that the 'most pressing foreign policy problem we face is to identify the circumstances in which we should get actively involved in other people's conflicts'.[21]

While the 'principle of non-interference' is still important and still stands, it 'must be qualified in important respects'. The most important qualification, he added, was that '[a]cts of genocide can never be a purely internal matter'.[22]

Although widely ignored by commentators, a more interventionist point was made by Blair in a visit to South Africa a few months before the Chicago speech. If a country is attacking, or threatening to attack its neighbours, Blair argued, 'the international community has a responsibility to act'.[23] Such a responsibility to protect the lives of innocents could be performed in a variety of ways: through the UN, such as in Mozambique, or through regional bodies, such as the Nigerian-led Economic Community Military Observation Group (ECOMOG) troops in Sierra Leone. Crucially, however, he declares that 'sometimes, if collective action cannot be agreed or taken in time, [the international community must act] through countries with a sense of global responsibility taking on the burden'.[24] Here, Blair is not only calling for the international community to intervene to prevent human suffering, but also for individual countries to do so. He underlines this by agreeing that although we cannot make ourselves the sole guardians of right and wrong, 'when the international community agrees certain objectives and then fails to implement them, those who can act, must'.[25]

From 1999, a key enactment of the Britain's ethical dimension to foreign policy was considered to be this responsibility to protect, and Britain's role of leadership was crucial. Cook, in 2000, submitted a series of six guidelines on humanitarian intervention to the UN Secretary General.[26] He subsequently claimed in 2001 that these proposals to help decide when the international community can intervene in a state's affairs were rejected by others in the UN, suspicious of greater intervention.[27] In September 2000, however, the Canadian Government established the ICISS in response to Kofi Annan's plea for an agreed approach and principles to 'humanitarian intervention'.[28] The subsequent ICISS report suggested moving from the language of 'humanitarian intervention' and the 'right to intervene' towards that of a 'responsibility to protect'.[29] Several recommendations along these lines were made to the UN General Assembly, Security Council and Secretary General.[30] For Paul Williams, these recommendations 'reiterated and developed' Cook's original suggestions the year before.[31]

It was via this intertextual route, however, that by 2005 the specific phrase, a 'Responsibility to Protect,' is incorporated into the British foreign policy text. Welcoming the Secretary General's range of suggestions for the reform of the UN (arising partly from the ICISS report) on behalf of the British Government, Bill Rammell hailed Annan's 'boldest recommendation' as the suggestion that all governments share this responsibility to protect the citizens of other states.[32] Similarly, Straw argues that although several decisions taken by the General Assembly, following Annan's recommendations, would make the UN more effective,

I believe that it will be the agreement on our Responsibility to Protect that will be seen in the future as the decision of greatest significance. If we follow through with that Responsibility to Protect, then never again will genocide, ethnic cleansing and crimes against humanity be allowed to take place under our noses with nothing done. The Responsibility to Protect is, of course, a reflection of our common morality. But it is also a recognition that the world in which we now live is too small for us to be unaffected by or indifferent to the innocent victims of murder and oppression.[33]

According to Straw, it should not be surprising that Britain is supporting such a policy in the UN, as they have been campaigning for a recognition of this responsibility for a long time. This specifically ties such a responsibility up with the rules of the international community stated previously. By March 2006, this concept of a 'responsibility to protect' is so thoroughly entangled with the British discourse that the agreement on it is seen as merely part of the development of Britain's foreign policy. Straw argues that the Labour government's values are

...the reason behind our determination to see a clear recognition that we have a 'Responsibility to Protect' all the world's citizens from genocide and crimes against humanity; and that there is a collective responsibility to act where states fail to fulfil this essential task.[34]

The UN Secretary General and the ICISS are not even mentioned. Britain's ethical dimension is presented as having been crucial. After all, what Blair had described as the 'most pressing foreign policy problem'[35] faced in 1999 was largely resolved by 2006, and with Britain's help and leadership. An agreement in the UN on a 'Responsibility to Protect' is presented as the achievement of what Britain had been pressing for: an agreement that there is a responsibility to intervene by force to protect humans from suffering. Yet, British foreign policy is still understood as *more* ethical than that of others'. To repeat an earlier quotation, Blair states that 'if collective action cannot be agreed or taken in time,' this responsibility must still be enacted 'through countries with a sense of global responsibility taking on the burden'.[36] It has very often been Britain that has shown this ethical 'sense' of a global responsibility to protect.

Britain's ethical leadership: Kosovo, Sierra leone, Afghanistan

From 1997, Britain engaged in a significant number of forceful interventions. Indeed, Kampfner in 2003 suggested the debatable statistic of five wars in six years – the bombing of Iraq (1998), Kosovo (1999), Sierra Leone (2000), Afghanistan (2001) and Iraq (2003) – to be 'without precedent in modern British political history and without parallel internationally'.[37] At least three of these 'interventions' were constructed as 'humanitarian', as part of Britain's leadership as a nation with the sense of a global 'responsibility to protect'. In other words, the actions in Kosovo, Sierra Leone and Afghanistan were represented as fitting within the framework of an ethical, responsible foreign policy – the doctrine of international community. There were clearly also other reasons for these interventions, but the responsibility to protect provided the ethical justification.

Blair's Chicago speech set out a redescription of the British foreign policy, but more immediately commentators saw it as justifying the intervention in Kosovo and attempting to compel Bill Clinton to use ground troops.[38] To this end, Blair talks about the 'unspeakable crimes' taking place, the 'tear stained faces' of refugees with 'heart-rending tales of cruelty'.[39] It is for these reasons that '[w]e cannot let the evil of ethnic cleansing stand. We must not rest until it is reversed.'[40] In a speech to the Muslim Council of Britain, Blair emphasises this with even greater force. He described meeting the Muslim refugees, 'victims of a terrible crime', in Macedonia as 'one of the most disturbing, shocking few hours of my life'.[41] These people, he says, 'are the reason for our military action,' and 'no civilised country could stand by and watch such brutality without acting'.[42] The intervention was, thereby, represented as an enactment of Britain's responsibility to protect the people of Kosovo. Their suffering was literally the reason for Britain's action.

Other reasons were, of course, given for the intervention, the most prominent being the credibility of NATO. 'What credibility would NATO be left with if we allowed that [Rambouillet] agreement to be trampled on comprehensively by President Milosevic and did not stir to stop him?',[43] as Cook put it. Blair emphasises the threat to NATO's integrity, arguing that, '[o]n its 50th birthday NATO must prevail... If NATO fails in Kosovo, the next dictator to be threatened with military force may well not believe our resolve to carry the threat through'.[44] Nonetheless, the need for NATO to succeed is still brought back to human suffering. As Cook said, it is 'for our own sake but also for the sake of the refugees',[45] while Blair stated that NATO must make the victory of justice over evil 'a reality for Kosovo's long-suffering people'.[46]

The intervention in Sierra Leone, in May 2000, was described as a forceful intervention to prevent Rwandan style genocide and maintain peace.[47] It was a limited action and was not justified in any way other than the responsibility to protect Sierra Leonian citizens. Kampfner quotes Blair as reacting angrily to suggestions that it was a neo-imperialist war; '[w]hen people say "run an ethical foreign policy", I say Sierra Leone was an example of that, not an example of not doing it. It is up in the high ground'.[48] Blair justified the action as an attempt 'to do what we can to save African nations from barbarism and dictatorship'; thus, he says, we can 'be proud of it'.[49] Britain, once again, is represented as taking a leading role in the international community, exercising its sense of a global responsibility to protect in the absence of collective action.

Afghanistan is a more complicated case than either Kosovo or Sierra Leone. The primary reason presented for the invasion of Afghanistan in October 2001 was the terrorist attacks on the World Trade Center and Pentagon. Afghanistan, and its Taliban regime, were said to be harbouring Osama Bin Laden and Al-Quaeda terrorist training camps. The Taliban refused, in Britain's representation, to comply with the will of the international community and hand Bin Laden over to the allied forces. Consequently, for Blair, 'our enemy's friend becomes our enemy too... in choosing to help the friends of terror, they are choosing to be enemies of ours'.[50] Yet, the humanitarian element of the intervention to overthrow the Taliban was also very much to the fore. Not only had the Taliban chosen to side with terrorism, this extremist regime had also made the Afghan people suffer for years. It is 'a regime without respect or justice for its own people.... They care little for human life.'[51] In contrast, Blair observed that 'we do care about the humanitarian plight of people in Afghanistan'.[52] The difference, once again, is Britain's sense of responsibility for suffering.

This responsibility to protect the Afghan people was at times emphasised so strongly as to appear the fundamental reason for the action in Afghanistan. Blair states that Britain is not fighting the Afghan people, '[t]hey are victims of the Taliban regime. They live in poverty, repressed viciously, women denied the most basic human rights and subject to a crude form of theocratic dictatorship that is as cruel as it is arbitrary.'[53] He ties the action in with the more explicitly humanitarian action in Kosovo, comparing the Taliban exactly with the 'hated regime' of Milosevic. 'We acted against Milosevic because what he was doing... was unjust';[54] similarly, it seems, Britain must lead the fight against injustice and human suffering in Afghanistan.

The representations of actions in Kosovo, Sierra Leone and Afghanistan, while often having other motivations and justifications, are explicitly connected in the speeches of British foreign policy makers. The link is that Britain as a leading member of the international community, and a prominent subject of international politics, has a responsibility to protect the innocent people of these nations. The connection with the invasion of Iraq is less obvious. Yet, while this intervention was declared an anomaly, breaking with Britain's ethical framework and the doctrine of international community, it becomes the most prominent example of how such an ethical responsibility to protect undermines itself.

Iraq: Exemplary anomaly

The invasion of Iraq in March 2003 was declared by the British foreign policy establishment to be a matter of enforcing the UN resolutions on Weapons of Mass Destruction (WMD). Blair explicitly stated that the 'United Nations Mandate on Weapons of Mass Destruction' was the 'reason we act'.[55] He emphasised that the aim of the invasion was never regime change but rather the disarmament of WMD. Justifying the war in October 2004, after it had emerged that there probably were not any WMD present at the time of invasion, Straw claims that Iraq's breaking of UN resolutions, and its refusal to demonstrate that it had no WMD, provided the legitimate reason for the invasion.[56] We can see that in the British government's representation, the reason for the invasion was not the same as in Kosovo, Sierra Leone and Afghanistan. The invasion was largely constructed as a legal matter: the enforcement of international law and the will of the international community.

Yet, this depiction is not entirely stable. A fascinating speech in July 2004 gives an overview of Blair's thinking on international affairs; it 'attempt[s] an explanation of how my own thinking, as a political leader, has evolved' over the past few years.[57] Directly linking his keynote speeches from 1999 onwards,[58] Blair states that Iraq was anomalous to his ethical framework of international community. He notes that 'humanitarian intervention' has been gaining currency and that he had tried to set this out in his Chicago speech.

> So, for me, before September 11th, I was already reaching for a different philosophy of international relations from a traditional one that has held sway since the treaty of Westphalia in 1648; namely that a country's internal affairs are for it and you don't interfere unless it threatens you, or breaches a treaty, or triggers an obligation of alliance. *I did not consider Iraq fitted into this philosophy*, though I could see the horrible injustice done to its people by Saddam.[59]

The invasion of Iraq did not fit into the doctrine of international community; it did not fall within the remit of Britain's responsibility to protect human life. The difference between the intervention in Iraq and that of the three other examples cited is said to be the difficulty of the decision it involved. He draws direct parallels, saying that 'Kosovo, with ethnic cleansing of ethnic Albanians, was not a hard decision for most people; nor was Afghanistan after the shock of September 11; nor was Sierra Leone. Iraq in March 2003 was an immensely difficult judgement.'[60] This difference is underlined during an interview three months late: the Iraq decision was difficult, Blair observed, while 'I felt that Kosovo was an open and shut case, I felt that Afghanistan in a sense with the Taliban was'.[61]

However, despite this major difference, Blair crucially brings the invasion of Iraq back into the doctrine and the responsibility to protect, and this is done in the same speech. Justifying Britain's action, he comes close to acknowledging that an intervention such as that in Iraq may be illegal under international law, but questions whether this should be the case. Using the rhetoric of rights and responsibilities, he argues that the doctrine of international community is no longer a vision of idealism.

> The essence of community is common rights and responsibilities. We have obligations in relation to each other. If we are threatened, we have

a right to act. And we do not accept in a community that others have a right to oppress and brutalise their people. We value the freedom and dignity of the human race and each individual in it... Emphatically I am not saying that every situation leads to military action. But we surely have a duty to act when a nation's people are subjected to a regime such as Saddam's.[62]

The decision on going to war with Iraq is, thus, brought back to the question of community and whether 'in a community others have a right to oppress and brutalise their people'. This means that we have a 'duty to act when a nation's people are subjected to a regime such as Saddam's'. He continues by tying this to the issue of human rights, the protection of which, as we have seen in the previous chapter, is the ultimate responsibility of any state as a subject in international politics.[63] 'The UN Universal Declaration on Human Rights is a fine document', declares Blair, '[b]ut it is strange that the United Nations is so reluctant to enforce them'.[64] Thus, in one speech, despite *declaring* Iraq to be different to Kosovo, Sierra Leone and Afghanistan, he effectively *describes* their sameness, the identity linking them all.

This identity is described in other speeches, especially by Foreign Secretary Jack Straw. Using Kosovo as the main comparison, Straw observes that '[a]s the humanitarian catastrophe was relayed live on our screens, the British Prime Minister's moral case for a military response became unanswerable'.[65] The difference between Kosovo and Iraq, however, was not that there was a humanitarian catastrophe in one and not the other but simply that in Iraq the catastrophe was not *visible*. Saddam has 'conducted his reign of terror off camera. So unlike Kosovo, Iraq has not pricked the world conscience through our television screens.'[66] Yet, the comparison with Kosovo remains. Straw acknowledges that although there 'are never exact parallels... I do remind my audience that many argued against military action in Kosovo. Who today would question the moral case for the Allied intervention which led to the fall of Milosevic?'[67] The implication is that the similarity between Kosovo and Iraq means the moral case for the latter is also unquestionable.

The responsibility to protect, while at times declared irrelevant, remains crucial to the representation of the invasion of Iraq. As Straw says elsewhere, until his 'long reign of terror is ended, Saddam Hussein will remain a scar on the conscience of the world, and a standing affront to the ideals which underpin the foreign policies of the UK, the United States and our European allies'.[68] The scar on the UK's conscience is not caused by the legal justification for war but by the nature of Saddam Hussein's regime, which, Blair says, 'represents the very antithesis of all the values we stand for'.[69] Iraq is described with many of the same adjectives as were used in relation to Milosevic's Serbia and the Taliban's Afghanistan: brutal, dictatorial,[70] barbarous,[71] evil,[72] depraved, cruel beyond comprehension and 'without an ounce of humanity'.[73]

Blair and Straw, thereby, bring their representation of the war in Iraq back into the structure of the doctrine of international community and the responsibility to protect. However, it still remains anomalous, or rather, *marginal*, to both. It is not always considered to be part of the doctrine and can perhaps best be used as a liminal case to show the particular characteristics of those that are central, the easy, open and shut cases of a responsibility to protect: Kosovo, Sierra Leone and Afghanistan. However, this very marginalisation of the Iraq invasion is what makes it interesting to a deconstructive reading. Culler observes that a common operation of deconstruction is to take what is apparently marginal to a text, such as a footnote, and transfer it to a place of centrality. This is because 'what has been relegated to the margins or set aside by previous interpreters may be important precisely for those reasons that led it to be set aside'.[74]

In 'Signature Event Context', Derrida performs such a reading of Austin's speech act theory, focusing on the possibility of the performative utterance (where something is accomplished through speech itself – e.g. 'I now pronounce you man and wife' said by a vicar in a marriage ceremony). Austin is interested in what makes a successful performative utterance, one that succeeds in accomplishing an act – such as marrying a couple. To analyse successful performatives, he excludes from consideration the possibility that every performative utterance can be quoted or cited outside the correct context, for instance, in a play. If an actor playing a vicar quoted the performative, 'I pronounce you man and wife' when on stage, this would not be a serious performative. Therefore, Austin pushes the possibility of citation to the margins as abnormal and parasitic.[75]

However, as Derrida asks, is the citation that Austin excludes from analysis as the 'anomaly' and 'exception' not 'the determined modification of a general citationality – or rather, a general iterability – without which there would not even be a "successful" performative?'[76] After all, language *must* have this general structure of iterability – the possibility for it to be repeated and transformed in different contexts – for it to be understandable. We must always be quoting, or citing; if we produced genuine 'singular and original event-utterances',[77] we would be understood by no one, thus, our performative utterance would be a failure. For any utterance to be a success, it must be a citation. A vicar can only be successful in his performative because he is citing other vicars and pronouncing words from within the iterable structure of language. In this way, Derrida takes what is marginal and makes it central, takes what is anomalous and makes it exemplary, while deconstructing the distinctions between these oppositions.

A similar reading can be given regarding the question of Iraq and the responsibility to protect. If the invasion of Iraq is marginalised and treated as a liminal anomaly to this responsibility, we must ask why. What reasons are there for this marginalisation? I suggest that the reason is precisely the difficulty of the decision emphasised earlier. The significance of this is that the difficulty of the Iraq decision stands for each and every intervention enacted as a 'responsibility to protect'. Rather than this difficulty marking it out as simply marginal to questions of ethics and foreign policy, it also signals its very centrality.

Iraq: Deconstructing the ethics of a 'responsibility to protect'

In early 2003, the moral case for war became the dominant government narrative of the decision to invade Iraq. Nonetheless, as suggested earlier, the responsibility to protect was always present within the government's discourse. For example, in September 2002, Foreign Office minister, Mike O'Brien, used Iraq as a fundamental issue in a speech on 'Morality in Asymmetric Warfare and Intervention Operations'. Here, he ties together the legal and moral justifications for war as an over-arching ethical question. He asks what response there should be to Saddam's use of chemical weapons against his own people and whether Britain could ignore Saddam's threatening the region and world by trying to develop WMD. However, these two questions are joined by O'Brien's final question of underlying importance: '[e]ssentially, how should we deal with the threat posed by Saddam's immorality?'[78]

Given that this is a leading question, as the responsibility to protect is represented as making an invasion of Iraq and the removal of Saddam necessary, why is the decision problematic? Crucially, because Iraq is represented as a *difficult* case (unlike Kosovo, Sierra Leone, Afghanistan), we have open discussion of the crux of the problem in *all these interventions*. In a speech to the 2003 Labour Party Spring Conference, Blair makes his biggest pitch for the decision to go to war in Iraq being based on an ethical responsibility to protect. Here, we see why Iraq was seen as problematic: Blair recognises for the first time that those who oppose the war have a 'moral purpose'.[79] But this does not mean that a decision to attack Iraq is immoral.

> The moral case against war has a moral answer: it is the moral case for removing Saddam. It is not the reason we act. That must be according to the United Nations Mandate on Weapons of Mass Destruction. But it is the reason, frankly, why if we do have to act, we should do so with a clear conscience... This is a regime that contravenes every single principle or value anyone of our politics believes in... So if the result of peace is Saddam staying in power, not disarmed, then I tell you there are consequences paid in blood for that decision too. But these victims will never be seen. They will never feature on our TV screens or inspire millions to take to the streets. But they will exist nonetheless. Ridding the world of Saddam would be an act of humanity. It is leaving him there that is in truth inhumane.[80]

Thus, Iraq is morally problematic because there is morality *on both sides* of the argument. Nonetheless, the morality of the decision is different to the reason for the decision. As already shown, the reason for the decision was to enforce the UN's will on WMD. In his speech to the House of Commons opening the debate on Iraq Blair emphasised this, saying that he 'never put our justification for action as regime change… But it is the reason, I say frankly, why if we do act we should do so with a clear conscience and a strong heart.'[81] Legality may supply the reason, but the ethical dimension, the reason we can be comfortable with the decision, arises from the responsibility we owe Iraqis. Just as there were other, not necessarily moral, reasons for invading Kosovo (the credibility of NATO) and Afghanistan (to prevent the operation of terrorist training camps), so WMD is a reason, but not the only one.

However, unlike in Kosovo, Sierra Leone and Afghanistan, regarding Iraq, it is acknowledged that there is an ethical argument for opposing the war. But where does this other morality come from? Crucially, it comes from the fact that enacting the responsibility to protect will inevitably mean that people are killed and injured. Acting responsibly and intervening to protect Iraqis will mean the death and injury of other Iraqis as well as invading troops. Literally, invading will mean both protecting and *attacking* Iraqis. Straw sums this up best. He notes in 2003 that if Britain has to invade, 'huge efforts will be made to ensure that the suffering of the Iraqi people is as limited as possible'.[82] Nonetheless, he says, we find ourselves in an 'eternal moral dilemma' because of the inevitable deaths of innocents.[83]

This eternal moral dilemma is brought about by the morality on both sides of the argument: that the responsibility to protect Iraqis is inevitably also a responsibility to attack and kill Iraqis. We are left to ponder why an eternal moral dilemma was absent from the representations of interventions in Kosovo, Sierra Leone and Afghanistan; why there was no concern shown, especially for the deaths of Sierra Leonians. Flesh and blood people who die as a result of the intervention simply do not exist in the Sierra Leone of British foreign policy. Yet, the Iraqi example, although it was marginalised because it was a difficult decision, can now be seen as central precisely because of the difficulty of the decision. It reveals the moral dilemma that *must* exist for each invasion.

Derrida analyses a situation where there is precisely such a dual responsibility in *The Gift of Death*. Noting the deep connection between the concept of responsibility and religion,[84] Derrida turns to the figure of Abraham, who unites all three 'religions of the book' (Judaism, Christianity, Islam). In Genesis 22, God orders Abraham: '[t]ake your son, your only son, Isaac, whom you love, and go to the region of Moriah. Sacrifice him there as a burnt offering on one of the mountains I will tell you about'. Abraham does this. Without asking any explanation from God, he binds his son on the altar and 'reached out his hand and took the knife to slay his son'. At this point, God steps in again, telling Abraham not to harm Isaac and that his faith was being tested.[85]

Questions of ethics and responsibility inevitably arise here. Did Abraham act responsibly? Did he make the responsible decision in preparing to kill Isaac? The reason this story is both scandalous and revealing in relation to responsibility in British foreign policy is that there is, as with Britain in Iraq, morality on both sides of Abraham's decision. Just like Blair and Straw, Abraham has two duties, not just one. If Abraham were only responsible to God, there would be no dilemma. Equally, if he only had a father's responsibility to protect his son Isaac, there would be no issue. But Abraham is absolutely responsible to both imperatives: to his God, the absolutely Other, upon whom he relies completely, but also to Isaac and his family, who he has a duty to protect. He cannot act absolutely responsibly towards both. The story is 'monstrous, outrageous, barely conceivable', nothing could be worse 'vis-à-vis love, humanity, the family, morality' and yet 'isn't this also the most common thing?' Isn't it what the 'most cursory examination of the concept of responsibility cannot fail to affirm?'[86] So, the revelation about responsibility affirmed by this story is simply that responsibility is paradoxical, riven with internal contradiction.

We can see the operation of this double moral claim, this dual responsibility, in the decision to invade Iraq (and with Iraq being exemplary, in all Britain's decisions to intervene). We can intervene to fulfil our 'responsibility to protect' certain others, but what about those who will be killed as a result of this intervention? What about our responsibility to protect them? But, if we act responsibly towards those others, what about those who we wanted to intervene to protect in the first place? Now we are acting irresponsibly towards them. For both Straw and Blair, despite its 'eternal' nature, this moral dilemma is swiftly resolved. Straw argues that for 'the sake of the Iraqi people… it is a challenge we must confront'.[87] Similarly, Blair in the long quotation earlier begins with the pained acknowledgement that the ethics of the Iraqi invasion are not straightforward. The case can be made either way. Ethical responsibility is owed on both sides, and 'consequences paid in blood' will be incurred on both. Yet, shortly after this observation, Blair asserts that one side of the argument is humane, and the other is, in truth, inhumane.[88]

The problem is that, in the claim that there is morality on both sides of the argument on Iraq, a crucial observation is made about the undecidable nature of ethical, responsible action. This observation then removes the very basis for Straw and Blair's resolution of that problem. The argument seems to be that an invasion will mean the death of US, British and Iraqi soldiers and civilians. Causing such death and danger would be morally wrong. But, equally, if Iraq is not invaded and Saddam not removed, he will continue to suppress and brutalise his people and WMD may be used by Iraq to destabilise the region or given to terrorists to attack Western democracies. Meanwhile for the Iraqi people, 'the darkness will close back over them again; and he [Saddam] will be free to take his revenge upon those who must wish him gone'.[89] This too would be morally wrong (and has 'consequences paid in blood'). But if both are morally wrong, no straightforward moral resolution is possible. There can be no straightforward 'responsibility to protect'.

To clarify, the point I am making is not that the invasion of Iraq was simply ethical. My argument is not, therefore, made in support of British foreign policy, nor of Blair's decision to invade Iraq. However, the more troubling aspect of the argument, its less palatable element, is that the invasion can also not be called merely unethical. The obstinate, uncomfortable position I advocate is that the invasion was both morally justified and unjustified, that it was ethical and unethical; it was both and neither at the same time. The ethics of the invasion, its responsibility, was caught in the eternal moral dilemma of morality itself, the dilemma of undecidability.

For Blair and Straw, the 'eternal moral dilemma' is, as has been shown, easily (and miraculously?) resolved. But this resolution cannot be of the order of responsibility, morality or ethics. As Derrida observes,

> I cannot respond to the call, the request, the obligation, or even the love of another without sacrificing the other other, the other others. *Every other (one) is every (bit) other [tout autre est tout autre]*, every one else is completely or wholly other. The simple concepts of alterity and of singularity constitute the concept of duty as much as that of responsibility. As a result, the concepts of responsibility, of decision, or of duty, are condemned a priori to paradox, scandal, and aporia.[90]

If '*[e]very other (one) is every (bit) other*' then there can be no reason for, as Straw and Blair do, resolving the dilemma in favour of one other or the other other. Any such resolution is problematic and, therefore, any assertion of a 'responsibility to protect' is, as Derrida observes, 'condemned a priori to paradox, scandal and aporia'.[91] This is precisely what makes the decision, as Straw himself affirms, an *eternal* moral dilemma. The moral of both stories (Abraham and Isaac and the invasion of Iraq) is morality itself: that morality must always be sacrificed to morality; responsibility to one other (Iraqi soldiers and civilians) must be sacrificed to our responsibility to other others (Western civilians, Iraqi dissidents and the Middle East region); ethical duty sacrificed to ethical duty. 'One must behave not only in an ethical or responsible manner, but in a nonethical, nonresponsible manner.'[92]

The crucial aspect of showing that the Iraq invasion is central to the responsibility to protect is that, unlike the other examples, the eternal moral dilemma is acknowledged as problematic. Previous interventions are represented as clear-cut, obvious, easy decisions. Yet, in fact, according to the British government's own reasoning, there is morality on both sides of each such decision. This illuminates the morality of responsibility, the responsibility of responsibility, as inherently undecidable.

Responsibility to save

Although 'humanitarian intervention' may have been *the* moral question of 1999–2003, the discourse shifted in 2004 to a focus on saving Africa as the major concern. Williams, therefore, observes that the 'UK's record on Africa became an important barometer of the depth of Labour's moralism'.[93] Although this shift was most easily marked from 2004, it began much earlier. As with many concerns in British foreign policy post-1997, Cook emphasised the issue long before Blair.[94] Similarly, Hain talked about 'a moral imperative' of supporting Africa in 1999.[95] Both Cook and Hain were suggesting that it was not only a moral imperative but also a matter of self interest, a theme Blair later adopted emphatically.

In November 2000, Blair hinted that Sierra Leone also demonstrated this different type of responsibility in British foreign policy. Britain, he asserted, must 'intervene, not excessively, but to do what we can to save African nations from barbarism and dictatorship and be proud of it'.[96] This section argues that such a 'responsibility to save' forms the second aspect of the way the British foreign policy text constructs its ethical dimension. The reference to 'African' nations, far from coincidental is integral to this responsibility.

Blair's 2001 party conference speech was described by political journalist Peter Riddell as highly 'moralistic', even 'messianic',[97] whereas according to Michael White, its 'sweep and moral fervour caught friend and foe off guard'.[98] In the most widely quoted section, Blair calls for the international community to act for the 'starving, the wretched, the dispossessed, the ignorant, those living in want and squalor' from Africa, to Gaza to Afghanistan.

> This is a moment to seize. The kaleidoscope has been shaken. The pieces are in flux. Soon they will settle again. Before they do, let us re-order this world around us. Today, humankind has the science and technology to destroy itself or to provide prosperity to all. Yet science can't make that choice for us. Only the moral power of a world acting as a community can.[99]

There is a responsibility to save and protect everyone, and this constitutes the 'moral power' of the world 'acting as a community'. However, in an earlier section of the speech, Blair called specific attention to Africa, using the famous lines: '[t]he state of Africa is a scar on the conscience of the world. But if the world as a community focused on it, we could heal it. And if we don't, it will become deeper and angrier'.[100] Here, the responsibility to save is a responsibility to heal, and the focus on Africa is clarified. As Blair claims in 2002, '[i]f Africa is a scar on the conscience of our world, the world has a duty to heal it, heal it we can and we must…'[101] The metaphor does not necessarily work (a scar is a natural result of the healing process, a sign that a wound has healed, rather than the opposite), but the point is clear: Africa is a standing affront to the ethics of the rest of the world, so it must be saved.

Regardless of these precursors, it was only in late 2004, and especially 2005, that British foreign policy began a concerted effort at presenting 'Africa' as a, or rather *the*, moral issue of concern. There are several possible reasons for this shift in ethical priorities: it could be seen as an effort to shift attention from the increasingly unpopular occupation of Iraq to a relatively uncontroversial 'ethical' issue; it also coincided with Britain holding the chair of the G8 and the EU Presidency simultaneously. In December 2004, Blair thus acknowledged that there is self interest in the desire to help Africa, but 'I also think it is a moral question'.[102]

In 2005, it became clear how Africa is presented as a moral issue. In line with the aforementioned argument, it is the *unnecessary* and *outrageous* death and suffering caused by *negligence* that marks it as such. Blair declares in a New Year's day *Economist* article, 'it can't be morally right, in a world growing more prosperous and healthier by the year, that one in six African children still die before their fifth birthday...'[103] Comparing it with the Asian tsunami, which happened just days before, Blair states that the difference is in the *preventability* of what is happening in Africa. Asked in a press conference whether it is a battle between good and evil in Africa, he replies that 'it is evil that you have preventable death on such a scale in Africa... That is an evil and what would be good is to do something about it'.[104]

It is crucial that, unlike the natural disaster in Asia, the death and suffering in Africa is preventable; indeed, this is what makes it a moral and political issue. Such a reading of the situation is presented as perfectly evident to anyone. As Blair observes, 'it barely needs saying, but it cannot be morally right that so many people die when their deaths could be prevented. That I think is obvious and we would all share that'.[105] This is, of course, not necessarily obvious. Although the tsunami itself was not preventable, many of the deaths were. For example, investment in an early warning system, better structural design of buildings, a more efficiently organised aid operation to outlying areas and education of coastal communities in survival techniques are just some of the options that could have prevented more deaths – now and in the future.[106]

Straw reinforced this representation of their preventability making African deaths a moral issue. Quoting statistics on the suffering of Africans and Africa's economic regression, Straw claims '[t]hat situation is a moral affront to us all'.[107] Lord Triesman, the newly appointed Minister for Africa (as of May 2005), claimed in the Tanzanian Parliament that 'it is a moral imperative that the world act now' in relation to Africa.[108] Crucially, the responsibility to save Africa no longer signifies *a* moral issue, but, as Blair says, there is 'no doubt at all that the biggest moral cause is Africa in the world today'.[109] In 2006, 'Africa is probably *the* great moral cause of our time'.[110] And why? '[B]ecause of the numbers of people who die, millions of people who die unnecessarily through conflict, or famine, or disease'.[111] So, just as the responsibility to protect civilians was a moral issue, and the most important foreign policy question from 1999–2003, the 'responsibility to save' Africa is *the* great moral cause of the time, or, at least from late 2004 onwards, in British foreign policy. And, in a similar fashion, the responsibility to save fits neatly within the foreign policy framework of subjectivity/objectivity and the doctrine of international community.

Development of the 'responsibility to save'

New Labour's foreign policy towards Africa is described as a departure from the old relationship. Although the concentration on the 'responsibility to save' Africa may have been present in the British foreign policy discourse before 2002, the precise contours of this policy were not fully worked through. By 2002, the operative word, emphasised over and again in the relationship to Africa, is *partnership*. Blair chose a visit to Africa in February 2002 to set this out in relation to Britain's policy of supporting the New Partnership for Africa's Development (NEPAD), an African-based initiative to promote African solutions to problems of underdevelopment, disease and poverty. Speaking to the Ghanaian Parliament, Blair talks about the need for partnership in development. This involves a 'fundamental shift in our approach to aid', not 'a hand-out but aid as a hand-up', not to,

> ...create dependence but to create sustainable independence, so that the relationship between the developed and the developing world is not one of donor and passive recipient but one of equal partners in building prosperity for all. This is aid as investment in our collective economic and political security.[112]

The problem with the old relationship appears to be that it aims to, or certainly has the effect of, creating dependence and passivity. In contrast, Blair's vision, through the support of NEPAD, is that of 'globalisation driven by a global ethic'.[113] Setting out his agenda for the G8, which Britain was chairing in 2005, Blair says that the '[t]he old donor/recipient relationship is patronising and unworkable'.[114] Old enactments of the responsibility to save are thus condemned as condescending and unethical. The new partnership ethical drive is essentially one of treating Africa as 'equal partners' to the 'developed world'.[115]

The responsibility to save is also emphasised as enacting a relationship of equality and partnership in 2004, when Blair announced his Commission for Africa. The Commission emerges from what Blair calls, 'the need to tackle the African problem as a whole'.[116] An initiative arising from the British Government, Blair describes it in a speech to the African Union (AU) as a commission of 17 people drawn from government, civil society and the business community in Africa and the developed world, to 'produce a comprehensive plan' for Africa.[117] This plan, published in 2005, was to be focused on 'how the international community can support African development in partnership together'. At the 'core' of this plan then is the 'real partnership between Africa and the developed world'.[118] Blair observed in June 2005 that the purpose of the plan for Africa 'is to try and put all the different aspects of the problem of Africa, not just that of aid and debt, but also that of governance and conflict to put all those items together in a comprehensive plan'.[119] The comprehensive nature of the plan means that

'Africa' is brought within the foreign policy remit, rather than just that of development.

In the concepts of 'equality' and 'partnership,' we can also see how Britain's representation of its ethical dimension to foreign policy, as a responsibility to save Africa, is drawn into the question of the rights and responsibilities of international community. Chapter 2 underlined that to be considered part of the international community one had to be capable of accepting one's responsibility. Although '[s]tates have the right to non-interference in their internal affairs', the rights of a subject, 'they also have responsibilities, towards their own people, and towards the international community and their international engagements'.[120] If a state ignores, neglects or is incapable of fulfilling these responsibilities, 'the international community may need to intervene'.[121] Literally, to be treated as a subject of international affairs, and allowed the rights that go with that, one has to accept and deal with one's responsibilities.

In June 2002, Blair notes that their new 'partnership' also has the character of a 'bargain': it is not a handout but rather a 'deal', with rights and responsibilities. The responsibility of the developed world to support NEPAD financially is 'dependent on African countries fulfilling their side of the bargain'.[122] Their side is outlined as an agreement to 'a whole series of initiatives on the rule of law, on proper commercial and legal systems, on rooting out corruption, on respect for democratic rights, and the processes of democracy'.[123] This is similarly the case with the Commission for Africa. In a joint press conference with George Bush in June 2005, Blair says that the African agenda is 'not a something for nothing deal', but rather a 'two-way commitment' in which 'we' (Britain and America, presumably) require commitments on governance against corruption and favouring democracy and the rule of law.[124]

NEPAD and the Commission, the entire 'responsibility to save' Africa, are all brought under the rubric of the doctrine of international community. It is a foreign policy designed to fundamentally move the relationship between Africa and the developed world onto a basis of the rights and responsibilities of subjects, of *equal partners*. As such, it replaces an unethical policy with an ethical one. 'Africa should not be seen as a victim but as a partner... This is about what we can do together, as equals, with mutual respect...'[125] The shift is represented as a movement away from Africa as a patronised, dependent, passive and unequal victim; an object of British foreign policy; a group of failing states incapable of responsibility and thus subjectivity. Now it is treated as a partner, an equal, a subject capable of fulfilling its responsibilities and being active participants in the international community.

Objectification of 'Africa': Supplementing partnership

Given the equality of the partnership espoused by British foreign policy, it may appear surprising that I have chosen to designate this a 'responsibility to save'. Would not a 'responsibility to partnership', a 'responsibility to bargain' or a 'responsibility to equality' be more appropriate? These are perhaps more descriptively accurate as well as having the advantage of not implying inequality. After all, someone who needs saving literally *needs* the one who saves. This is acknowledged by Blair, who, as observed earlier, dismisses the old relationship between Britain and Africa as passive, disrespectful, dependent and patronising.

There is an unexamined power relationship in operation here similar to that of Rosenau's 'penetrated political system'[126] discussed in Chapter 1: a state who saves others is seen as having an abundance of something a state who is saved lacks. If Britain, as Blair claims, 'save[s] African nations from barbarism and dictatorship,'[127] it is because Britain has an abundance of what Sierra Leone lacks: well-trained security forces, established rule of law, limited corruption, economic prosperity, for instance. In fact, the subtitle of 'responsibility to save' is appropriate and precisely for this reason. As Doty argues, debates and narratives surrounding foreign aid, democracy and human rights promotion in Africa are 'instances in which we can gain significant insight into the representational practices that inform contemporary encounters between the North and the South'.[128] In fact, the responsibility enacted and espoused towards Africa shows specifically the unequal relationship which Britain is said to be avoiding with its 'new' partnership. Effectively 'Africa', while *declared* an equal subject, is *described* as a passive, unequal, homogenous object of British foreign policy.

This becomes clearer when examining the connection between Britain's two main 'Africa' policies: the support for NEPAD, on the one hand, and the Commission for Africa's comprehensive plan on the other. During a revealing interview in South Africa, Blair is asked about this relationship. The interviewer notes that many people saw Britain's establishment of the Commission as 'being quite arrogant because there was already a plan – called NEPAD – which was set up by Africans, for Africans'.[129] Why then, 'the need for another plan, which was spear-headed by Britain?'[130] Blair replies that this was far from arrogant,

> ...because I mean the NEPAD process, which I was also heavily involved in, and obviously President Mbeki was the main mover in it, the whole purpose of that was to see what Africa could do for its own development. But I think everybody recognises, and indeed this is how our conversation began, that the outside world also has a responsibility and obligation to act... So I think you need the combination of the developed and the developing world working together.[131]

The relationship between the two then seems to be that NEPAD was Africa's effort at a solution, while the Commission was the *developed* world's comprehensive plan. The explanations given by junior ministers such as Ian Pearson and Lord Triesman (Minister for Africa) are even more revealing.

While touting 2005 as the 'Year for Africa' in Japan, Foreign Office minister Ian Pearson argued that African governments 'must take the lead in Africa's development, and they are' through NEPAD.[132] He describes this as 'their [progressive African leaders'] own blueprint for tackling the continent's problems'.[133] However, the role of the Commission is 'that Africa cannot on its own achieve the take-off point in development. It needs our help – in terms of trade access, Overseas Development Aid, debt relief and investment…'[134] Lord Triesman repeats this, again in June 2005: '[t]he Commission argues – and we agree – that Africa cannot, on its own, achieve the take-off point in development'.[135]

In Derridean terms, we can see the Commission operating as a 'supplement' to NEPAD; the British plan supplementing the 'African'. Derrida's conception of the 'supplement,' as outlined in Chapter 2, contains two meanings.[136] First, it is an insignificant and inessential extra, a surplus to what was already complete in and of itself. Thus, the Commission is merely a surplus to NEPAD, an ultimately useless addition to the African plan that was complete in and of itself. In 2002, Britain's foreign policy of supporting NEPAD, supporting progressive African leadership in finding solutions to 'Africa's' problems, was enough. It was fulfilling a responsibility to save by a genuine partnership.[137] It was sufficient to Africa's needs while being an ethical, non-patronising way of helping an equal. The additional setting up of the Commission in 2005 was unnecessary.

Second, however, the very possibility of this surplus suggests that which is supplemented is incomplete. Otherwise, the addition of a supplement is futile. Such a 'supplement supplements. It adds only to replace. It intervenes or insinuates itself in-the-place-of.'[138] Thus, at the very beginning of Blair's 'Year of Africa'[139] (2005), the support of NEPAD is no longer sufficient. In his New Year *Economist* article, Blair declares that '[t]ruly a *new* partnership is required'.[140] The partnership involved in NEPAD, it seems, was not enough. This is why the Commission was set up: to produce a *truly* comprehensive plan. As Blair observes, 'we put together that comprehensive plan for Africa and it is the only thing that will give the continent a hope'.[141] If the Commission will produce a fully comprehensive plan four years after NEPAD, then NEPAD *must have been deficient*. It must have lacked something or been incomplete in some way. It was not enough for Africa to 'achieve the take-off point' in development.[142] 'Africa' needed 'us' (variously conceived as Blair, Britain, the developed world or the international community) to bring hope in a comprehensive plan of true partnership. Quite literally, the Commission adds 'only to replace' NEPAD. It replaces the deficient, lacking, incomplete African effort with British completeness, plenitude and abundance.

Derrida's reading of Rousseau in *Of Grammatology* makes the distinction between what Rousseau 'declares' (what he wishes to say) and what he 'describes' (what his discourse ends up saying, what effect it produces contrary to intention).[143] Thus, we can say that, as observed earlier, British foreign policy declares African nations to be subjects, to be 'equals' in a 'partnership', capable of accepting their responsibilities as members of the international community. While this is declared, however, what is described works against this. Africa is described as precisely the opposite, as an object, incapable of accepting responsibility, lacking a comprehensive plan, and incapable of coping alone. NEPAD requires supplementation by the Commission. Although British foreign policy declares a 'responsibility to partnership' between equals, a 'bargain' or a 'deal', it describes an unequal, patronising and morally problematic 'responsibility to save'.

Of course, to a certain extent, we do not even need the logic of deconstructive supplementarity to reveal how British foreign policy makes 'Africa' into an object. 'Africa' is simply treated as a homogeneous lump from the beginning of the period of foreign policy under study. In all the speeches mentioned earlier, it is not specific problematic nations of Africa (such as the Sudan and the DRC, for example), or even 'certain African states' that are being talked of, but simply 'Africa'. Blair's speech to the AU announcing his Commission is entitled 'Speech on Africa'. This is ironic given that a stated aim of the Commission was to 'draw attention to Africa's diversity of cultures'.[144]

Such a gesture of concealing difference also hides the fact that saving each and every African state or individual would be impossible.[145] Revealing difference would necessitate choice and decision as to which African state should be saved. In turn, this would mean that one responsibility (to Algeria, Burundi, the Central African Republic, Côte d'Ivoire, the DRC and Somalia, which were all suffering significant turbulence at the time but were largely ignored)[146] would have to be sacrificed to another (Sierra Leone), just as in the responsibility to protect. Treating 'Africa' as a homogenous, singular entity deceptively suggests that no such choice, or ir-responsibility, is required.

In this way, 'Africa' as a whole is represented as an object, in contrast to 'Asia', 'South America', 'North America' or other land masses, that would never merit such undifferentiated treatment. At this point, it would be possible to produce statistics that show how internally diverse Africa truly is and how there is no 'problem of Africa' as Blair continually declares.[147] However, this is the not the critique currently undertaken. Rather than bringing in other discourses, a close examination of the British foreign policy text illustrates how the discourse undermines itself.

Of greater importance, in this sense, is the way that Blair's 'Speech on Africa' acknowledges the status of 'Africa' within British foreign policy. Declaring 2005 a year of decision for Africa, Blair argues that a comprehensive plan finally exists, having 'at its core a real partnership between Africa and the developed world'.[148] The price of failure, he says, is immense. 'The prize for success would be an Africa standing proud in its own right in the international community.'[149] The important thing to note is how this supports the logic of the supplement regarding NEPAD and the Commission for Africa. The aim, the goal, the prize is Africa 'standing proud in its own right in the international community' – implicitly, it currently cannot do so. 'Africa' (or certainly African nations) is either not considered part of the international community, because it cannot fulfil the responsibilities of a subject, or is seen as within the international community, but not 'proud[ly]' so, nor 'in its own right'. If it can be seen as within the international community, it is only there because of Britain's magnanimous responsibility to save. It is acknowledged that Africa, and NEPAD, require Britain, and the Commission, to survive and eventually become true subjects.

Pity: Deconstructing the responsibility to save

With the supplementation of NEPAD by the Commission, of African efforts with British, we can see that the ethics of a responsibility to save appear stuck in the reversal phase of deconstruction. The responsibility to save rather than being a moral, ethical principle is revealed to be precisely immoral and unethical. However, things are not so simple. If we look at this 'responsibility to save' as primarily a matter of pity, we can see that, once again, responsibility deconstructs within the British foreign policy text. The 'responsibility to save' is always already both moral and immoral, responsible and irresponsible action.

As was discussed at the beginning of this chapter, obligation and responsibility in British foreign policy primarily arises from preventable and outrageous human suffering and death. Blair talks about making those suffering from Africa, to Gaza, to Afghanistan 'our cause'.[150] Witnessing this kind of 'human tragedy' makes us 'obliged to accept moral responsibility,' according to Cook.[151] In this representation, what moves us to this obligation is the fact that, through witnessing it, we essentially *suffer with* those that undergo such human tragedy. Its very preventability and outrageousness makes them that witness it suffer as well. This sensation of sorrow at another's suffering, of suffering with them, is the very definition of the word 'compassion', coming from the Latin *compati*, meaning 'suffer with'.[152] What is described then, without being declared explicitly, is a responsibility to save arising from compassion in the face human suffering.

Compassion seems an unambiguously ethical basis for responsibility. Yet, we are already alerted to its unethical aspect in the discursive treatment of Africa examined earlier, and we can trace this through the fact that compassion is merely one designation of the word 'pity'. 'Pity' comes from the Latin, *pietas,* via the Old French *pite* meaning a feeling of 'compassion' at the suffering of others.[153] The language of compassion is also necessarily a language of pity. Through pity 'you want, if possible – and there is no more insane "if possible" – *to abolish suffering*'.[154] But compassion is not the only aspect of 'pity'. We can also see a more unpalatable facet, that noted by Nietzsche, regarding its irrevocable link with 'contempt'. When seen as both a matter of compassion *and* contempt, it is easier to make sense of an Africa apparently marked by a 'lack' which requires supplementation.

Nietzsche claims that pity is 'felt as a sign of contempt because one has clearly ceased to be an object of *fear* as soon as one is pitied'.[155] In *Daybreak*, he expands somewhat, saying that pity is as good as contempt because we get no enjoyment from seeing a 'contemptible creature suffer', but to see an enemy, who is your equal, suffer is an 'enjoyment of enjoyments'.[156] This is because you admire your enemy; to see him suffer is to increase your respect for his resilience. This respect, because he is your enemy, is also a form of fear. To show pity is to show that you do not see the person as capable of handling the pain, thus you do not fear him, indeed that you must save him because he is incapable of helping himself. Pity is an acknowledgement of a person's incapacity and lack and, therefore, deeply humiliating for the person pitied. To pity a person is to see him or her as incapable where you are capable, as beneath you. In the terms used in the current discussion, to pity is to view as an object who is done-to, rather than a subject who does. To pity is to view with *contempt*.

This brings us back to the discussion of subjects and objects. Here, the African object is pitied, meaning both that it is viewed with compassion and contempt. Both of these arise from its status as an object, its lack and incapacity for responsibility. However, as I revealed in Chapter 2, this representation is destabilised by the lack which is also at the heart of each and every subject. Rather than being completely successful and capable, the state subject (such as Britain) at every point fails to achieve full presence through a complete guarantee of security. The subject is also always already incapable, already lacking. It is always becoming-object, just as the object is in the process of becoming-subject. Pity, as compassion and contempt, then, is not just felt for the African other, but also for the self. Hence, Nietzsche observes that '[w]here pity is preached today' you will hear the 'genuine sound of *self-contempt*'.[157]

In this way, the possibility of morally saving 'Africans' is undermined by its necessary corollary: to do so is to objectify, patronise and treat 'Africa' with contempt; it is also to treat the self with contempt. This is illustrated by the treatment of 'Africa' as a homogeneous problem, and African efforts at development (NEPAD) being insufficient and requiring British supplementation (the Commission for Africa). The responsibility to save, like the responsibility to protect, reveals both a moral responsibility to help and suffer with one's fellow man but, equally necessarily, an immoral, irresponsible contempt. The responsibility to 'intervene... to do what we can to save African nations from barbarism and dictatorship'[158] both seeks to bring African nations into the international community as subjects capable of accepting responsibilities ('[t]he prize for success would be an Africa standing proud in its own right in the international community'),[159] and reproduces their patronised 'object-hood', their status as a 'scar' to be healed by the developed world ('[i]f Africa is a scar on the conscience of our world, the world has a duty to heal it, heal it we can and we must...')[160] The 'responsibility to save' cannot be simply either responsible or irresponsible, ethical or unethical. It can only ever be both and neither at the same time, undecidable as to its true nature.

It is now clear that neither the taking of responsibility nor its enactment can be stabilised in an ethical representation. However, the construction of EU subjectivity and the way it represents its responsibility are different in key respects to that of the British text. Responsibility for the EU, as a 'family' and a 'home', is primarily exercised as hospitality. In the next chapter, I turn to look at whether the effects of an unstable 'EU' subjectivity are more secure than those of the 'British'; whether an EU understanding of ethical foreign policy contains greater possibility for success.

4   Hospitality

Welcoming the other in EU foreign policy

Hospitality is not a notion that is of obvious importance in a first glance at international relations (IR) or international political theory and has never been a focus of foreign policy analysis (FPA). This is partly because it is a liminal concept, existing on the border between the 'domestic' and 'international' but disturbing the difference between the two. Yet, if we look more closely at the structure of IR theory, we can see that it is in fact fundamental.[1] In his collection of essays, *Inside/Outside*, R. B. J. Walker looks at how IR theory came to be divided from political theory. In the 'pre-modern' period, he claims that the identity of Christian universalism in Europe predominated over the differences caused by state particularism. Sameness was given greater stress than difference. In the modern period, however, the opposite came to be the case as Christian identity gave way to state differences, 'with difference here becoming a matter of absolute exclusions'.[2] Universalism could, from then on, only be pursued *within* the state; the international arena was dominated by difference and particularlisms.

This was how a spatial separation came to be constructed between the inside and outside of the state. Yet, there was also a crucial temporal division: within the state, ethical goods such as political community and justice were the natural pursuit of a citizenry under a sovereign authority; outside, the 'lack of community can be taken to imply the impossibility of history as a progressive teleology, and thus the possibility merely of recurrence and repetition'.[3] This then produced the separation between *political* theory inside the state, and mere *international relations* outside. A proper ethical and political community was understood to be possible only within the state; outside, these goals were negated or deferred.[4]

As a liminal concept that works on the border of the way that traditional IR has been thought, hospitality still allows the enactment of ethics as it welcomes the outside into the inside. Meanwhile, hospitality is of immediate and obvious importance to international political theory as a sub-discipline that is defined by contesting and cross-examining the separation between inside and outside.[5] However, when hospitality is examined in IR, such as in a confrontation with Kant,[6] the emphasis is placed on granting hospitality to *individuals*, especially, the refugee.[7] Critics of this Kantian cosmopolitanism generally follow this line that limits hospitality to individuals.[8] In the European Union (EU) foreign policy text, however, the focus is upon welcoming in nation-states. In broader terms than Kant or many of his followers allow,[9] we can see hospitality as simply an openness to the other, the stranger, who comes from outside and is received into our home.

There are three EU foreign policies examined in this chapter, all of which are based, to varying degrees, on such a hospitable openness to the other. First, there is the cornerstone of EU foreign policy during this period: enlargement.[10] This is represented as the most simply hospitable foreign policy, literally a welcoming of other countries into the EU home. Second, there is the policy towards the Balkans, which develops from an offer of 'virtual membership' into a matter of conditional hospitality through enlargement. Finally, there is the far more circumscribed hospitality of the European Neighbourhood Policy (ENP). This is represented as friendly and generous, while not *fully* welcoming the other into the EU. These policies deconstruct to show that the EU can only ever be welcoming and unwelcoming, ethical and unethical toward the other.

However, first, a brief discussion of the ethical in EU foreign policy and its basis in a responsibility of proximity is necessary. This responsibility sees its main enactment in the concept of hospitality, which, like any notion of hospitality, is based on the EU as a 'home' or 'family'. The familial imaginary of the EU is both *geographical* (bounded by the 15, and by 2004, the 25 member states' borders) and *moral* (based on a range of ethical and political values seen as 'European'). Welcoming others into this family home can only be the height of ethical foreign policy for the EU. As Patten put it: '[w]hat better way could there have been of treating a neighbour than inviting them into our home?'[11]

Responsibility, hospitality and the 'European home'

There is much overlap between how the EU regards the ethical in foreign policy and the British discourse. Prodi claims that what distinguishes Europeans is their 'sense of responsibility',[12] and this stress is placed on a responsibility to protect and save human life. In the most coherent and extensive statement of the ethical in EU foreign policy, Solana notes that humanitarian intervention is a 'modern way to describe a very ancient practice. To help out one's fellow human being in a situation of distress'.[13] This 'simple gesture' is first of all connected to the European welfare state by Solana, but he then expands this beyond both nation-state and EU borders:

> However, European solidarity goes far beyond the frontiers of the European Union... *Catastrophes happen.* Some we put down to 'natural causes'; others we blame on the darker side of human nature – be it embodied in a person or a regime... the consequences are the same: people suffering, lives at risk... *The essence of humanitarian relief is the*

job of saving lives and of helping the suffering... Bringing relief is always worth it – and almost at whatever cost when human lives are at stake. But even an intrinsically ethical action must be carried out according to rules and principles, and cannot be standard free.[14]

He acknowledges that such catastrophes have been happening since before the end of the cold war, and all that has changed since then is that we see more of it. But this 'does not alter the enormous responsibility we have in the face of those tragedies'. It would, he declares, 'be morally untenable, sometimes unthinkable, to sit idle, without reacting to such human misery and distress. Therefore we are compelled to act'.[15]

Although there are similarities, the key difference between the British and EU representations of ethical responsibility is the stress placed upon proximity. In British foreign policy, there is no distinction made between the responsibility for those close to us and those far away[16]; the starving, wretched and dispossessed 'from the deserts of Northern Africa to the slums of Gaza, to the mountain ranges of Afghanistan: they too are our cause'.[17] In contrast, Patten argued in 2000 that the Common Foreign and Security Policy (CFSP) is crucial in ensuring that the EU is able 'to shoulder its share of global responsibilities, beginning – but not ending – with its own backyard'.[18] Responsibility, wherever it may end, begins with those closest to the EU.

Similarly, reflecting on a year in office, Solana states that the Balkans have been the top priority for EU foreign policy, while its second priority is the Mediterranean as, 'like the Balkans, this region is on our doorstep'.[19] Such prioritisations are justified by proximity over and over again.[20] Enlargement gives the EU even more responsibilities, but once again this is 'especially as regards our immediate neighbours'.[21] Speaking to the European Parliament, Prodi declares that 'we assume a clear responsibility in the region... But our responsibilities stretch beyond our region'.[22] Nonetheless, it is proximity that brings a *clear* responsibility.

Solana appears deeply uneasy when pushed on the EU's *wider* responsibility in 2003. In an interview with *Die Zeit* about the European Security and Defence Policy (ESDP) operation to protect key facilities in the Ituri region of the Congo, he is asked what the 'European interest' in the Congo is. Solana states that while the EU has an interest in regional stability, it 'furthermore bear[s] a responsibility in the face of human suffering. We must not simply shut our eyes to it'.[23] Yet, the full extent of this responsibility is left unclear. Asked if it extends to the whole of Africa, the response is, '[n]o, of course not. We are not the Africa Corps'.[24] A follow-up question involves whether this responsibility extends to Africa today, Latin America tomorrow and 'the following day the rest of the world?'. Once again, the response is ambiguous and uneasy. 'No. We do not feel called upon to become a global police force. But we do bear a responsibility for the world, whether we like it or not'.[25] While the responsibility owed to the Mediterranean region and the Balkans is seen as natural, clear and obvious, the question of wider responsibility is answered equivocally at best.

Patten ties this wider responsibility in with the development of the EU; yet, he always ends up with the prioritisation of proximity. In a speech on the EU's relations with Latin America, he notes that as 'Europe develops further, it will have to take ever more account of its global responsibilities and challenges'. With increasing globalisation, it is 'no longer possible to shut out the rest of the world'. However, he immediately follows this by ignoring Latin America: 'Europe is bound to give a very high priority to relations with its closest neighbours'.[26]

The fact that the EU does not really have a strong ethical or responsible representation of its foreign policy towards the *far* abroad, the *foreign* foreign (rather than the 'European' foreign) is illustrated by the triviality accorded to it in Patten's memoirs. 'As for other countries and continents, it would be wearisome to tour the world, describing visits here, there and everywhere, recounting small victories and whitewashing small defeats'.[27] As a speech writer, he used to call such speeches a *tour d'horizon* but now prefers Denis Healey's term – 'a "tour de gloss"'.[28] Thus, there is uncertainty regarding the EU's wider responsibility. Although the EU does bear a responsibility 'for the world, whether we like it or not',[29] it is not yet fully capable of accepting it. It appears that the EU lacks confidence in its status as a truly global subject. The concentration remains on the EU as a regional actor, with primarily regional responsibilities.

Hospitality and the common European home

The priority for the EU's ethical foreign policy is its 'neighbours' and those on its 'doorstep', and thus enacting this responsibility is represented as an offering of hospitality. The specific policies that I examine come together in the idea of the European family/home, and the EU foreign policy discourse during 1999–2004 is replete with hospitable metaphors of families and homes. It is important to examine how the 'architecture' of this home is represented, as it forms the basis for the way the EU sees itself and how it enacts its hospitality.

The 'home' is, of course, crucial to any idea of hospitality. Its significance is outlined by Derrida in an interview given in 1993 (though published in English only in 2003). Although the International relations context of the interview, the massacres and ethnic cleansing of the Bosnian conflict, reveals that the concept of a national home can be used in an insidious way to violently exclude and kill others, Derrida nonetheless defended the 'home'. This is because the 'unconditional desire [for the home], which is impossible to renounce' also 'should not be renounced', for without the home, 'there is no door nor any hospitality'.[30] The singularity of the home should not be given up because, while it can be a violent 'closedness', it is also the very 'condition of openness, of hospitality and of the door'.[31]

On a purely practical level, the possibility of my welcoming someone, of offering hospitality, is predicated on my having a home to welcome them into. Reflecting upon hospitality demands, or presupposes as Derrida says elsewhere, 'the possibility of a rigorous delimitation of thresholds or frontiers',[32] a separation from otherness.[33] A home must not only be separated and closed but also, as we shall see in relation to the EU, have windows and doors, such that the other can be welcomed in. For hospitality to be possible, there must be an inviolable home, but that home must be constituted by closure as the very possibility of openness. And for Derrida, 'hospitality' in this sense is as close as one can get to a synonym for ethics.

> Insofar as it has to do with the *ethos*, that is, the residence, one's home, the familiar place of dwelling, inasmuch as it is a manner of being there, the manner in which we relate to ourselves and to others, to others as our own or as foreigners, ethics is hospitality; ethics is so thoroughly coextensive with the experience of hospitality.[34]

The 'home' is crucial to the very possibility of both hospitality and ethics. Without it, we have nothing to welcome the other into, nothing to give the other.

Although the European 'home' becomes central, it is prefigured in the EU text by the connected metaphor of 'family'. During one of his first speeches as President of the EU Commission in October 1999, Prodi declares the ambition involved in the enlargement project: 'for the first time in history we are unifying Europe! We are bringing together not only countries but, above all, peoples into a new and much larger European family'.[35] In an interesting narrative of the CFSP, Patten notes how the EU has acted to encourage and support candidate countries in their process of reform towards becoming free-market democracies. It has worked at 'smothering flash points', teaching these countries tolerance of criticism and diversity.[36] 'In short', he says, the aim has been to help 'these countries become normal, and take their rightful place in the family of European nations'.[37]

In 2002, Prodi adds the 'home' to his metaphor of the family, suggesting that the policies of enlargement and cooperation with neighbouring countries 'will lead to a new architecture for the whole continent. A new structure for our common European home'.[38] Patten had already championed this spatial imagery early in 2000. Speaking to the Foreign Affairs and Legal Committees of the Albanian Parliament, he praised Albania's democratic reform and hospitality to Kosovan refugees. 'In short, you have returned to the European family and you look, rightly, to the rest of Europe to welcome you home… The challenge is to maintain these efforts, to stay on the right road – the road to Europe'.[39] There is clearly a distinction being made here between the European *family*, which Albania has returned to through its democratic reform and hospitality, and a European *home*, which Albania has not yet reached. Rather, it is on the *road* towards that home.

This 'road to Europe' will take up great prominence in the discussion of EU policy towards the Balkans later, but other spatial metaphors are also used. Patten characterises EU policy towards the Balkans as 'about building peace and security, not just in our backyard but in our front yard too'.[40] The difference is not quite clear, but he adds that its importance is because peace and security is 'an integral part of our European common home'.[41] Perhaps here there is an indication that the Balkans are potentially part of the common home but are currently its front or backyard. This confusion is a constituent part of the EU's ambiguous representation of the Balkans: occasionally, they are treated as part of the European family, though not yet the home, whereas at other times, they are simply a neighbouring region, along with Russia and the 'Mediterranean' – a term largely designating the Middle East.[42] However, by the end of 2002, the Balkans are being sent a 'clear message' of hospitality by Prodi, who says that 'the EU's door is open and we hope to invite them in as soon as possible'.[43] Solana further emphasises this hospitality, telling Bosnians that if they chose reform, 'the door of Europe is open to you'.[44] Similarly, though they are not yet being invited in, he tells Serbians that their 'new democratic leadership opened the door for Serbia to join the European mainstream'.[45]

The potential resolution of the Balkans' liminal status illustrates how the European family home, as well as having a road that leads to its door, also has a neighbourhood, which is sometimes described as a backyard. These countries, including 'our future eastern neighbours and the whole Mediterranean area', are described as a 'ring of friends… from Morocco to Russia to the Black Sea'.[46] This representation of such countries as 'neighbours' and 'friends' of the EU is repeated over and over again in the speeches of Prodi from 2003 onwards.[47] It is significant that, first, the spatial metaphor designates them as *neighbours* to the European *home* – i.e. not within the home, but outside – and, second, the relationship metaphor describes them as *friends* to the European *family* – i.e. not part of the family, but close to it.

Although there is an evident geographical element to who is 'in' the EU family home, who is on the road to it and who is consigned to the backyard/neighbourhood, there is also an ethical element. As Derrida observes, hospitality is about ethics as the *ethos*, as 'the residence, one's home, the familiar place of dwelling, inasmuch as it is a matter of being there, the manner in which we relate to ourselves and to others'.[48] The 'home' or residence constitutes us, forms our subjectivity. For the EU, this ethos, this 'home', is not just about geography, but also about European values and ethics. In setting out Europe's role in a future system of world governance, Prodi argues in March 2000 that any such system must be based on 'shared values such as justice and fair play, sustainability and subsidiarity, transparency and democratic accountability'.[49] Why should these specific values be at the heart of the EU's foreign policy? Because they are part of the EU's ethos, part of what makes the EU the EU, a constitutive element of the common European home.

The European Union already enshrines and promotes precisely those values. They are a part of Europe's distinctive political and ethical heritage, and they reflect in large measure our humanist tradition and the moral legacy of the three Mediterranean faiths. That is why I want Europe to be at the forefront of global progress, shaping the world of tomorrow... It also means making progress on enlargement, unifying our continent around ethical and political values and influencing our neighbours to share those values.[50]

Building on this speech a week later, Prodi argues that 'social and ethical values such as tolerance, inclusiveness, social justice and respect for other cultures... are what give Europe its sense of corporate identity'.[51]

These ethical and political values are explicitly associated with the European family and the enlargement policy of the EU. Prodi claims that the reconstitution of the 'extended family of European nations and, above all, peoples' is not about homogenisation but about 'bringing together diverse people who are heirs to a common civilisation'.[52] The peoples in this family share 'unchanging fundamental values such as democracy, respect for human rights, the protection of minorities and the rules of law. Values that give us unity in our diversity'.[53] These 'values' are, says Solana, what the EU's foreign policy is about. The EU, he claims, is 'founded on the values of tolerance, democracy and respect for human rights... Our foreign policy should be nothing less than the projection of those values'.[54] Similarly, in the wake of what he calls the 'crisis' of the EU's inability to agree a common position on the war in Iraq, Prodi dismisses the possibility of a return to nineteenth century balance-of-power politics. '[I]t would be contrary to the very nature of the Union, which is based on dialogue, solidarity, multilateralism and an ethical dimension to politics'.[55]

Enlargement, the Balkans and the two laws of hospitality

For the EU, although there is a responsibility to protect and save human life, the greatest ethical obligation is owed to those closest to it in geographical (and moral value) terms. This responsibility of proximity is exercised through hospitality while the concept of the 'common European home' as a community of political and ethical values defines the subjectivity of the EU and controls which others can be welcomed inside. However, the simplicity of this hospitality is problematised by examining two EU foreign policies with an ethical, hospitable dimension: the enlargement toward 10 Central and Eastern European countries completed in 2004 and the potential enlargement toward the Balkans.

Enlargement could be considered problematic as a 'foreign' policy. After all, Patten himself observes that 'the EU was in a sense created as an alternative to foreign policy'.[56] Then, to bring other peoples and nations into the EU could be seen as an ending of foreign policy rather than a tool of it.

Nonetheless, enlargement is represented by the EU as very much a foreign policy. Indeed, Patten claims in 2002 that 'in Central and Eastern Europe, we are using the prospect of EU membership as a specific and successful tool of foreign policy'.[57] Later, he even describes it as 'the most successful foreign policy pursued by Europe'.[58]

This highly successful policy is also represented in moral terms because it is about welcoming others into the EU family of ethical and political values. It is, as Prodi puts it, a matter of the 'Slavonic world... rejoining the common European family'.[59] This, for Solana, makes enlargement, a political, economic and 'moral imperative'.[60] The EU, he says elsewhere, has 'a political and moral responsibility' to support these countries seeking to enter the EU.[61] Patten, in 2000, calls the enlargement 'morally right'[62] and emphasises the democratic nature of the ethical family home the countries of Central and Eastern Europe are being welcomed into.

> Enlargement is a profoundly important moral and strategic cause for us. It is the chance to unite our continent at last; the opportunity to entrench liberal plural democracy within Europe's borders, and to bring fully into the European democratic community our fellow Europeans who were trapped on the wrong side of history.[63]

Prodi, as ever, goes one step further, suggesting that the economic reasons for enlargement are secondary to the 'political and ethical reasons'. Enlargement, he declares, 'is the fulfilment of the European project'.[64]

If we conceive of hospitality as, primarily and simply stated, an openness towards the other, what could be more ethical than the EU's policy of enlargement? When Patten asks if there could be a better way of treating the neighbour than inviting them into our home,[65] we should clearly take this 'better' in an economic, political and moral sense. Given that 'our home' is represented as a space of political and economic good governance, where human rights and other ethical values flourish, enlargement can be viewed as a transparently ethically successful foreign policy. It is ethics and responsibility primarily conceived in terms of an open hospitality to otherness.

Discussion of the Balkans is ever present in EU foreign policy from 1999 to 2004. Patten talks about 'events in the Balkans' being 'etched' into every European's conscience.[66] Prodi affirms this in claiming that it is the 'moral duty' of the EU 'to take care of the Balkan countries'.[67] Solana describes the EU's experience of the Balkans as not only 'sobering' but also as providing an 'opportunity. It is a test of our commitment to the region, to a wider Europe, and to a mature common foreign and security policy.'[68] Patten emphasises this representation, saying 'the region offers the defining test of our nascent CFSP'.[69]

Viewing the Balkans as a test for EU foreign policy means it is a test of the EU's constructed subjectivity as an international actor. Testing the maturity of the CFSP is also a test of the EU's capacity to take responsibilities, to accept its international duties, or at least its regional duties. And nowhere could this test be stronger than in the region where '[a]s Europeans we cannot avoid a heavy share of responsibility for what happened', especially in Kosovo.[70] Therefore, the way the Balkans are handled in this period is formative for how the EU constructs itself as a subject. The development of EU foreign policy into the coherent picture painted earlier is important – the Balkans as on the road to the EU, knocking at the door of the family home. However, the reasons for this 'road bound' status illustrate Derrida's observations on the divided and problematic nature of 'hospitality' itself.

From 1999 to 2002, the EU discourse, as stated earlier, was somewhat ambiguous on the status of the Balkans in the EU's spatial imaginary of its home and family. In 1999, Prodi talked about the importance of 'mak[ing] it clear to Albania and the countries of the Former Yugoslavia that we see them as part of the European family of nations'.[71] Initially, they are offered 'virtual membership'.[72] This was designed to ensure that they felt part of the family 'and that once they have met the criteria for membership we shall welcome them into the EU, provided certain important steps are taken beforehand'.[73] Nonetheless, in 2002, Prodi still occasionally refers to the Balkans as a 'neighbouring region', such as Russia and the Mediterranean.[74] Similarly, Patten talks about extending peace, stability and prosperity to 'our Balkan neighbours'.[75]

Therefore, though the EU foreign policy text retains ambiguity on the ethics and hospitality that would be offered to the Balkans,[76] it begins to settle into the spatial metaphors mentioned earlier. As Patten stated in 2000, Albania is looking to Europe to be welcomed 'home' and they must 'stay on the right road – the road to Europe'.[77] Solana begins to talk about the Balkans as on a 'journey' that '[w]e must help them to complete'. We must also, he says, 'help the straggler [Serbia] along'.[78] The metaphor of the 'road to Europe' is used often by Patten, and it develops further. For example, in a speech to Bosnians, Patten suggests that the EU can 'help build that road... we can flag the staging posts, and applaud you as you pass them', all of which means they will ensure 'BiH [Bosnia and Herzegovina] never has to walk the road to Europe alone'.[79]

Speaking of a metaphorical 'road to Europe', which has staging posts, as well as of a 'straggler' on a journey, represents progress towards membership of the EU as a linear track. On this track, you can be more or less advanced. Each step taken forward is towards the European home, towards becoming European. The only other options are to move slowly, like Serbia, stop, or even move backwards. But sideways movements appear to be impossible. Other roads are not an option. As members of the European family of nations, the Balkans can only move unilinearly towards, or away from, the home; at the end of this one road is the door, which they are assured is open to them.[80]

What has been barely mentioned so far, however, is the conditionality that is placed on the EU's hospitality to the Balkans. Progress down the European road means precisely progress on meeting the conditions for entry into the home, and thus membership of the EU. The Stabilisation and Association Agreements made with each of the Balkan countries are represented as commitments by the EU to help them 'along what I call the "road to Europe"; and commitments on the part of the countries themselves to thoroughgoing reform'.[81] In a generalised representation of the conditions that the Balkan countries must meet, Patten says that, 'if they chose democracy, if they chose open economics, if they chose the rule of law, we would want to bring them closer to the European family'.[82]

Although the EU's responsibility for the Balkans is 'etched' in their conscience, the responsibility for actually gaining entry to the European home is shifted to the Balkan countries themselves. Patten tells Bosnians that 'we have to redouble our efforts' towards this reform. He specifies that this 'we' is meant 'in its most *inclusive* sense. But it is a *we* whose main burden actually falls on *you, you the leaders and people of Bosnia Herzegovina*'.[83] Similarly, when asked by a Macedonian journalist what answer the Former Yugoslav Republic of Macedonia (FYROM) can expect from the EU on its application for membership, Solana replies '[t]hat question is not for me to answer, it is for the people and politicians of your country'.[84] The responsibility for the EU's hospitality is placed on the shoulders of the Balkans. *They* are now responsible for the EU's ethical foreign policy. This puts the subjectivity of the EU, as that which is able to take responsibility by acting hospitably, in question. It is no longer the EU which takes responsibility, or acts ethically, but rather the Balkans.

In 2001, Patten translates this into his spatial metaphor once again:

> The [Stabilisation and Association] Agreements are the vehicle that helps you along the road, the road to Europe. The speed at which you travel along that road is up to you. The faster you reform, the more you show that our values, the values the EU represents, are your values, the faster we will be able to cover the distance – politically, at least – between Brussels and Skopje, or Brussels and Belgrade, Sarajevo, Tirana, or Zagreb.[85]

In other words, to place yourself on the road to the European home, you must demonstrate that you are already part of it, in terms of the values (democracy, free markets, human rights, rule of law) set out earlier, in section one. These are the conditions that must be met. As Solana puts it, '[t]he path to Europe is paved with concrete reform, not just good intentions'.[86]

The two laws of hospitality

Clearly, the enactment of the EU's ethical dimension towards the Balkans is represented differently to that of their enlargement policy. What is the status of this far more conditional hospitality? Is it still ethical? Can we still call it hospitality? On a basic level, as suggested, hospitality is simply openness towards the other. This does not get us very far however: the EU may seem open to the Balkans but certainly not as open as it is to the countries of Central and Eastern Europe. What is needed, therefore, is a closer reading of the concept of hospitality, for which we can turn once more to the work of Derrida.

The simplicity of hospitality defined as an openness to the other is problematic because it hides within it a crucial distinction between what Derrida calls the two laws of hospitality: or rather *the* law, and the law*s*.[87] The unconditional law of absolute hospitality,

> ... requires that I open up my home and that I give not only to the foreigner... but to the absolute, unknown, anonymous other, and that I give place to them, that I let them come, that I let them arrive, and take place in the place I offer them, without asking of them either reciprocity (entering into a pact) or even their names.[88]

Absolute, unconditional hospitality then calls for us not just to invite the guest into our home without asking questions but to allow them to come without invitation (a hospitality of visitation as opposed to invitation).[89] We must not just give them a bed to sleep in and food to eat, but *our* bed and *our* food.

As such, unconditional hospitality must break with hospitality by right, or duty, what Derrida calls the juridico-political law*s* of hospitality, which are always conditional.[90] They are conditional because, like the asylum and immigration laws in any country, they put a variety of conditions upon hospitality (you must have the right documentation, a visa, a job to go to etc.), ask a variety of questions (your name, your origin, your purpose for entry etc.), may partake of an economy of reciprocity (such as a visa waiver agreement between states) or demand an invitation (such as a work permit).

The hospitality offered to the Balkans by the EU is heavily conditional: it asks questions, is involved in a reciprocal notion of responsibility and demands an invitation. These countries must demonstrate what Patten and Prodi call their 'properly European vocation'.[91] This can only be done by showing that they *are* European, that they belong in the European home. Far from an absolute hospitality, where no questions are asked of the other prior to their being welcomed into the home, the EU literally asks thousands of questions (in fact, over 2,500).[92] When the FYROM applied for membership of the EU, when one could say it was knocking on the door of the European home, the door turned out to be not as open as was previously suggested. Prodi inducted a ceremony in 2004, handing over a questionnaire to the FYROM government. 'We expect', he said, 'to receive replies to an impressive number of questions... which will allow the Commission (together with other information) to formulate its Opinion if the country is ready to undertake the rights and obligations of membership to the EU'.[93]

Entry into the common European home demands an invitation, which the EU Commission will give an opinion on whether or not to offer.

To be absolutely responsible, the EU would have to enact an unconditional hospitality, to ask no questions, to set no conditions upon entry and to demand no reciprocal responsibility. Each condition that is set upon entry into the home is a nullification of hospitality, a violent exclusion that attempts to make the other into the same before entry is granted. It makes hospitality the responsibility of the Balkan countries rather than that of the EU; a responsibility to become European, to no longer be other, to no longer be outside, before being allowed inside. Quite literally, it makes hospitality a hostility to otherness. The conditional hospitality of enlargement, with its selection of the same and exclusion of the other, cannot help but be both hospitable and hostile. It is hostile towards the other who is absolutely excluded, and hostile to the otherness that must become the same to be included.

Yet, the absolute, unconditional law of hospitality is, as Derrida himself acknowledges, impossible to practically implement or organise. One cannot derive a politics from it.[94] In one sense, it is absolutely naïve and utopic. Such a pure hospitality 'can have no legal or political status. No state can write it into laws.'[95] Nonetheless, the retention of unconditional hospitality is essential. Without 'at least the thought of this pure and unconditional hospitality, of hospitality *itself*', there could be no conditional hospitality or way to determine its rules.[96] As Patten says, quoting Samuel Butler, '[e]xtremes are alone logical, and they are always absurd; the mean is alone practicable and it is always illogical'.[97]

Conditions upon an unconditional, such as those placed on the Balkans' entry into the European home (the EU), can only arise as contaminations of the pure ethical concept. Yet, to retain the name of that concept (hospitality and ethics) these contaminations must also retain an orientation toward it. To remain logical, to still *be* hospitable, one must retain a reference, a gesture, to the extreme or absolute form of hospitality. But any dilution of this extreme can be nothing but illogical and thus inhospitable. For the EU to only give hospitality to the Central and Eastern European countries (as happened in the 2004 enlargement) is less hospitable than to give hospitality to the Balkan countries as well; but we can only say this because we refer to the unconditional form of hospitality as absolute openness. Hospitality to all countries would be closer to the ideal. The unconditional is the condition of the conditional. In other words, unconditional hospitality as a complete openness to the other is a necessary reference point for a conditional, selective hospitality. Without the unconditional *law* of hospitality, the *laws* would be just that, *laws*, rather than laws *of hospitality*. The laws are impossible to determine without reference to *the* law.

Hospitality, on which the EU bases the ethical dimension of its foreign policy, is both divided against itself and yet necessarily joined in one concept. The two laws, as Derrida puts it, are at one and the same time, heterogeneous and indissociable.[98] They are heterogeneous because they are mutually antagonistic; one always seeks to displace the other. Conditional hospitality denies the possibility and utility of the unconditional; unconditional hospitality denies that the conditional is hospitality. As heterogeneous, movement from one to the other is not possible without an 'absolute leap'.[99] But they are also indissociable, as,

> I cannot open the door, I cannot expose myself to the coming of the other and offer him or her anything whatsoever without making this hospitality effective, without, in some concrete way, giving *something determinate*. This determination will thus have to reinscribe the unconditional into certain conditions. Otherwise it gives nothing. What remains unconditional or absolute... risks being nothing at all if conditions... do not make of it some thing.[100]

Just as the law*s* need *the* law, and politics needs absolute hospitality, so *the* law of absolute hospitality *needs* politics and law*s* of conditional hospitality. One can see the irony in a concept of absolute hospitality giving nothing; thus, it requires a reference to its bastardised form which gives concretely – if never giving enough. Nonetheless, despite this indissociability, the necessary heterogeneity remains. One does not nullify the other. They are both true at the same moment. Hence, the hostility contained within the conditional law*s* and the hospitality contained in *the* unconditional law of hospitality are one and the same. This is why Derrida coins the term *hostipitality* to reveal the way hostility and hospitality are joined within the same undecidable un-ethical concept.[101]

Consequently, we can see why there is confusion over whether the EU's foreign policy towards the Balkans is still hospitable and, as such, ethical. A close reading of hospitality reveals the way it both enables and disables itself. It is enabled as the two laws work together indissociably, but it disables as their heterogeneity means they work against each other. It is important to note, however, that although the policy towards the Balkans reveals this problem, it is no less a constitutive part of the hospitality shown towards Central and Eastern European countries through enlargement. Solana notes in early 2000 that although the EU has a 'political and moral responsibility' to support the countries that will accede four years later, the EU should nonetheless not weaken its criteria or the standards they must reach for membership.[102] It was because the conditions upon this hospitality were so strong that, despite enlargement being 'priority number one for this Commission since its very beginnings [in 1999]',[103] it was only in 2004 that they gained entry to the European home.

The undecidable nature of hospitality, or *hostipitality*, is equally applicable to both the enlargement and Balkan foreign policies of the EU. Because the conditions set by the EU's hospitality are contaminations on a pure concept, we can neither say that the hospitality offered by EU foreign policy is simply ethical or unethical. In making reference to the pure ethicality of hospitality, they retain an ethical element. But the set conditions (the need to have entrenched democracy, human rights, free markets and the rule of law, the need to answer over 2,500 questions) remain contaminations on this pure ethicality and, in this sense, remain unethical. Both the enlargement and Balkan policies can only be seen as hospitable and inhospitable, inclusive and exclusive, ethical and unethical, and yet neither one nor the other at the same time. The hospitality, and thus ethics, of EU foreign policy is inherently undecidable.

Deconstructing the European home: The ENP

My argument thus far has relied heavily on the idea that hospitality requires some notion of an 'at-home' for its possible performance. While the home can be a way to close off the outside, to exclude, it is also the very 'condition of openness, of hospitality, and of the door'.[104] Yet, this key point is far from being straightforward. To leave the matter here would be to ignore the further aporias and contradictions within the concept of hospitality, contradictions that deconstruct the very possibility of the home. This raises the issue of the third key EU foreign policy with an ethical dimension – the neighbourhood policy – a policy that undermines the very possibility of the European 'home'. Although the two laws of hospitality problematise the possibility of a simply ethical or hospitable foreign policy, this deconstruction destabilises the basis of hospitality itself: the home. As such, it is also a deconstruction of the EU's subjectivity.

While the previous two EU foreign policies discussed have been explicitly hospitable, with varying degrees of conditionality, the ENP is an often explicitly *inhospitable* policy. I would suggest, however, that the EU's policy towards its 'neighbourhood' retains a reference to hospitality and more importantly describes the limits of its hospitality. This reference to hospitality means that what becomes the ENP is still considered ethical in its intent in the EU discourse. However, the limits it places on hospitality, and the way the policy is described, reveals even more starkly the inseparability of hospitality and hostility – the undecidability of hospitality as *hostipitality*.

As early as 1999, Prodi was stressing the importance of working with the EU's Eastern and Southern 'neighbours' to produce peace, stability and prosperity: a 'new European order'.[105] The aim of this cooperation with the 'new neighbours' the EU has gained from enlargement is also, however, 'to spread our ethical and political values through the wider Europe'.[106] One impulse for the future ENP is thus presented as the desire to spread the principles of the European home/family. In this sense, it could potentially be seen as hospitable. However, the other key impulse is the desire to stop enlargement, to prevent more hospitality, to close off the European home and preserve its integrity. This latter representation comes to the fore towards the end of 2002 as Prodi sets out the reasoning for a new 'neighbourhood' policy:

When we look to the East and the South, it is very difficult to make out the new frontiers of Europe. This, of course, is nothing new: it has been hard to decide where Europe ends in these two compass directions for thousands of years. However, this does not mean that we can just keep on enlarging Europe. The cost would be too great, since it would effectively mean abandoning the European political project. At the same time we cannot draw a neat demarcation line, as some Mediterranean countries – Malta and Cyprus – are preparing to become members of the Union, others, Turkey are candidates for membership, and all are linked to Europe by ties of tradition, special situations and interests.[107]

Although this foreign policy goes through various names (the 'Wider Europe' initiative,[108] the 'Proximity Policy'[109]), in January of 2004 Prodi announces the new ENP, a 'partnership based on shared values and enhancing economic development, interdependence and cultural links *for those neighbours for which accession is not on the agenda'*.[110] In other words, the ENP is about extending, or offering *something,* to those that are explicitly being excluded from the European home.

In his memoirs, Patten translates this policy into the metaphors he uses so frequently.

So, if we can persuade our citizens that enlargement should continue, where do we tell them that it should stop? Do we simply continue adding rings of friends and neighbours until we get to the Caspian Sea or the Pacific? What do we say when Israel, Iraq or even Azerbaijan come knocking on the door? Plainly there has to be an end to the process somewhere, and we have tried to put it firmly in place with a so-called Neighbourhood Policy... These agreements offer the countries that are parties to them a share in our market and in some of our policies... in return for implementing democratic and economic reforms. But membership of the EU is not on the table. *Our partners are welcome to set up their stall in the marketplace, but not to set foot in the town hall.*[111]

The spatial metaphor is once again revealing as to how the ENP fits into the EU's hospitable foreign policy. When Israel, Iraq or Azerbaijan come knocking, the aim is to be able to answer them (though the emphasis on 'even' Azerbaijan is somewhat puzzling). And the answer, this sharing of 'everything except institutions', means that these neighbours can make the most of EU values, prosperity and stability, but only come as far as the 'marketplace'. They are barred from the centre of the European home, the 'town hall'.

The way the ENP is represented by Prodi recalls the 'road bound' policies towards the Balkans noted earlier. Prodi gives three almost identical speeches in September 2004 to students and 'representatives of civil society' in Azerbaijan, Georgia and Armenia, summing up the benefits of the ENP. For example, he claims that '[b]y promoting democracy, the rule of law, human rights, the market economy and conflict settlement, the ENP will help to improve life for Azerbaijanis'.[112] Yet, he says, the provision of such help will 'require Azerbaijan to demonstrate it shares values with the Union in practice as well as in principle... You will not be surprised that our assistance will be conditional'.[113] Just as the Balkans had to demonstrate that they shared European values, that they were capable of reforms on democracy, the rule of law, human rights and the market economy, so it is with Azerbaijan and neighbouring countries.

It is important, declares Prodi, that the EU plays its part in this cooperation. But 'ultimately, Azerbaijan's future relationship with the EU and Azerbaijan's own future will depend on you yourselves – on your own determination to make your country work'.[114] In another repetition of the Balkans policy, the responsibility for EU hospitality is shifted to the neighbouring countries themselves. Now it is 'ultimately' Azerbaijan, Georgia and Armenia's responsibility to meet the conditions of the EU's hospitality. Neighbouring countries, just like the Balkans, are being offered a limited form of hospitality on the understanding that they first become like the EU; that they cease to be other and become the same, even if these countries do not get the same in return as the Balkans.[115]

Yet, while the stable representation of the policy towards the end of 2004 is interesting, what is crucial to this discussion of hospitality is the way it is spoken of during its development. In 2002, Prodi talks about a 'duty' to formulate a clear response to other countries' expectations, to find a new system of relations between the enlarged EU and 'an encircling band of friendly countries stretching from the Maghreb to Russia'.[116] But first, there is a need to answer the question, '[w]here *does Europe stop?*'[117] This is explicitly not about separating countries, '[w]e want to tear down old divisions – *to integrate, not separate*'.[118] This gives the policy its reference to hospitality. Yet, limiting this hospitality, he repeats that, 'clearly we cannot keep on enlarging the Union indefinitely... We need to maintain the EU's *internal equilibrium and cohesiveness*' and retain the EU's capacity 'to act on its basis of shared values and objectives'.[119] In other words, they must maintain the integrity of the European home, based on what he calls a 'broader idea of *"belonging"*'.[120] Thus, Prodi calls for a framework of cooperation with the EU's neighbours, 'where we share everything but *institutions*'.[121]

These themes of the 'ring of friends', as opposed to *family*, and the sharing of 'everything but institutions' are repeated over and over again.[122] Prodi justifies this limited hospitality in various ways that all come back to the same theme: continued enlargement would risk 'water[ing] down the European political project and turn[ing] the EU into just a free trade area on a continental scale'.[123] Although this is exclusionary, it is, as has been stated, crucial to hospitality. If the European home was 'watered down' and did become merely a free trade area, it would no longer be the European home discussed earlier: an area of shared ethical and political values. And if there was no home, then *there could be no hospitality*. As well as being about openness, hospitality presupposes what Derrida calls this 'possibility of a rigorous delimitation of thresholds or frontiers',[124] a separation from otherness.[125] The policy of the ENP shows precisely the inseparability of hospitality and hostility. The delimitation of borders, the cordoning off of the European home is both crucial to hospitality and a violent, hostile exclusion. The ENP then, in a similar yet different way to the enlargement and Balkan foreign policies, can only ever be undecidable: both ethical and unethical, as well as neither ethical, nor unethical.

Deconstructing the European home

Although this hostile, exclusionary aspect is more explicit and acknowledged than in the policy towards the Balkans, it is also clear that there is discomfort surrounding it. The ENP is considered to be about tearing down divisions, integrating rather than separating. Hostility and hospitality are continually mentioned together; yet, the hospitable aspect is stressed as if to try and convince neighbouring countries that the policy is not hostile. In a speech tackling the subject of where 'Europe' ends, Solana emphasises that, while '[a]ll roads should not lead to Brussels', the EU's new 'borders must be lines that connect not lines that divide'.[126] The difficulty of drawing these lines in relation to the ENP, however, reveals a further aporia of hostipitality. This aporia goes to the very heart of the EU's ethical, hospitable foreign policy, undermining the possibility of the European home itself.

In his memoirs, Patten warns that although the ENP is 'an imaginative try' at solving the question about where to draw the line around the European home, two events will make it difficult to 'hold the line'.[127] These are the agreement with Turkey to begin accession negotiations and the Ukrainian Orange Revolution (when Ukrainian citizens forced the state to award the election to a pro-European candidate after initially undemocratically appointing a pro-Russian). Patten recounts how, in his first meeting with a foreign minister from the Ukraine in 1999, he was asked why Turkey was seen as a European country and Ukraine was not.

> What, he [the Ukrainian foreign minister] asked, was so special about Turkey's European vocation and so deficient about Ukraine's? I stumbled through an unconvincing answer, one that convinced me even less in retrospect when I discovered that two of my officials present at the meeting had parents who had been born and worked in what is now Ukraine, but which then had different borders.[128]

It is revealing that Patten finds it difficult to respond convincingly to the question, but the most interesting aspect of Patten's story is the presence of two EU foreign policy officials who have Ukrainian parents. As we have seen, the integrity of the 'home' is based upon the ability to draw lines and delimit otherness. Yet, in the act of drawing this line, Patten reveals that the other is already inside. The Ukraine is clearly represented as the other, a 'friend' and 'neighbour' to the EU as opposed to being part of the 'family' or in the EU 'home'. Yet, as this line is drawn, as a clear threshold to the home is delimited, the friend is revealed to be already family, the neighbour already in the home.

This raises profound questions about the possibility of demarcating a 'home' in the first place. Yet, these questions are not merely specific to EU foreign policy. Derrida observes that they are already installed in the language of hospitable discourse itself. In French, the subject of hospitality is the *hôte*, which means both 'host' and 'guest'. Literally, the *hôte* is both the giver and receiver of hospitality. To translate it as either simply one or the other, either 'host' or 'guest', is impossible. The *hôte*, as host, is the subject that welcomes the *hôte*, as guest; but the *hôte* is both at the same time.[129]

This issue could merely be dismissed as one of translation, a problem created by the vagaries of the French language.[130] Yet, we can see its operation in the earlier example of the Ukraine taken from the EU foreign policy discourse. The EU is the 'host', and Ukraine the potential 'guest', which the EU is granting a highly circumscribed form of hospitality through the ENP. But the Ukrainian foreign minister questions this status, suggesting that the Ukrainian 'European vocation' is far from deficient – perhaps Ukrainians are better considered a 'host'? To allow the operation of hospitality, however, Patten must assert the thresholds and boundaries of the home and the difference between 'guest' and 'host'. Yet, the subject of hospitality as *hôte* reasserts itself in his realisation that his officials are Ukrainian. Discomfort is brought about by the fact that the EU finds itself to be also the 'guest' of the 'host', the Ukrainians, within what it thought was its own, common European home.

Up to this point, my critique has mainly surrounded precisely this limited form of hospitality that the EU enacts. The only argument against an unconditional form of hospitality is that we cannot organise it or derive a politics from it.[131] Yet, this problem of the *hôte* applies even more strongly to absolute, unconditional hospitality, which every hospitality (including that offered in the enlargement, Balkan and neighbourhood policies) that deserves the name must refer to. As outlined above, this means giving place to the other in our own home. This is not simply a matter of allowing them to occupy part of our home, giving them shelter and asking no questions, but it literally means that the *other takes our place*. If they take our place, then we are no longer in the simple position of host. Indeed, effectively, the positions have been reversed – we are now a guest.

In this way, our home is no longer simply 'ours'; hospitality makes us, as host (*hôte*), literally a guest (*hôte*) in our own home. My home then is only 'mine' in so much as it is also the other's. The question of hospitality is no longer just about us giving hospitality to the other, it is about hospitality being granted to ourselves in our own 'at-home', which is always the home of the other.[132] In a supplementary irony then, though the home is a prerequisite for hospitality, hospitality itself makes the very concept of the 'at-home' impossible. As Derrida says, hospitality 'is a name or an example of deconstruction. Of the deconstruction of the concept, of the concept of the concept, as well as of its construction, its home, its "at-home." Hospitality is the deconstruction of the at-home'.[133] In other words, the unconditional form of hospitality, which EU hospitality must retain a reference to for it to be conceived as in any way ethical, undermines the very possibility of the home: the condition of hospitality itself.

The European home, as discussed above, is fundamental to the operation of hospitality, and yet now we can see it is also disabled by this very hospitality. Importantly, this deconstruction and putting into question of the possibility of the self and the home cannot be felt as benign. When these fundamental aspects of our identity, our very subjectivity, are put into question, invaded by others, hospitality can only be felt as a radical form of persecution. As such, the subject of hospitality, the *hôte*, is not only both host and guest, but both are also *hostage*.[134] Our home is no longer where we can relax, feel free to be ourselves, but where we are persecuted. It is no longer our space, indeed it never was, but rather the space of the other. The other can arrive at any time, without invitation, and take what he likes in our place. The 'at-home' becomes where we are held hostage. But this is the case for everyone: the structure of substitution, where everyone is *hôte*, as guest and host, 'make[s] everyone into everyone else's hostage'.[135]

As I have argued, hospitality cannot be separated from hostility, but now we can see that this is true for both its conditional and unconditional forms. In a conditional form of hospitality such as that of enlargement, the necessary filtering and choosing (of who and what is included) necessitates a violent exclusion of the other. This exclusion occurs on a spectrum from those geographically distant (such as Latin America and Asia, who are absolutely excluded), to neighbourhood countries (who are largely excluded), to the Balkans (who are excluded until they stop being other and become the same). Thus, in what may appear the ethical concept *par excellence*, hostility, violence and injustice are inevitably installed.[136] For unconditional hospitality, however, the hostility is even more extreme. After all, our very sense of self, our subjectivity, our being-as-we-are, is persecuted, questioned and occupied. Hence, even unconditional hospitality is always already hostipitality. That which we have conceived as coextensive with the ethical relation to the other is hostile and unethical. EU policies, even those such as enlargement that are more hospitable, cannot be anything but hostile. Enlargement, whatever the conditions or lack thereof that it sets, will inevitably fall into the ethical undecidability of hostipitality.

What is most important about unconditional hostipitality, however, is that it deconstructs the possibility of the home and thus the subjectivity of the EU. The EU conceives its home as a place of shared ethical and political values. As such, it seeks to keep countries such as the Ukraine outside the European home because it is not seen as representing those values. Yet, the

ENP reveals that, contrary to its intention, hospitality has already been offered and accepted. The Ukraine is already in the home; it is already part of the family. This is shown not only by the Orange Revolution, which Patten views as demonstrating its European-ness,[137] but also by the presence of Ukrainians within the institutions of the European home. The outside is already a constitutive part of the inside, and the delimitation of frontiers that are so crucial to the possibility of the home (and thus hospitality) is always already impossible.

The last three chapters have traced the deconstruction of the 'ethical' in British and EU foreign policy around three points of incision: subjectivity, responsibility and hospitality. Each deconstructs and undermines itself, revealing its constitutive undecidability; but where do we go from here? Does deconstruction leave us in a moral wasteland where all ethical action is fundamentally impossible? Should we abandon or ignore possibilities for ethics as foreign policy because it has shown itself to be an unachievable goal? Through the concept of 'negotiation', I will argue, we can and must retain the ethical (as well as a certain subjectivity, responsibility and hospitality) through what Shapiro calls a 'degree of unreading, unmapping, and rewriting'[138] of the foreign policy text.

5   Negotiating Undecidability
Ethics, politics and the perhaps

There are two obvious responses to the undecidability of ethical concepts: either acknowledge them and resolve that an ethical foreign policy is *impossible* and perhaps even dangerous in its impossibility; or, ignore the contradictions and paradoxes and act *as if* we know who/what 'we' 'are', what responsibility and hospitality mean and how they can be enacted. Both these responses are rejected as *fundamentally* unethical: the first because it acknowledges itself as such; the second because, as Derrida says of responsibility, any inadequate thematisation of the ethical is itself an irresponsible, unethical thematisation.[1] It mischaracterises and misleads, allows one to think one has acted responsibly when the opposite is true and limits our awareness of other, perhaps more responsible, possibilities. But what other response, what other solution, is there for the undecidability of ethical foreign policy?

Although I am not proposing a solution, I am looking for a way to move forward. This forward movement cannot be conceived teleologically and, thus, would be better described as a problematic and contingent movement through the paradoxes of ethics as foreign policy rather than a movement toward a fully ethical foreign policy. As such, perhaps it is better characterised as a 'living with' undecidability and aporia,[2] a way of operating within a context of irresolvable contradiction. This movement through, or living with, is made possible by introducing the Derridean concept of *negotiation*. This is not 'negotiation' as traditionally understood. It does not 'imply a diplomatic operation that takes place in political-institutional contexts. It is an operation that takes place in every sentence: no, in every word, practically, that I publish'.[3]

Negotiation in this sense is an incessant movement between the poles of contradiction within a concept, such as unconditional and conditional hospitality. It does not seek to dialectically *resolve* these contradictions in a third term, for instance, a *real* hospitality. The contradictions are interminable, and there can be no simple 'third way' or 'middle ground'. Rather, negotiation suggests the possibility of particular context-specific decisions. These are taken without renouncing either of the poles of a contradiction – the unconditional or conditional, the incalculable or calculation – but without merely following either. As such, negotiation makes no claims to achieve an ethical foreign policy, and it cannot produce a responsible relation to otherness, but rather it opens a possible way of living with the logical contradictions of ethical foreign policy.

This movement must, of necessity, remain irresolvably problematic and subject to perpetual re-negotiation. In other words, this movement must maintain the undecidability of the problem as this is the condition of ethical and political responsibility as well as the decision itself.[4] It is, literally, a continuing-to-live-with undecidability. In this way, the possibility of negotiation is not that of an ethical foreign policy but an *ethico-political foreign policy*. Instead of resting on *an* ethics or *an* ethical, negotiation keeps ethics always political, always open to question. As such, it retains openness to the unexpected and unanticipatable arrival of the other, the possibility of the impossible ethical foreign policy.

As Derrida observes, a necessary part of thinking the ethical and political is a 'questioning *without limit*'.[5] Initially, such a questioning reveals aporias at that the heart of traditional systems of thought, aporias that have been effaced by British and European Union (EU) attempts at ethical foreign policy. Through negotiation, however, we potentially open a far greater range of possibilities for thought. The retention of what Derrida calls the unconditional '"hyperbolic" ethical vision' of his concepts keeps us always 'torn', but it allows the possibility to 'inflect politics', to change things, to think differently, to invent.[6] This possibility will, however, always remain an experience of the *perhaps*.[7] Here, the word 'perhaps' is the best figure of the French *peut-être*, literally *peut* meaning 'can' or 'may' and *être*, to 'be'.[8] All concepts that retain this hyperbole (justice, responsibility, subjectivity, hospitality and the other) cannot simply be but always *may be*.

After I have provided the broad outlines of negotiation, I suggest examples of what could be possible, perhaps, in a negotiation of ethics as foreign policy for Britain and the EU. In this vein, I outline the potential for *ending* British foreign policy, or rather, ending the automatic affirmation of 'Britain' as a subject of foreign policy. I then make a case for the accelerated accession of Turkey to the EU; a Turkey that remains very much 'Turkish' and only awkwardly 'European'. Far from neat policy proposals, these are only indicative sketches as they stand outside the immediacy of the context in which negotiation can happen. These illustrations, therefore, remain *suggestive* rather than *prescriptive,* outlining possibilities and impossibilities, some of which remained unthought in British and EU foreign policy.

Negotiation: calculating openness and closure

Deconstruction has been criticised in the past for revealing logical contradictions and moral conundra without indicating any way to resolve them.[9] The problem is that, for Derrida, '[e]thics and politics ... start with undecidability'.[10] They can only begin when 'I am in front of a problem and

I know that the two determined solutions are as justified as one another. From that point I have to take responsibility which is heterogeneous to knowledge'.[11] But how do we take such a responsibility? Surely, the ethical and political necessity of preserving undecidability means that there can be no decision as this would end undecidability?

Derrida engages this issue in his discussion of a justice beyond law. Justice is separated from the law in the same way as unconditional hospitality is separated from its conditional form; or absolute responsibility to all others is separated from a legal, or moral, responsibility to an other. These concepts are entirely heterogeneous; yet, they are also indissociable: law, responsibility and hospitality must retain a reference to justice, responsibility and hospitality to keep their name. The unconditional requires conditions to be able to give anything at all. Crucially, this aporetic heterogeneity and indissociability 'cannot and should not serve as an alibi for staying out of juridico-political battles'.[12]

> Left to itself the incalculable and giving idea of justice is always very close to the bad, even to the worst for it can always be reappropriated by the most perverse calculation. It's always possible. And so incalculable justice *requires* us to calculate... Not only *must* we calculate, negotiate the relation between the calculable and the incalculable, and negotiation without the sort of rule that wouldn't have to be reinvented there where we are cast, there where we find ourselves; but we *must* take it as far as possible, beyond the place we find ourselves and beyond the already identifiable zones of morality or politics or law.[13]

Rather than allowing us to stay out of ethical and political controversies because of the incalculability of ethical concepts, this very incalculability, in fact, gives us a duty to get involved, to calculate a response and to make a decision. The openness of these ethical concepts also requires that there be a closure as, 'left to themselves', they can produce unethical consequences and even the 'worst' consequences. After all, unconditional hospitality leads to the violation of the home and thus the death of hospitality itself; and a responsibility to all others (as 'ever other (one) is every (bit) other'[14]) produces paralysis before the impossible choice of precisely whom to act responsibly for. 'Hyperbolic'[15] ethical concepts would be at the mercy of figures of the 'worst' such as genocide, ethnic cleansing and Nazism.

But what makes these figures of 'the worst'? How can we decide what constitutes the 'worst' calculation? For Derrida, this is a matter of always trying to oppose 'those events that we think obstruct the future or bring death', those elements of otherness 'that put an end... to the affirmative opening for the coming of the other'.[16] In other words, the 'worst' calculations are those that close, precipitously and finally, against our ability to be open toward the other. Opposing the 'worst' is a matter of respecting a guiding principle of deconstruction: '[i]t is better to let the future open – this is the axiom of deconstruction, the thing from which it always starts out and which binds it, like the future itself, to alterity'.[17] An ethical, responsible relation to the other, to alterity, begins with such openness – one might even say it begins with hospitality.

This openness to the other, to alterity, to the future, is both necessary to an ethical vision and fundamentally dangerous;[18] it cannot be considered an a priori good thing because it brings with it the possibility of the 'worst'.[19] But, equally, such danger does not alleviate the fact that any closure upon otherness remains a closure and, therefore, contrary to the openness of deconstruction. Thus, the calculation of closure needs to be thought, or negotiated, specifically as a way of opening towards otherness at the same time. The calculation of closure must have the character of an opening.

Yet, how are we to calculate what is incalculable? This is where the concept of negotiation becomes central: the relation between the incalculable and the calculable, between openness and the closure of a decision, must be negotiated. The word 'negotiation' arises from the Latin *neg-otium,* meaning 'no-leisure'. Derrida sees this '[u]n-leisure' as the 'impossibility of stopping or settling in a position... establishing oneself anywhere'.[20] Its best figure is that of a shuttle, going back and forth between different positions: the incalculable and the calculable, the universal and particular, the unconditional and conditional, the open and the closed.

As a restless shuttling, negotiation does not allow either of these poles to become a resting place, thereby preserving undecidability. Yet, the continual movement does not negate the fact that negotiation involves decision. It must always decide, cut and close. Otherwise, there would be no possibility of *moving through* the undecidability of ethics as foreign policy. But such a decision cannot resolve the aporetic undecidability of subjectivity, responsibility and hospitality as this is the condition of ethics, politics and the decision.[21] Negotiation can be seen as an ethico-political movement that aims, through a decision, to preserve the possibility of itself, its own undecidability.

The decision that may result from a negotiation then cannot hope to *achieve* justice, ethics, responsibility or hospitality. These must always remain part of the otherness, the future, that negotiation tries to stay open toward. This inability to attain a genuinely ethical foreign policy is implied in the common understanding of 'negotiation', which is associated with compromise and impurity. But, as Derrida notes, there is no crisis in acknowledging that '[n]egotiation is impure'; just as the obligatory closure of a negotiated decision must have the character of an opening, so the necessary contamination resulting from negotiation arrives 'in the name of purity'.[22] Rather, negotiation seeks 'intermediate *schemas*' between the two poles of the undecidable,[23] intermediate schemas that aim to avoid the 'worst' or indeed seek to find the 'better' or 'least bad' closure. Nothing, Derrida observes, counts more than the quotation marks that must always surround this 'better' which is 'not good, it is only a stopgap, but one that *it is necessary to seek*, that it is necessary not to stop seeking'.[24]

The barest details of a negotiation would then describe it as an oscillating movement between the poles of an undecidable concept (openness and closure, unconditional and conditional, incalculability and calculation) that looks for the 'better' place to cut, close and decide while still retaining undecidability. All this appears very abstract, but the problem with illustrating how it could work in, for example, British and EU foreign policy is that much like deconstruction[25] a negotiation depends entirely upon context.

> An essential aspect of negotiation is that it is always different, differential, not only from one individual to another, from one situation to another, but even for the same individual from one moment to the next. There is no general law, there is no general rule for negotiation. Negotiation is different at every moment, from one context to the next. There are only contexts, and this is why deconstructive negotiation cannot produce general rules, 'methods'. It must be adjusted to each case, to each moment without, however, the conclusion being a relativism or empiricism. This is the difficulty. That there is something like an absolute rule of negotiation that can only be adjusted to political, historical situations.[26]

All we have is the 'something like an absolute rule' of negotiation that any decision must strive to maintain openness. This is what Derrida calls the 'categorical imperative, the unconditional duty of all negotiation', which is 'to let the future have a future... to leave the possibility of the future open'.[27]

Because of this sensitivity to circumstance, we cannot possibly say how a negotiation would work in any given situation as we are necessarily outside the specificity of that context. Thus, far from suggesting a set of neat policy proposals for British and EU foreign policy, I aim to provide examples of what *could* be possible, *perhaps*, regarding the negotiation of ethical foreign policy. In providing these, I will also draw out some more of the implications of negotiation.[28] However, these are only indicative sketches and do not seek to stand in any kind of judgement over the ethics displayed in British and EU foreign policy: they do not state what 'should' or 'should not' have been done, which construction of subjectivity would have been better, which decision more responsible or policy more hospitable. As illustrations, they remain suggestive rather than prescriptive, outlining possibilities and im-possibilities, some of which remained unthought in British and EU foreign policy.

Ending British foreign policy

To an extent, a sensationalist suggestion of ending British foreign policy can only be a misnomer: foreign policy, like ethics, as a question of relating to otherness is not something that can be 'ended'. As I sought to illustrate in the previous chapter, there must always be a delimitation of frontiers between a 'self' and an 'other', an inside the 'home' and its outside. Without it, there would be no possibility of ethics or foreign policy. The notion of ending *British* foreign policy is nonetheless worth pursuing, especially when foreign policy is more traditionally defined – as a state-based practice whose intended target is beyond that state's borders.[29] It is this conventional understanding that could be abandoned or, rather, moved beyond by negotiating a more open subjectivity that would widen the notion of a responsibility toward others. A negotiation would perhaps reject the generalised and automatic affirmation of 'Britain' as a subject in international affairs, opening subjecitivty – precisely who/what is constituted as responsible – to constant re-assessment.

In response to a call from the other (whether Kosovan refugees, Sierra Leonian civilians or down-trodden Afghan women), a subject is affirmed in British foreign policy as being capable of taking responsibility for protecting and saving that other. At various times, this subject has been 'Britain', the 'United Nations' (UN), the 'international community', the 'international coalition' and so on. Currently, although it may later be supplemented by another signifier of subjectivity, if there is a call from an other, there is an automatic assumption that Britain will be constituted as a foreign policy actor, as a subject, capable of taking responsibility. After all, as Patten observed, Britain, unlike the EU, does not need to explain what it is and where it fits into the world.[30] It has a foreign policy establishment (a government ministry, civil servants, ministers and diplomats worldwide) in place to deal with international issues precisely as 'Britain'. While there is sometimes an acknowledgement that the 'international community' is something that must be constructed or built,[31] the subjectivity of 'Britain' is treated as an unquestioned reality.

Negotiating an end to British foreign policy is about suggesting that 'Britain', as a subject capable of taking responsibility in international politics, is too closed, too exclusionary. It does not open enough to the future, to the coming of the other. This closure toward otherness means that policies can be conceived without the participation and contribution of the other, or become programmed outcomes rather than context-specific decisions. Literally, to claim that 'Britain', or 'the UK', can take responsibility, either for saving Africa or for protecting Iraqis, also constitutes a contemptuous pitying of 'Africa' and an exclusion of a responsibility to other Iraqis (among others). Other subjectivities should therefore be sought, or rather constructed and invented, subjectivities that are more open to otherness, to the future and thus to ethics.

Of course, other subjects are affirmed in British foreign policy. Perhaps there is a future in these, a future to be negotiated. However, as they stand, subjects such as the 'international community' or the 'international coalition' could also be more open than they often appear in the British discourse. For instance, the 'international coalition' was used as a supplement to the 'international community'; it allowed countries such as Syria[32] and Saudi Arabia[33] to appear to be included, while they were actively excluded from the international community. However, within this chapter I cannot provide potential negotiations of all moments of undecidability in British foreign policy. Suffice to say that negotiating an end to British foreign policy would potentially open up these other subjects to debate and contestation. After all, as they appear in the British foreign policy text, subjects such as the 'international community' and 'international coalition' have their discursive borders patrolled, being distinguished and defined, precisely by the interpolators of that text: 'Britain'.

A crucial aspect of negotiation is that it aims to *invent*, to think new possibilities, the unprecedented and the unthought.[34] In fact, however, this suggestion of abandonment is far from unprecedented but rather an inventive iteration – meaning both repetition and change – of existing ideas from within the British foreign policy text. In January 2001, then Foreign Office minister Peter Hain put the issue on the agenda by publishing a pamphlet entitled 'The End of Foreign Policy?'[35] His basic point in this initiative was that an increasing number of 'foreign policy' issues were, in fact, far more complicated than traditional notions of diplomacy and foreign policy could deal with: climate change,[36] the elimination of poverty, the trade system, global epidemics, drug abuse, terrorism,[37] refugees[38] and competition for necessary staples such as water and fish.[39]

None of these problems can be solved by traditional diplomatic solutions. In simplistic terms, Hain argues that it is impossible to 'find the villain'[40] in each case. Rather, in all the aforementioned examples, but more specifically with the drug trade, the 'villain' is not 'a corrupt government, careless corporation, faceless bureaucrat or greedy gangster – but the millions of daily choices made by individuals with either too little knowledge of or too little concern for the consequences'.[41] Thus, there is no single source to confront. Rather, the origins of the aforementioned problems 'straddle both national and sectoral boundaries in haphazard ways'.[42] There is neither a single government department nor a single national government or international institution charged with solving these problems. Also, no policy could be effective on, for example, climate change without the participation of all national governments, major multinational corporations (MNCs) such as General Motors or Microsoft, non-governmental organisation (NGOs) such as the World Wide Fund for Nature and Greenpeace and international and regional organisations such as the World Trade Organization (WTO) and the EU.

Hain's argument is, of course, very different to mine: he claims that there *was* a traditional notion of foreign policy, but this reality is changing. Not only is it changing, this change is also for the better. In contrast, I am arguing that a potential negotiation of ethical possibility within foreign policy could involve abandoning what was always already a construction: Britain as a coherent subject capable of taking responsibility in international affairs. However, the outcome of the two suggestions could be similar. After all, Hain proposes that 'Britain' is fragmenting; all the issues listed earlier are breaking down the inside/outside, domestic/international, logic upon which 'foreign policy', as it is generally understood, is built or even produces.[43] The 'target' of policy aimed at the drug trade, climate change and refugees is not in any simple sense beyond a state's borders; it is always already inside *and* outside, while breaking down the possibility of distinguishing between the two. As Hain puts it, 'at the heart' of the new complexity 'lies the blurring, sometimes to vanishing point' of the 'familiar distinction' between 'domestic and foreign policy'.[44] Thus, his speculative and open conclusion is that,

> Perhaps Foreign Ministries will be renamed 'Departments of Global Affairs' – as the concept of the 'foreign' becomes ever harder to define... In the process we will see an end to traditional foreign policy and the evolution of a new foreign policy based upon global linkages, recognizing natural limits, and embracing global responsibility; a foreign policy for a world in which there is no longer any such place as abroad.[45]

A Department of Global Affairs appears designed to match the breakdown of the inside/outside distinction. It could feed into a much more fluid conception of subjectivity, a concept where there is no necessary, automatic or natural subject and thus no predetermined notion of the 'foreign' or 'otherness'. Rather, the symbolic abandonment of the Foreign and Commonwealth Office (FCO) could reinforce the openness of a negotiation. A newly conceived Department of Global Affairs may seek to enable the work of local groups and councils, businesses, MNCs, NGOs, charities and international and regional organisations.[46] An openness to input from a wider range of multilevel, multinational sources could seek to be an active embodiment of a deconstructive negotiation.

However, it would be wrong to finally close the door on the subjectivity contained in affirming British foreign policy. It is crucial to emphasise the importance of 'Britain' no longer being *automatically* affirmed as a subject of international affairs, as if it were natural. Such a de-reification is necessary and would perhaps enable the chain of signifiers for subjectivity[47] to be halted at subjects with greater openness; indeed, perhaps new ones could be invented. But negotiation must seek to leave the decisions undecidable and open to the specifics of a context, thus, it is important to qualify my argument. Conceivably, there could be occasions in which, to avoid the coming of the 'worst', 'Britain' is necessarily affirmed as a subject, capable of taking responsibility. For instance, were there to be a repetition of the internal warfare, killing, mass rape and maiming that occurred in Sierra Leone in 2000, would it be more or less open to the other to allow for the possibility of affirming 'Britain' as a subject? This *ad hoc*, little publicised intervention has seemingly been relatively successful.[48] If there were no other claims to responsibility, if the UN, the African Union (AU), maybe even the EU, claimed an incapacity to take responsibility, would it be better or worse to reconstitute British foreign policy?

Any such decision would have to be taken and negotiated in the imminence of the context. After all, a singular negotiation cannot allow itself to become a 'policy', in the sense of a 'known formula of universal application'.[49] Rather, it must always allow for difference and the possibility of a different outcome according to the specificity of circumstance. In this sense, a negotiation is radically different to a 'policy' that can be transferred between contexts. Rather, each moral norm or rule that is affirmed through a negotiation must be reinvented and rejustified each time – the decision must be made *as if* the rule were being invented there and then. Such a decision then is not the mechanical following of a policy rule or moral norm but a new invention each time.[50] Thus, although it is crucial to de-reify British foreign policy and remove its automatic and apparently natural status, it is also important to keep the door open for its reinvention.

Negotiating difference

Although the publication of Hain's pamphlet could be seen as a moment of openness in British foreign policy, what followed was a closure. A new ministerial team, led by Jack Straw, took over at the Foreign Office in 2001, with a specific interpretation of the events of September 11. Almost exactly a year after Hain launched his pamphlet, new minister Denis MacShane gave a speech at the same venue announcing 'The Return of Foreign Policy' – a definite riposte to Hain.

> [W]hat 9/11 has done – though the process was already under way beforehand – is to strengthen governments and [place] alliances between states firmly in the driving seat of foreign policy... What I think 9/11 has done is expose the rise of non-state actors, whether malign or well-intentioned and the need for governments to be sure-footed in dealing with them... The fashionable view of the 1990s, that foreign policy can be dictated by meetings between special interest groups, has been exposed as dead-end thinking... So the idea that foreign policy had come to an end or that the role of diplomacy would be replaced by experts in the post-national issues of concern to the world has not lasted. Foreign policy is back.[51]

Through a peculiar formulation, governments are put firmly back in charge of a traditional foreign policy: the events of September 11 has shown that both malign (presumably he means Al-Quaeda) and well-intentioned (presumably the likes of Amnesty International) must be put in their place by solid governmental control. There is, once again, a definite inside and a definite outside, a clear domestic and a clear foreign. It is through the 'democratic state and its government' interacting with the outside 'through dialogue, negotiation' and 'international agreements' that 'we will help improve the quality of life for our fellow-citizens', on the inside.[52]

Significantly, it is also in this period that the notion of failed and failing states comes to the fore in British foreign policy. As I have argued elsewhere, the dualism of succeeding and failing states relies upon, and is also the basis for maintaining, a firm line between the inside and outside, domestic and foreign.[53] One of the reasons that Hain's idea of ending foreign policy had to be closed down was that it attempts to permanently displace the line between the domestic and foreign. But, as we saw in the government's reaction to the terrorist attacks in the United States in 2001 and Britain in 2005, the maintenance of this line is essential. Without it, such acts of terror cannot be dismissed as 'foreign'; they cannot be portrayed as emerging from the 'secular dictatorship and religious extremism' of the Middle East,[54] or as Straw puts it in relation to September 11, 'evil acts... co-ordinated from failed states in distant parts of the world'.[55] Rather, there would have to be some acknowledgement that an element of terrorism is always domestic, that the line between foreign and domestic cannot be maintained and that the ultimate failure of the subjectivity erected in British foreign policy is a *general* condition.

A de-reification of British subjectivity in international affairs, symbolically demonstrated by the abandonment of the FCO and official British foreign policy, arguably produces a negotiation of the succeeding/failing state subject dichotomy. After all, if the inside is always outside, the foreign always domestic, the successful subject is always also a failing object. With failure a general condition of subjectivity in international affairs, there must be a constant questioning of the extent to which the other can be 'known': the other previously simply known as a failing subject or as an object. But this negotiation would not rest with the generalisation of subject failure. To do so could have either the effect of reducing differences to nothing, and thus Somalia and the United States become simply the *same*, or it could generate a hopeless 'throwing up of one's hands' – the problems of all subjects are too *different*, too other to be known. Negotiation of the failing state subject thus operates between the two poles of sameness and difference, without giving in to either.

Such a negotiation could lead to at least two suggestions: a rejection of pre-emption and the discursive 'responsibility to save' in favour of a differentiated, politicised view of subjectivity; and the invention of a 'responsibility to respect'. To begin with, the discourse of the failing state enables British foreign policy to treat others as objects that can simply be 'known' in terms of its problems and their solutions. This allows the notion of pre-empting state failure, a fore-knowledge that the subject will become an object,[56] meaning that British foreign policy can automatically 'diagnose' and 'cure' the failing state-object. This logic of pre-emption is very clear in both Blair and Straw's speeches,[57] but such pre-emption jettisons any notion of the *politics*, or undecidability, of foreign policy. It is in danger of discarding negotiation and the ethico-*political*.

Indeed, a policy of pre-emption risks making the matter decidable: it has *already* been decided, *before* the context arises. Negotiation seeks to operate precisely without such certainty or fore-knowledge about the other. It seeks to retain, or reanimate, the *political* contestation of foreign policy, much in the way that Jenny Edkins has done with the concept of famine relief which, as she observes, 'is not a technological or managerial matter that can be resolved by better theories or techniques'.[58] Removing the matter from 'British foreign policy' *per se*, allowing the issues involved in 'state failure' to be considered by wider, broader subjectivities, means that the privileging of the state could itself become problematic. It could certainly no longer be assumed. The formerly natural privileging of the 'state' and its 'success' as a subject would, thus, be politicised and thrown into question.

This opens the possibility that the other could be conceived *differently* and not necessarily just in terms of the *same*. As Mark Duffield observes, where some see state failure, it is possible to see 'innovative and long-term adaptations to globalisation'.[59] Rather than a failure of a particularly Western notion of state subjectivity, these could be 'the development of forms of political authority that are no longer based on territorial integrity or a bureaucratic system or even on consent'.[60] These new forms of authority may still be undesirable; certainly, in the case of Sierra Leonian gang leaders this is very likely, but they should not be dismissed as failure simply because they are not the same. Such a transition *could* be made easier if the subject conducting foreign policy itself was not a state. If the subject in its subjectivity – a regional, intergovernmental or supranational body for example – called into question notions of the domestic and foreign, success and failure, policies would be open to more negotiation.

Negotiating the end of British foreign policy could not only abandon preemption and introduce a politicised, differentiated view of subjectivity, it may also enable a replacement of the 'responsibility to save' with a less pitying 'responsibility to respect'. Through the notion of the failing state subject, British foreign policy essentially constructed an (almost exclusively African) other to the international community. This other was an object worthy of pity, worthy of *being saved* with the symbiosis of contempt and compassion. But this necessitated that Africans should be helped to become the *same*. They should not be allowed to remain other and *different*. There is compassion for the potentially same but contempt for the currently other.

Negotiation oscillates between these poles of sameness and difference, searching for the better place to close in each context. If help or aid is to be offered to the other, it should be offered precisely to the other *as other*, as *different*, as not in the process of becoming same. In other words, there could perhaps be the negotiation of a 'responsibility to respect' by the subject of foreign policy, whoever or whatever that may be. After all, if all subjects are failing, the basis for a contemptuous 'responsibility to save' is largely removed. Perhaps a first sign of this negotiation would be allowing an internal differentiation of the 'African' other. Chapter 3 discussed the way British foreign policy refers almost exclusively to 'Africa', or the 'problem of Africa',[61] as if it were a homogenous lump. Although this is perhaps a minor point, a negotiation of sameness and difference could be at least illustrated by references to specific problems of specific regions, communities or states within Africa. Allowing for such a differentiation would place in doubt the possibility of the Commission for Africa's goal, a 'comprehensive plan for Africa'.[62] A 'comprehensive plan' suggests that a policy as a general rule for application is the target, one that does not affix itself to the cultural, religious, socio-economic specificity of each context.

This is not, however, to say that policy in this area is entirely bad or that it should be abandoned wholesale. Perhaps the New Partnership for Africa's Development (NEPAD), as an African policy produced by Africans, despite its generality, could be supported as a negotiation of a 'responsibility to respect'. Perhaps it is merely the Commission for Africa that should be abandoned because of its potential institutionalisation of contempt. Notwithstanding this potential, there are also significant concerns over NEPAD as a 'vehicle driven by a small group of African leaders who chose their destination without consulting their own citizens. It was also noticeable that the vehicle was built according to the specifications of Western development consultants'.[63]

The other, however, cannot always be respected in its otherness. After all, negotiation does seek to avoid the 'worst', or that which closes toward the future. And, as was shown by the Rwandan genocide, with up to a million people slaughtered, what could be the 'worst' is not to be underestimated; as Straw says, it 'still haunts us today'.[64] Campbell sums this up in relation to Bosnia, stating the need to 'reclaim politics from pity and enable the exercise of responsibility while at the same time paying respect to those small steps that have already been taken'.[65] 'Britain', however, as an apparently necessarily closed subjectivity, with its 'natural' statist, inside/outside, succeeding/failing subject assumptions, is perhaps not the subjectivity to enact such a negotiating reclamation of politics from pity.

Negotiating minimum closure

No illustration of negotiation can say in advance which construction of subjectivity would prove a 'better' affirmation. Indeed, nor can it judge in retrospect. Any such judgement must remain political, undecidable, even in the unique specificity of the context. What I am proposing is that 'Britain', or the 'international community' as Britain constructs it in its foreign policy text, is probably too closed to the possibilities of ethics or the ethico-political. After all, Britain's construction of the 'international community' as a subject actively excludes 'Africa'.[66] However, which subjectivity is affirmed must remain to be decided, or rather to be negotiated, as the most open in that context while closing to try to exclude the 'worst'.

Arguably, and ironically, there was precisely such an attempt to affirm an open subjectivity in British foreign policy post-September 11. While one part of the foreign policy text (interpreted by MacShane) was declaring that state-based foreign policy was back, another part spoken by Blair was doing the opposite. Generally speaking, the 'us' affirmed by Blair's foreign policy was the 'international community', abortively the 'UN', and became increasingly the 'international coalition'. Specifically *British* foreign policy was largely abandoned. When Blair spoke, he seemed to speak for, or as, the international community or coalition. The attacks of September 11 were characterised in British foreign policy as attacks upon the entire international community, 'on the basic democratic values in which we all believe so passionately and on the civilised world'.[67] Even in EU foreign policy, Chris Patten described them as attacks 'on the values we all share... the values which the whole of the international community has to uphold'.[68]

The problem, however, is that such representations appear to require the subsequent objectification of Afghanistan as a failing state to *assert* the 'international community' as a successful subjectivity, capable of taking responsibility. Yet, paradoxically, this assertion is only necessary because the subject has blatantly been proven a failure – the international community was incapable of taking responsibility for its citizens' security and welfare. What we need to ask is whether such a closure of subjectivity has the character of an opening. It seems reasonable to suggest that if the failure of subjectivity demonstrated on September 11 were characterised as an inevitable possibility, inherent within and constitutive of the subject rather than a negation of that subjectivity, greater openness could have been negotiated. That is to say, if terrorism were acknowledged to be part of, rather than a threat to, the viability of a subjectivity, perhaps there need not have been an extra closure against an other in the British foreign policy text.

Straw characterised September 11 as a 'strategic opportunity', which '[w]e owe it to those who founded the international community to seize'.[69] Perhaps he was correct, and a negotiation of subjectivity could have kept the international community open to the unthought ethical possibility: an openness to Afghanistan itself. It should be considered that a minimal closure against otherness would have involved the inclusion of Afghanistan. This may seem peculiar given the grotesque nature of the Taliban regime, even by some non-Western standards. As Stephen Chan observes, 'it was a state whose strictures were so severe that it seemed universally unpopular'.[70]

However, there is some indication (from as conventional an approach as the English School of international relations (IR) theory) that, particularly in the figure of Mullah Zaeef, the Afghan ambassador to Pakistan, there were grounds to believe the Taliban were adjusting to the apparently 'civilising' conventions of international society. As Paul Sharp argues, Zaeef's brief diplomatic career demonstrates how traditionally Western attributes of diplomacy (flexibility, justification and explanation of actions and so on) were becoming part of the way the Taliban did business.[71] Without the assertion of the international community's exclusionary subjectivity, there could, perhaps, have been a negotiation of time to allow such conventions to work. After all, there were attempts afoot to make Bin Laden available for trial in a third country,[72] which would have proved a significant cultural compromise given that '[n]either Sharia nor Pashtun conventions of hospitality would permit Bin Laden's surrender to a secular power, particularly on prudential grounds alone'.[73]

An openness to the possibility of Taliban membership of the 'international community' would have involved further significant negotiation of sameness and difference; yet, Afghans themselves may have been beginning such a negotiation. An additional benefit could have been a prompting of reflection upon which others any subject is responsible for protecting. British foreign policy itself argues that a responsibility to protect some human lives through violent intervention involves abnegating a responsibility to protect human lives that will suffer and die as a result of that intervention.[74] A more open subjectivity may also, one can only speculate, involve acknowledgement of a moral responsibility for more others. The assertion of the international community seemed to come at the unquestioned expense of Afghan soldiers, civilians, the new category of 'un-lawful combatants' (which included Zaeef, who was eventually transferred to detention in Guantanamo Bay),[75] as well as allied casualties. Perhaps maintaining an open, negotiating subjectivity would have at least demanded no *additional* closure toward the other, no additional denial of responsibility as was arguably demonstrated subsequently in Afghanistan and later Iraq. The closure of the subject as affirmed by British foreign policy, despite its apparent openness (through its inclusion for example of Syria, Saudi Arabia and Pakistan), could then have been negotiated further to maintain a responsibility for *more* others. Perhaps the active policy of *doing nothing* in relation to Afghanistan would have been the best negotiation of the ethico-political after September 11.[76]

However, to a certain extent, this discussion is parenthetical. Ending, or at least de-reifying, the institution of British foreign policy would have done little to affect the policy toward Afghanistan and Iraq; as has been made clear, 'Britain' was not the subject affirmed by the British text. Yet, the same logic of negotiating a minimal closure, or maximum openness, of subjectivity is applicable to what may be more commonly seen as domestic policy. Much of the discussion has thus for related to the construction of September 11 as a threat to the subjectivity of the 'international community'. But the terrorist attacks on London in July 2005 were constructed precisely as a 'foreign' threat[77] against the subjectivity of 'Britain'. The closure on this occasion was not so much against an external as an apparently *internal* other, against British-born extremists. This would appear to make the government's response to the London bombing a matter for the Home Office rather than the Foreign Office. However, as a practice of discursively constituting and relating to otherness, foreign policy can also happen domestically. Such otherness can be 'at home' as well as 'abroad'.

A negotiation of the end of the formal reification of British subjectivity in foreign policy would mean, similar to that of the 'international community' mentioned earlier, an acknowledgement of failure as inherent within the possibility of success. The greater openness generated by shuttling between the necessary failure of insecurity and success of security could be used to negotiate less automatic closure against otherness seen in the crackdown on human rights. Such precipitous closures, which would be brought under considerable scrutiny by any such negotiation, would include the increases, and attempts to increase further, the period of detention without charge of terrorist suspects;[78] the tactics used in the 'Forest Gate' raid; and particularly the Metropolitan Police's 'shoot to kill' policies (in *Operation Kratos* and its companion *Operation Clydesdale*).[79]

These policies, especially those involving 'shoot to kill', have come under closer scrutiny, but only following the shooting of Jean Charles de Menezes.[80] The aim of a negotiation of British foreign policy in this context would be similar to that of the 'international community' following September 11: a broader responsibility toward more others, a responsibility that closes against fewer others, those who will suffer as a result of a policy *as well* as those who may suffer without it. However, there is no guarantee that a negotiation, a decision that seeks openness through closing according to the specificity of the context, will not cause death and suffering. After all, the killing of de Menezes, the very policy that has been used to show the ultimate violence toward the other in British foreign policy, could easily be the result of a negotiation.

Although there are many unanswered questions relating to the shooting,[81] it was certainly not the simple result of a policy. The response was framed in terms of *Operation Kratos*,[82] or with its parameters, as senior Metropolitan Police sources described it.[83] But Barbara Wilding (then Deputy assistant commissioner and chair of the Met's suicide bomber working party) makes clear that the two policies in place for suicide bombing scenarios (*Kratos* and *Clydesdale*) did not cover the events surrounding de Menezes' shooting. Rather, it was 'somewhere in between' the two.[84] Far from rigidly following a predetermined policy, the shooting bears many hallmarks of negotiation: it appears a context-bound decision, without clear knowledge, to close against one other presumably to act responsibly to other others. The only way to have ruled out this killing would have been the opposite of negotiation: a strict policy of *not* shooting to kill. The shooting of de Menezes then, while a potential example of the 'worst', an outrageously unethical closure, an irresponsible extra-judicial killing, will always be a risk of negotiation.[85] Yet, it is possibly 'better' than a strict policy of not shooting to kill.

Negotiating risk

Negotiating an ethico-political foreign policy will not be in any sense 'safe', and it is 'everything but a position or assurance'.[86] This is part of the reason for Derrida choosing the word 'negotiation', meaning 'no-leisure'. By maintaining an openness to the future, negotiation also maintains an openness to the coming of the 'worst'; even the attempt to avoid the worst through intermediate schemas aims to be a closure that maintains openness. Although this risk and danger has been brushed over in the sections earlier, it should not be ignored, and the possibility of (i.e. ir-responsible), un-ethical killings, such as that of de Menezes, is only one such hazard.

Most importantly, leaving the affirmation of a subjectivity open to be negotiated in the immediacy of a context is an unwieldy and awkward prospect. There is no criterion to judge where it is better to close, where to stop the chain of signifiers, whether new subjectivities should be constructed or whether existing constructions can be affirmed. Yet, equally, any decision must be made as a matter of urgency. Although negotiation oscillates between imperatives, this cannot mean a deferral of the decision; rather, the decision must be made '*with the utmost urgency*. And by *urgency*, I mean the necessity of not waiting, or rather, the *impossibility of waiting* for the end of reflection.'[87] The decision must always be made *now*, in the immediacy of the moment. Thus, when the call comes from the other, as it appeared to from Sierra Leone in 2000, or 'Africa' more generally post-2003, the subject capable of taking responsibility must be affirmed and respond immediately. There can be no ethical justification for deferral and delay.

This urgency applies to the knowledge informing our decision of which subject to affirm as well as its timing. Negotiation is specific to context and, therefore, strives to take the whole of this context into account. Yet, even if it were possible to do this (which it is clearly not),[88] even if comprehensive information were available about Sierra Leone for example, the moment of decision 'must not be the consequence or the effect of this theoretical or historical knowledge'.[89] In a sense, the negotiated affirmation of a subject must be taken *without knowledge*. It must not be taken in ignorance; indeed, 'one needs to know and one needs to know as much as possible and as well as possible'.[90] But between this knowledge and the decision, 'the chain of consequence must be interrupted'.[91] That is to say, the relationship between knowledge and the decision cannot be one of cause and effect; the decision cannot result as a simple consequence of knowledge. Such a complete knowledge, if possible, would *give* the decision; it would make the matter *decidable*. In contrast, to retain undecidability and thereby our responsibility for making the decision, there must be doubt as to the openness of the subject, whether 'Britain' closes too precipitously toward African states and the AU in Sierra Leone, or through supplementation of NEPAD by the Commission for Africa.

The cumbersome nature of ending British foreign policy clearly has its risks and drawbacks in terms of responding efficiently and effectively. It is arguably 'safer' to continue with the automatic affirmation of 'Britain' as subject, as capable of taking responsibility for others through its foreign policy. After all, 'it' can react immediately as it is seen to be more 'natural', if less ethically open, than other possibilities. It also has the infrastructure, the diplomats, contacts and missions to make a quick response possible. However, such a 'safety' is not without danger: danger of irresponsibly reinforcing the humiliation of an objectified, failing 'Africa'; danger of allowing the indefinite detention of suspects to assert a necessarily insecure subjectivity. This, for Derrida, is even worse than the first option as it risks 'the worst along with good conscience' that one has done the right thing.[92] In contrast, negotiation allows no good conscience but prompts us to think other options, other possibilities, other inventions of ethics as foreign policy. A negotiated risk, while irreducibly risky, can be experienced 'both as a threat and *as a chance*',[93] a chance of avoiding the worst and even inventing the 'better'. Ending the reification of 'Britain' as natural subject, I would argue, is also a risk with a *chance*: a chance of a wider, more respectful responsibility toward more others.

A second significant danger or threat is that opening the formation of a new 'British foreign policy' to otherness risks it being perverted. In Hain's terms, the new type of foreign policy would be collated by a 'Department for Global Affairs',[94] but how would one prevent such a Department from falling prey to the influence of illiberal, extremist groups? Without a strong notion of what 'Britain' *is* in world politics, what British foreign policy stands for and, therefore, which MNCs, businesses, organisations (international, regional and national), pressure groups, charities and foreign states should be included in and (more importantly) excluded from the process, a Department of Global Affairs could be colonised or hijacked.

This risk is essentially one of hospitality, as will be discussed further in relation to negotiating Turkish accession to the EU. However, in one sense, it misunderstands the *negotiation* of ending British foreign policy. Such a negotiation will always try to guard against the worst calculation – it is a negotiation of inclusion *and exclusion*. Yet, the potential for danger here is far greater than if a strong notion of 'Britain as subject' were perpetuated. But this is also a risk with an opportunity: an opportunity to include others in the policies that will affect them; an opportunity to act responsibly and respectfully, therefore, toward a wider range of otherness, while not toward all otherness.

Perhaps there is another risk here that could be mentioned, though it is only hesitantly included: the danger of a lack of accountability in foreign policy. David Chandler and Volker Heins claim that the notion of an ethical foreign policy is attractive to Western politicians because it means they can escape national democratic accountability by appealing to a wider, universal constituency.[95] But with a Department of Global Affairs, open to the influence of otherness, who is to be held accountable for foreign policy? Who is it that answers to the question 'who'? If a policy goes wildly wrong, if it turns out to be deeply unethical and irresponsible by causing more suffering and death than it prevented, who is to be blamed? The risk associated with negotiation here is that perhaps no one can be. Perhaps responsibility is diffused amongst all.

But what would be the purpose of holding someone to account in this manner? If it is that unethical practices should be noted as such and irresponsible entities placed beyond where they can do further damage, this is important to reclaim. However, if the issue is rather one of holding a single entity accountable such that all others can have a clear conscience, perhaps such a risk is worth taking. Such a clean conscience is not something a deconstructive negotiation would be in the business of pursuing; indeed, a hallmark of negotiation is the *impossibility* of a clean conscience.[96] If negotiating an end to British foreign policy risks this particular loss of 'accountability' then it seems no particular risk at all.

An ending of British foreign policy, defined as terminating the apparently 'natural' and immediate affirmation of 'Britain' as a subject of foreign policy, could perhaps allow a greater openness to the other. This could involve a negotiation of policies such as a 'responsibility to respect', which may allow for help to be given to the other as other, rather than as becoming same. It may also provide the opportunity for a more minimal closure against both external others, such as Afghans and Iraqis, and internal others, such as suspected domestic terrorists and Jean Charles de Menezes. In all this, however, ending its foreign policy also leaves 'Britain' open to risks, such as terrorist attacks and genocidal massacres. The hope is that such a threat could also be considered an opportunity.

Accelerating Turkish accession

In contrast to the apparent sensationalism of 'ending' British foreign policy, accelerating Turkish accession into the EU may seem a rather obvious and banal suggestion. However, any potential negotiation of ethical hospitality in EU foreign policy will necessarily be a matter of negotiating between a hospitality offered toward the other and a hospitality offered toward the same – a negotiation of what the same 'is', of how the EU sees its 'self', its own subjectivity. The demand for this is even greater because the other (for instance, Ukraine) is always already within, making the EU a stranger to itself. As Michael J Shapiro notes, any ethical, cosmopolitan hospitality 'must begin at home', through an 'ethic of hospitality... to one's collective self'.[97] A negotiation of EU foreign policy and the suggestion of accelerating Turkish accession is thus far from banal: it is about a de-reifying and de-essentialising, an 'unmapping' and 're-writing',[98] of the European 'home' without abandoning it.

But what would be involved in such a potential negotiation? What would a 'de-essentialising' of the European 'home' look like? As I discussed in Chapter 4, this 'home', as represented in EU foreign policy, contains both geographical and moral elements. First, those granted hospitality must be considered geographically European, hence the responsibility toward the proximate 'family'. Second, the EU represents its 'home' as based on 'political and ethical' values such as justice, transparency, democratic accountability,[99] respect for liberty, human rights, fundamental freedoms and the rule of law,[100] tolerance, inclusiveness and respect for others.[101]

A negotiation of EU foreign policy must question precisely these predicates of the 'home'. A negotiation seeks an im-possible invention of the ethical, something that 'exceeds my own being, my own possibility, my own potentiality'.[102] Such an invention would be something like a decision I myself am incapable of making. If a subject is defined as a set of capacities, attributes, or predicates, such an invention would be one that breaks from this definition; thus, it could no longer be of *me*, but is more like 'the decision of the Other'.[103] Such an invention for the EU would therefore involve a hospitality that is impossible for the EU as it defines itself, a hospitality that the EU could not seem to offer in its own terms.

In a territorial sense, a radical invention of ethics as hospitality would perhaps mean moving away the questions of the European Neighbourhood Policy (ENP) and Ukraine; instead, countries that are precisely *not* territorially adjacent to the EU and yet share their ethical and political heritage could be considered. What about the accession of Canada, New Zealand or, perhaps, Brazil? John Redmond notes the 'practical consideration[s]' that make it 'difficult for New Zealand to function as a member of the EU'.[104] But could such practical problems not be solved, especially for the sake of an ethical vision that the EU claims to embrace wholeheartedly? Similarly, a negotiation of the values of the European 'home' might permit an invitation to those nearby who, while not necessarily sharing 'European' values, are perhaps in more need of hospitality (for reasons of security, prosperity, stability and so on). Could Israel, Lebanon or even, perhaps, Morocco be extended a hospitable welcome?

These are, of course, highly unlikely speculations. But they are precisely the possibilities of the impossible that remain to be thought through a negotiation of ethics as EU foreign policy. Furthermore, through consideration of the apparently impossible, space is created for what is argued here: a negotiation of an EU ethico-political foreign policy could, perhaps, accelerate Turkish accession to the EU. Possibly the best illustration of a negotiated ethics practised as hospitality is the welcoming of a Turkish other, an invitation to a Turkey that remains dangerously Turkish and other, to become a transformative part of the European 'home'.

Turkish accession to the EU

Unlike ending British foreign policy, Turkish accession to the EU has been part of the EU foreign policy text for many years. An openness to abandoning British foreign policy was demonstrated only once; Turkish accession has been a live issue since 1963. As such, accelerating Turkish accession is far from an invention of the unprecedented. However, as Patten put it in 2004, the question of Turkish accession 'has been asked, and received halting, embarrassed and obfuscatory answers for more than thirty years'.[105] Revealingly, Patten goes on to give a halting and obfuscatory speech in which he restates the clichéd argument that Turkey 'lies on the cusp between the current EU and the Islamic world'.[106]

Turkey has long been a liminal, problematic figure for Europe.[107] However, in 1963, Turkey was granted associate membership of the European Economic Community, and then, President of the Commission, Walter Hallstein, famously declared that 'Turkey is part of Europe', demonstrating that full membership was likely in the future.[108] In 1970, it was agreed that a customs union would come into affect by the end of 1995; yet, the Commission and Council were broadly negative about Turkish membership. Harun Arikan argues that this period saw the EU conduct a 'containment strategy, designed to delay indefinitely the prospect of membership while keeping Turkey within the economic, security and political sphere of influence of the EU'.[109]

In 1997, the European Council Summit in Luxembourg saw negotiations open with all applicant countries except for Turkey, leading to a Turkish withdrawal from the process in protest. Helpfully, Jose Casanova translates this into the hospitable terminology of the EU's ethical foreign policy: Turkey, he says, has been 'patiently knocking on the door of the European club since 1959, only to be told politely to keep waiting, while watching latecomer after latecomer being invited first in successive waves of accession'.[110] A compromise was reached at the Helsinki European Council in 1999, with the EU accepting Turkey as a candidate for full membership. However, a negotiation schedule was not granted until the Copenhagen summit in December 2002. This is the context of the period of EU foreign policy under consideration. It led to one of the Prodi Commission's self proclaimed 'most important' decisions:[111] the 2004 assessment that Turkey was in compliance with the Copenhagen criteria for membership and the recommendation that negotiations on accession be opened.[112]

Throughout the 1999–2004 period of EU foreign policy, Turkey was described as unlike other potential members of the European family: '[t]he situation of Turkey calls for special treatment'.[113] By 2002, although talks continued with Bulgaria, Romania and Turkey, '[f]or the first two countries the way ahead is already mapped out. For Turkey it is less well charted.'[114] In 2004, while moving toward the Commission's positive opinion on beginning accession negotiations with Turkey, Prodi especially begins to treat Turkey as more 'normal'. For instance, he claims that the 'Commission will apply the same principles to Turkey as to all other candidate countries'.[115] Yet, when the decision came, the Commission offered a 'yes', but a 'qualified yes that is accompanied by a large number of recommendations on following up and monitoring the situation in Turkey'.[116]

During this period, the wider debate has seen a rehashing of familiar themes. While a crude formulation, those opposed to Turkish accession 'simply see Turkey as too big, too poor, too far away and too Islamic'.[117] Emphasis has been placed on a whole range of issues denoting Turkish difference: Turkey's population size (both in terms of the voting weight Turkey would carry in the Council and in terms of migration), the predominance of Islam, limits on Turkish democracy, human rights abuses, the continued denial of the Armenian 'genocide', the unresolved question of Cyprus, the treatment of the Kurdish minority, the ongoing conflict with Greece and the structure of the economy.[118] This comes together for German historian Hans-Ulrich Wehler, part of the vanguard against Turkish accession, in the argument that Turkey is simply not European, or Western, enough.[119]

In contrast, those in favour of accession have argued, along Hallstein's line, that Turkey simply *is* European. Turkey, it is argued, has a clear 'European vocation'.[120] The very name 'Turkey' is, after all, European, adopted in 1923 when the Republic was set up from the Italian version, *Turkiye*.[121] Turkey has taken on Swiss and German law, the Latin alphabet and French administration. Although Norman Stone acknowledges that this does not constitute Europeanness, to 'make so much use of the European model does mean that [Turkey] must have had the genes in the first place'.[122] As Prodi puts it, to those in favour, it is a 'fact that Turkey belongs to Europe'.[123]

Ironically, there is a common ground between these two irreconcilable positions: both agree that for Turkish accession to be legitimate, Turkey must somehow 'be' European; one side claims it is, and the other claims that it is not. My argument for accelerated Turkish accession as a potential negotiation of the ethical in EU foreign policy opts for neither of these essentialist positions. It turns them on their head, suggesting that Turkey should not be allowed to accede *as* European, but rather that it should accede *as other*, as *not* European, as *Turkish*, to the extent that it can *be* any of these things. What could appeal to a negotiated ethico-political invitation to Turkey is the opportunity to invite the other in as other, rather than as the same. This would be an invention of the policy of Turkish accession, something that the EU could not decide to do because of the (territorial and moral) way it defines its 'self'. Rather, such a decision could only come from the other, an other that is explicitly not simply European, neither territorially nor in moral values.

There are, at times, suggestions of openness to such a negotiation of the ethico-political in the EU foreign policy text. In territorial terms, when debating the formation of the ENP, Prodi observes that the borders of the EU are not permanently fixed. To the East and South, 'it is very difficult to make out the new frontiers of Europe. This, of course is nothing new: it has been hard to decide where Europe ends in these two compass directions for thousands of years'.[124] In terms of values, Patten hints that what appeals most about Turkish accession is that it is not precisely the same but retains at least some element of otherness. 'How welcoming should we be to a neighbour that has demonstrated the falsity of the case that Islam and democracy do not mix?'[125] He continues by observing that 'we cannot help but be conscious of the symbolism, at this time, of reaching out a hand to a country whose population is overwhelmingly Muslim'.[126] Indeed, Patten would later redefine Turkish accession as an opportunity, one which would change the EU and the way it defines its 'self', giving it a new purpose and dynamism.[127]

Such openness has since been largely closed down and greater restrictions placed on negotiations for Turkish membership. Although not in the time-span I cover, it is interesting to note that EU enlargement commissioner Olli Rehn observed in 2005 that 'Turkey will not become a member of the union today or tomorrow ... It will be a long, difficult and tortuous road'.[128] As Casanova puts it, the 'closer Turkey gets to meet [sic.] the political conditions, the more the unstated cultural conditions of already belonging to European civilization tend to gain prominence in the debate'.[129] In other words, the EU's apparent openness to the Turkish other is closing; hospitality is becoming increasingly dependent on the other becoming same. By the end of 2006, negotiations were partially frozen, and Redmond argues that the best Turkey can now hope for is some kind of special status or partial membership of the EU.[130] For this reason, the suggestion that accelerating Turkish accession could constitute a negotiation of the ethical in EU foreign policy comes at an ideal time.

Negotiating decisions

The ethico-political in EU foreign policy is about both the negotiation of hospitality (the conditional and the unconditional) and the 'home', or the 'self', into which the other is welcomed. In relation to accelerating Turkish accession, we must first of all seek an oscillation between the imperatives of conditional and unconditional hospitality, searching for the better decision, the better cut or closure, the better *hostility*. This means that all forms of hostility, all questions asked and conditions set by the EU must be thrown into doubt and interrogated relentlessly as to the possibility of their abandonment.

The first challenge a negotiation would perhaps pose is toward the intense questioning of applicant countries. As Derrida observes, the unconditional law of hospitality demands that we ask nothing of the other, neither for the reciprocity of entering into a pact nor even their names.[131] In sharp contrast to this, Prodi describes the 'questionnaire' handed to Croatia and FYROM upon their applications to join the EU as 'over 2,500 questions on the political, economic, and administrative situation in the country', the answer to which 'will form the basis for the Commission's opinion on the starting of accession negotiations'.[132] Although an unconditional hospitality is out of the question, the emphasis on the number, range and invasiveness of the Commission's questioning appears to stress the EU's general level of hostility to otherness.

There is a danger that the EU's policy of hostility/hospitality through enlargement and the ENP become too ossified, precisely *as a policy*: a matter of applying the same rules and conditions to each applicant country. A negotiation must, therefore, question the unilinear 'road' to EU membership that the Balkans has been 'placed' upon.[133] The representation of the 'road' as a single track, the same for all applicants, suggests that 'hospitality' may have become a dogmatic hostility, a range of conditions set automatically for each applicant, regardless of specific characteristics, history and needs.

The risk is that this hostility is to be equally applied to Turkey; as Prodi said, Turkey will be treated the same as any other applicant country. He is at pains to continually stress that the Commission uses 'the same criteria and methodology that so successfully has been used for all the other candidate countries... These criteria were not invented for Turkey, but apply equally to all countries'.[134] For most critics who back Turkish accession, it is actually the *lack* of uniformity in the conditions which is the problem. Arikan, for example, argues that the conditions placed on Turkish entry are far more strict than those placed on others.[135] In contrast, it is such uncritical uniformity that negotiation discards. Of course, Turkey should be treated differently to Bosnia Herzegovina and Croatia; to the extent that Turkey 'is' anything, it is different to these other entrants. Treating Turkey differently, however, does not mean being more hostile, as has generally occurred. In fact, the opposite could, and perhaps should, be the case. But it is precisely the simple transference and application of conditions from one case to the next, without serious debate or questioning, that is anathema to negotiation.[136]

If such conditions and questions are permanently interrogated, negotiation opens up the possibility that the road to the EU could, in fact, be multilinear. These conditions and questions could, for example, prove too closed to allow for others arriving and travelling on different paths toward the European 'home', or knocking on different doors, depending upon their need. Turkey certainly seems to have travelled a different path, one that is other both to Western Europe and the Central and Eastern Europe which has been 'trapped on the wrong side of history'.[137] Such flexibility and multilinearity of hospitality has been demonstrated by the EU in the past. Spain and Portugal travelled neither the Western nor Eastern path and could not have complied with many of the criteria applied to the Balkans or Turkey. As Redmond puts it,

> Spain's post-Franco democracy was not fully secured when Spain acceded to the EU in 1986; in fact, Spain was allowed to join in large part to safeguard Spanish democracy and to allow it to develop and become fully established... Turkish accession 'can be done' – it just needs the same vision and political will that has been displayed at key moments in the Union's past.[138]

The history of the EU demonstrates the falsity of claims to unilinearity. Negotiation of the conditions on hospitality has occurred to allow what might be called a 'Southern' road into the EU, as well as the 'Eastern' and 'Western' roads. Why not also a 'Turkish' road? And why not make such a road less conditional rather than more so?

The point is that negotiation never allows conditions on hospitality to go unchallenged. Importantly, however, the emphasis on the number and invasiveness of the EU's questions also suggests that the EU is seeking some-thing very specific for its hospitality: assurance. If enough questions are asked and the conditions have been prepared sufficiently, the decision whether or not to offer hospitality will be based on a comprehensive knowl-edge. This would be an ethics of certainty. The knowledge would literally give, or produce, the ethical decision as a pre-programmed response.

However, far from an assurance of ethical foreign policy, this knowledge-based *production* of 'decisions' risks a closure toward the other in the name of an impossible guarantee against the 'worst'. As observed earlier, although knowledge is important for any decision, it can only help so much. It cannot give the decision; if it does, it is not a decision but the product of a technical procedure. The undecidable has been made decidable, and ethics and hospi-tality have been reduced to that which they must exceed. Openness to a truly ethical decision involves negotiation breaking the simple chain of cau-sation between the knowledge and decision. Contrary to the apparent desire of EU officials then, knowledge cannot *produce* an ethical and hospitable decision.

Any decision to welcome Turkey into the EU would, therefore, need to be precisely that: a *decision*. It should be a singular, individual and context-bound closure, which tries to remain as open as possible. This does not mean that the existing rules should be entirely ignored. Rather, norms and rules need to be both conserved *and* destroyed in a negotiation.[139] Each use of a rule or question must be justified within the specific context; a decision to preserve a rule should have the character of a reinvention or at least a rejustification each time to avoid becoming a mechanical application.[140] Therefore, questions *must* be asked, and conditions *must* be set; without them, hospitality and ethics would not be possible. But the questions must be questioned, and conditions must be conditional. This demand of negotia-tion opens up the space for a different treatment of a Turkey that arrives on a different road, to a different door: a welcoming of Turkey as other.

Negotiating Europeanisation/Turkification

Negotiating the conditions placed upon hospitality will always be a matter of negotiating the subjectivity of the host. Allowing the other inside the home means that the host is no longer at-home-with-itself. The home changes, it is not what it was before the entry of the other and the apparent comfort of the subject is disturbed, threatened and changed. It is this aspect of ethics as an openness to otherness, the fact that it also means a *becoming other*, that the EU tries to guard against with its strict conditionality. The EU's ethical enlargement discourse suggests that hospitality can only be granted to the other that has become the same. This is demonstrated by the need for the Balkan countries to prove what Patten and Prodi call their 'properly European vocation'.[141] The other must make itself safe and unthreatening by purging itself of difference.

This standard is applied directly to Turkey: having asked what the EU is, or rather, what it takes to be a member of the EU, Chris Patten suggests that this 'naturally' raises two questions: 'Is Turkey European?' and '[d]oes Turkey respect our principles?'[142] The first question is an especially blatant dismissal of difference, but if Turkey is not able to answer yes to both, it cannot be treated ethically and welcomed into the EU. If hospitality is to be negotiated, however, the oscillation between conditional and unconditional hospitality must be between hospitality to the other *as other* and hospitality to the other *as same*. And it is this which makes Turkish accession such a key moment for ethical EU foreign policy. Unlike most countries seeking a hospitable welcome, Turkey is not represented as straightforwardly European. If it was, Patten would not ask the question. Solana points out that '[f]or almost a century, Turkey has been resolutely affirming that it is a European country';[143] clearly this remains unconvincing.

Turkish accession is an interesting case for ethico-political negotiation precisely *because* Turkey is not European, precisely *in so far as* it remains other. And for the possibility of a genuinely ethical, hospitable foreign policy, it is to the other *as other* that hospitality must be granted. If one welcomes the same into the home, there is no hospitality or ethics – the same is always already part of the home, constituting it as safe, as *home*. In contrast, hospitality being offered to the truly other is risky, and even if no harm comes to the host, it will no longer be what it was. This is acknowledged at times; Patten notes that with Turkish accession, 'we potentially pave the way for a very different EU – and that should be squarely and honestly confronted'.[144] Replace 'potentially' with 'definitely', and Patten is quite right.

Once again, negotiation opens up all conditions placed on Turkish entry (and especially Turkish entry) to a radical interrogation. This does not mean that all conditions are abandoned; that Turkey should gain entry with no safeguards for human rights; that the military's continuing role in Turkish politics goes unchallenged; that treatment of minorities such as the Kurds be simply ignored. Negotiation guards against the 'worst' and will, therefore, always place conditions upon hospitality. Rather, it claims that there is an ethical case for a relaxation of the Copenhagen criteria or their replacement with context-specific criteria. In such a negotiation, the apparent 'facts' of Turkish difference, its overwhelmingly Muslim population, its size, geographical position, traditions, the role of its military, its demographic make-up, regional disparities, infrastructure and rural population[145] would contribute to the case *for* a relaxation rather than for further restriction.

Beyond questioning, there must also be a negotiation of how the subjectivity of the EU will necessarily be transformed by Turkish accession. In what way will the EU become other to itself? As Nilufer Gole observes, even if the issue is narrowed to religion, '[t]he encounter between Europe and Islam is a two-way relation that transforms both sides, both European and Muslim self-presentations'.[146] There has been too much concentration on the Europeanisation of Turkey, attempting to make Turkey less other; perhaps we should also be negotiating a 'Turkification' of the EU. Such a 'Turkification' has already been put under pressure by the fact that Turkey could be the last country to enter the EU and, as such, will have the least influence on its development.[147]

Some recognition exists that both subjects would be changed by a Turkish accession. However, there is always a danger that this negotiation be presented as Turkey becoming more European and Europe simply becoming more 'universal', as suggested by Riva Kastoryano:

> For the Turkish side it is a matter of meeting the conditions to become part of European multiculturalism, from its plurality to its equality. On the side of the member states at stake is a true universal opening, and their effort to influence public opinion on this view of Europe. For this, it is necessary that good wills agree to embrace the idea that Turkey as member state is not a 'threat' to European identity, but to the contrary a trump in its representation of universality.[148]

Such a 'true universal opening' is of course denied by the 'conditions'. Turkey must meet to 'become part of European multiculturalism'. Any true universal opening, a genuine unconditional hospitality, would make no such demands and would very much be a threat to European identity. To welcome a Turkish other to salve liberal European consciences, providing a trump to all criticisms of its universality, is explicitly not what a negotiation searches for.

A 'Turkification of the EU', while an inelegant phrase, is a way of representing the general need for the EU to embrace becoming other to what it is, or what it claims to be. Yet, it must always retain the importance of 'home', if not the possibility of its completeness. It does not necessarily mean that the EU should become more 'Turkish', if there is such a thing. However, the negotiation of EU subjectivity could do worse than to take its lead from the recent attempts to renegotiate the subjectivity of Turkey. This reconceptualisation of Turkey, as both other to, but also *within* Europe, is arguably what has occurred in Islamic Turkish parties over the last decade. Traditionally, Islamic groups in Turkey have seen EU integration as 'the last stage of the assimilation of Turkey's Islamic identity into the Christian West', part of 'a Kemalist plot to convert Turkey to Western civilization'.[149] This was the position of the Welfare Party (*Refa Partisi* – RP) as late as 1995.[150] However, in 1997, the Turkish military flexed its muscles, forcing the RP to give up its increasingly Islamic activities. The party was then closed down by the Turkish Constitutional Court for anti-secularism.

The RP's successor, the Virtue Party (*Fazilet Partisi* – FP), was formed from the RP's ashes in December 1997. However, the FP broke from Turkish Islamic party tradition and declared its support for EU membership as well as democratization, human rights and personal liberties, civilian superiority over the military and the rule of law.[151] In June 2001, the FP found itself also banned for anti-secular activities, but the former RP Mayor of Istanbul, Recep Tayip Erdogan, formed the Justice and Development Party (*Adalet ve Kalkinma Partisi* – AKP), which consisted of the FP's reformist wing.[152] The AKP's triumph in 2002 and landslide victory in 2007 has been partly attributed to their reformist agenda started by the FP and the RP before them.[153]

BuhaneHin Duran claims that the relative ease with which the military forced the dissolution of the RP government in 1997 was a watershed moment for Islamic politics in Turkey. The conversion in relation to the EU, as well as the liberalising changes it made to make itself more acceptable to the EU, were 'directly related to the expectation that Turkey's membership... would facilitate the realization of Islamist demands that had been suppressed by the secular state'.[154] Islamist parties required EU freedoms to avoid being periodically crushed. Ironically, Turkish Islam negotiated a change in its own subjectivity, making itself more like the EU, in order to gain access to the EU and thereby *retain its otherness*. The otherness of Turkish Islam could not be retained in Turkey; it had to become other to itself to remain other to the EU.

Such renegotiation of the same and other must be undergone by the EU as well; 'Turkification' is also necessary. The AKP makes this demand, arguing that the EU must also go through a process of redefining what is 'European', such that it can recognise the possibility of being Muslim, Turkish and European at the same time.[155] This negotiation is necessary to retain the EU's openness to ethics. But it will not be without its problems.

> Islamism in Turkey will challenge and complicate this process of constructing a new, common European identity that is politically viable. If Turkey is included, Islamism can no longer be considered a minority problem of multicultural Europe. Instead, it will take the form of a multicultural and multi-religious identity problem affecting all European citizens.[156]

This is the promise and threat of ethics, and it is part of the inherent risk of negotiating hospitality. This danger of ethics cannot be made safe and should not be under-emphasised. But it is a risk that retains a promise, a chance of the impossible possibility of ethics.

Negotiating risk

Negotiation does not seek to deny the danger involved in offering hospitality and maintaining an openness to the ethical. This, as Derrida notes, is why Kant set limits on hospitality, because 'he knew that without these conditions hospitality could turn into a wild war, terrible aggression'.[157] Yet, even Kant's hospitality risks war and aggression. As soon as you allow the other, as other, into the home, the home is put at risk. However, in relation to Turkey, the EU has specific worries, some legitimate, some evoking old prejudices and playing on contemporary fears.

> The fantasy is that the Turks are again at the gates of Europe, ready to overrun its cities with hordes of unemployed males who are not capable of integration; having stopped them once in 1389 in Kosovo and then again in 1529 and 1683 before the gates of Vienna, Europeans are now committing collective suicide by inviting them into the Union, a view suggested by Jorg Haider's Freedom Party.[158]

Sadly, it is not just in the Austrian Freedom Party that such views are expressed. Following the bombing of a synagogue in Istanbul in 2003, Angela Merkel reminded her colleagues that allowing Turkish accession would bring further Islamists and Al-Qaeda members into the EU.[159] Such a representation relies on a convenient memory loss with regard to the terror- ist cells in Hamburg and other European centres planning the September 11 attacks, not to mention the Madrid and London bombings.[160] This reason- ing for the exclusion of Turkey can only be further undermined by the Former US head of Homeland Security, Michael Chertoff, and his observa- tions that *Europe* is currently seen as a major platform for terrorists threatening the United States.[161]

Nonetheless, in large part, the riskiness of welcoming the Turkish other is precisely how other they appear. In purely practical terms, Turkey's popula- tion of 71.1 million would make it the second largest country in the EU (second only to Germany at 82.5 million).[162] Crucially, this would mean that Turkey would require more, or at least equal weighting, of votes to the Brit- ain, France and Italy in the Council of Ministers. This would give Turkey a significant power to disrupt and change the work of the EU, especially with the extension of majority voting in the Lisbon Treaty.[163] Other practical concerns with the population of Turkey are with regards to its relative pov- erty, lack of infrastructure and sizeable rural population.[164] All these will require a transfer of funds away from existing members of the EU towards Turkey. However, these factors have also occurred with several other recent entrants; 'Turkey would not be the first country to join the EU that was not fully prepared' in this sense.[165]

Perhaps more concerningly, as Patten and Solana remind us, if Turkey were to accede, the EU would suddenly share a border with, among others, Syria, Iran and Iraq.[166] A case could be made that, though Merkel's argu- ments are politically motivated slurs, terrorist groups could have easier access to the EU with such a border (though they have not needed one thus far). Should this be considered a security risk, however, it would perhaps be more than assuaged by the size of the Turkish military. Currently, the EU has around two million men and women under arms; Turkey has just over one million, making it the second largest armed force in NATO.[167] This would constitute a potential 50% increase in the EU's military capability, at a time when the EU is seeking to have its ESDP and CFSP taken seriously. Perhaps this, like the population question, would give Turkey too much say within the EU on military matters. But that too would make little difference if it were not for the cultural otherness of Turkey, beyond the many other factors.

A major aspect of its cultural otherness is the predominance of Islam in Turkey and also in its ruling party. There remain concerns about the Islamism of the AKP. The overt religious activities of the AKP are kept in check by the military, which has shut down the AKP's two immediate predecessors and prompted a Constitutional Court vote in July 2008, which came within one vote of shutting down the AKP itself. Critics argue, however, that the AKP reveals its true colours in more subtle ways. For example, Prime Minister Erdogan's rhetoric has been suffused with references to religious books and legends, something that has been emulated throughout the AKP.[168] Critics also point out that Erdogan has history in this regard: as Mayor of Istanbul, he was sent to prison and had to give up his post for reciting a well-known poem in public that summoned the faithful to battle.[169] Perhaps more worryingly, Erdogan has also been quoted as saying that democracy is 'a train to be taken on the way to the final destination, and that the vehicle would be left when it had outlived its usefulness'.[170]

This may well be the reason that the EU wants to place such heavy conditions on Turkish membership. It is certainly a factor in the negative European press reaction toward the AKP election victory in 2002.[171] And the quotation attributed to Erdogan earlier plays directly to the fears that Europe would be 'committing collective suicide'[172] by offering hospitality to Turkey. If the AKP embraced democracy for such instrumental purposes, could they not be doing the same with the EU? Why place the EU in danger by allowing a huge, Islamic other inside that has only a pragmatic use for the EU's fundamental values? After all, if the EU's home becomes a place where it is held hostage, this removes its ability to act ethically and to offer hospitality. And what if Turkey is just *too* other? What if hospitality does indeed lead to 'wild war' and 'terrible aggression' within the European home?

It should be noted that Erdogan has also emphasised that the AKP is a 'conservative democratic' political movement, modelling its link to Islam on the German Christian Democrats' link to Catholicism.[173] This appears to play down the threat of the AKP's Islamism, representing itself deliberately as more European. However, although much of this fear may well be overblown, the riskiness of ethics, the danger of negotiation, must not be minimised. Ethics as hospitality always risks a violation of the home, and by relaxing the conditions upon Turkish entry, by accelerating Turkey's accession and by opening the EU *more* toward the other and, therefore, possibly the 'worst', this danger and insecurity is increased.

Once again, however, it is important to stress that a negotiated risk, while irrevocably dangerous, can be experienced 'both as a threat *and as a chance*'.[174] Were Turkey to be excluded merely because of this otherness, it would demonstrate a violent lack of ethical awareness that itself risks the 'worst'. But unlike a negotiative openness, there is no chance, no opportunity, no possibility of inventing the 'better' in this closure. I am merely proposing that in this context, perhaps, an openness to the Turkish other is a 'better' way of living with the undecidability of ethics.

This recalls an argument made by a group of thinkers brought together to advise Romano Prodi on the 'Spiritual and Cultural Dimension of Europe'. In Spring 2002, Prodi asked the Institut für die Wissenschaften vom Menschen (Institute for Human Sciences) in Vienna to reflect on this issue and report back to him. The argument emerging in their report, published in 2004, was that such negotiative openness toward the other is at the heart of what it means to be 'European'.

> Europe and its cultural identity thus depend on a constant confrontation with the new, the different, the foreign. Hence the question of European identity will be answered in part by its immigration laws, and in part by the negotiated accession terms of new members. Neither of these... can be determined a priori on the basis of fixed, static definitions, such as a catalogue of 'European values'... If Europe is not a fact, but a task, neither can there by any fixed, once and for all defined European boundaries, be they internal or external. Europe's boundaries too must be always renegotiated. It is not geographical or national borders, then, that define the European cultural space – it is rather the latter which defines the European geographical space, a space that is in principle open.[175]

Although this Reflection Group was instituted by Prodi, its open, negotiating attitude toward the subjectivity and identity of Europe is probably not what he was looking for. After all, around the time the group was forming, Prodi was publicly asking: 'Where does Europe *stop*?'[176]

Nonetheless, although the group's report may underplay the riskiness of their strategy, they also make an important point regarding the perpetuity of its negotiation. Accelerating Turkish accession does not mean that hospitality can rest, that ethics have been enacted. Rather, the tension remains between openness and closure. The EU can never know whether it has opened *enough* toward otherness, or whether it will in the future. If Europe is 'in principle' an open space and is to remain so, the terms of each new accession must be negotiated in each individual context. This means that Europe will never stop and neither can the negotiation of its ethico-political foreign policy of hospitality. Perhaps there could even be reason to invent new offers of hospitality: offers to those geographically distant, but close in values, such as New Zealand or Canada; offers to those geographically close, but distant in values, such as Lebanon or Israel.

Yet, there are further possibilities of the impossible for an ethical foreign policy of hospitality. In critiquing Kant's limited notion of hospitality,

Shapiro notes that it 'lack[s] a sensitivity to peoples and nations that [are] not organised in the form of states'.[177] Perhaps a genuine invention of the ethico-political foreign policy the EU has sought to enact could be to advance hospitality toward *peoples* who are not *states*. Perhaps the EU could usher into the European home those truly in need of its protection; perhaps the EU could welcome the Kurds. Such suggestions for the time-being at least remain im-possible, which is not simply the opposite of the possible. But along with ending official British foreign policy, these potential negotiations are attempts to provoke ethico-political foreign policies in the absence of the genuinely ethical.

6   Conclusion

Where I am, I don't know, I'll never know, in the silence you don't know, you must go on, I can't go on, I'll go on.

Samuel Beckett[1]

I'm an optimistic Sisyphean when it comes to ethics and foreign policy. I hope to end up with the stone a bit higher up the mountain than when I started.

Lord Howe of Aberavon[2]

A famous King in Greek mythology mentioned in both the *Odyssey* and the *Iliad*, Sisyphus was, as Albert Camus puts it, 'accused of a certain levity in regard to the gods'.[3] When it was time for Sisyphus to die, he outwitted Thanatos, the personification of death, shackling him until he was freed by Ares.[4] Sisyphus also persuaded Persephone, Goddess of the underworld, to allow his return to the land of the living to ensure the correct sacrifices were conducted for his death. He then failed to return to the underworld and lived on.[5] By way of punishment for this levity, Sisyphus was condemned by Zeus to endlessly roll a large stone up a mountain. Odysseus describes this punishment when he sees Sisyphus in the land of the dead:

> Also I saw Sisyphos. He was suffering strong pains,
> and with both arms embracing the monstrous stone, struggling
> with hands and feet alike, he would try to push the stone upward
> to the crest of the hill, but when it was on the point of going
> over the top, the force of gravity turned it backward,
> and the pitiless stone rolled back down to the level. He then
> tried once more to push it up, straining hard, and sweat ran
> all down his body, and over his head a cloud of dust rose.[6]

Sisyphus has become synonymous with pointless and wasted activity; the Gods thought 'that there is no more dreadful punishment than futile and hopeless labour'.[7] Thus, Camus makes Sisyphus his symbol and hero of the absurd: 'His scorn of the gods, his hatred of death, and his passion for life won him that unspeakable penalty in which the whole being is exerted towards accomplishing nothing'.[8]

Despite never speaking of ethics in the section of his autobiography devoted to his time as British Foreign Secretary (1983–1989),[9] Lord Howe's description of ethical foreign policy is deeply evocative. Like the Sisyphean goal of reaching the top of the mountain, the undecidability of an ethical foreign policy makes it risky, uncomfortable and ultimately unachievable. The concept of negotiation seeks a movement through the undecidability of ethics as foreign policy rather than a movement towards its decidability; it concentrates on *how* the stone could be rolled rather than *where* it will end up. Nonetheless, I remain, like Lord Howe, *optimistically* Sisyphean; the unrealisable goal of an ethical foreign policy persists as the animating concern of this book. As Camus declares in the final line of his essay, '[o]ne must imagine Sisyphus happy'.[10]

The deconstruction of ethical foreign policy is not *opposed* to its possibility. Rather, my reading, which aimed to expose this deconstruction, is inspired by a desire for an ethical, responsible relation to otherness. This conclusion summarises my main arguments of the last four chapters and draws out their central contributions by reasoning them through the possibility of an 'ethical foreign policy *to come*'. But what is meant by this awkward phrase 'ethical foreign policy *to come*'? To answer this question, an outline of Derrida's use of the term 'democracy to come' is necessary.

Promise and perfectibility of the to come

Derrida introduces the concept of the 'future-to-come' as something that resolutely resists clear definition or summary. The temptation to ask 'what *is* the future to come?' is itself part of the problem as this calls on the future to present itself and make itself present. As such, it would no longer be to come.

> The future-to-come, whose grammar is necessary here and imposes the very injunction of its 'it is necessary,' has precisely the impossible-to-anticipate figure of that which comes, which is coming, which remains to come. Irreducible to calculation, program, project, subject, object, and anticipation, what is coming can receive indifferently the names 'event' and 'other'. What remains to be thought remains to come and thus resists thinking. The word 'thinking' thus takes in, without being able to house or contain, this inappropriable resistance of the other.[11]

The future to come then links with what is meant by using the word 'other' as both are impossible to anticipate or fully apprehend. Unlike a future-present (a future that *will* be present), a future-to-come is something we cannot predict, anticipate or name. Thus, the future-to-come is always an experience of the *perhaps*,[12] that which cannot simply *be*, but *may be* (*peut-être*).

But what does it mean to speak of a concept, or a practice, as having a 'to come'? Derrida describes various concepts and institutions as having this quality, including justice,[13] the gift,[14] reason,[15] communism,[16] international law and international institutions.[17] However, the dominant description comes in relation to democracy. In *The Other Heading*, Derrida observes that to speak of its 'to come' means democracy is 'never simply given... but rather something that remains to be thought... that must have the structure of a promise'.[18] Prefixing 'democracy' with a 'to come' does not, therefore, mean what we may currently understand as a representative, generally liberal, form of parliamentary government. It is not pointing to 'the future of a democracy that is going to come or that must come or even a democracy that *is* the future'. To speak of the 'very concept of democracy as a concept of promise' means it will not *be present* in the future.[19]

Derrida, thus, conceives the promise of the 'to come' as *messianic*.[20] The experience of the promise, the experience of waiting for democracy to come, is likened to that of a religion that awaits the coming of the messiah.[21] However, the crucial difference between the promise of the 'to come' and religion is the *lack* of a messiah. The 'to come' is an experience of 'messianicity without messianism',[22] *without* a messiah. A concept of the future to come is beyond anticipation, apprehension and fore-knowledge. Thus, unlike religion, experiencing the promise of a concept that is to come is about 'a waiting without horizon of expectation',[23] without any expectation of when, who or what will come. It is less like waiting for God than *Waiting for Godot*.[24]

Nonetheless, despite the lack of a messiah as the future-present of democracy, or rather because of this lack, the promise of the messianic without messianism still remains 'affirmative' and 'empancipatory'.[25] Instead of being simply achievable and possible, the promise of democracy to come is *beyond* apprehension, knowledge and programming, beyond all our current designations of democracy as liberal or representative. This promise gives an affirmative injunction to strive for its achievement, for its *avenir*, despite the im-possibility of this accomplishment. As Derrida puts it, the 'expression "democracy to come" does indeed translate or call for a militant and interminable political critique'.[26] The experience of democracy to come is both like, and unlike, that of Vladimir and Estragon, who simply wait for Godot without leaving their spot. The '*to*' of the "to come" wavers between imperative injunction (call or performative) and the patient *perhaps* of messianicity (nonperformative exposure to what comes, to what can always not come or has already come)'.[27]

Thus, current affirmations of today's 'democracy' are far from enough; the performative *to* calls for an indefinite contestation of democracy's contemporary forms in the name of 'democracy to come'. This is what Derrida enacts in affirming international institutions and international law while pointing out their significant failures and inadequacies.[28] All the outdated concepts on which institutions such as the UN are based, such as state sovereignty, require rethinking through an interminable political critique:

Which does not mean that international institutions are to be condemned. We ought to be glad they exist, imperfect as they may be, and their perfectibility attests to their future, their still-to-come. Their current existence, even when it leaves something to be desired, represents an immense step forward.[29]

The promise of concepts and institutions with a 'to come', their messianicity without messianism, is demonstrated by their perfectibility, by their capacity for improvement and even 'progress'.[30] As Alex Thomson argues, with the concept of 'democracy-to-come', Derrida 'does confirm the possibility of there being more democracy rather than less'.[31] Yet, this progress, this 'step forward',[32] is only possible as a heavily circumscribed movement of contestation and negotiation that seeks, but cannot achieve, *perfection*.

The perfectibility of democracy to come should not, however, blind us to its corollary: an equally necessary *pervertibility*. Remaining open to the future to come is hazardous: '[t]he future can only be anticipated in the form of an absolute danger'.[33] Because we cannot apprehend what may come, it 'can only be proclaimed, *presented*, as a sort of monstrosity'.[34] This is what Penelope Deutscher observes when she implies that the perfectibility and pervertibility are equally potential corollaries of the 'to come': in the process of perfecting and improving, 'this improvement itself contain[s] the risks of perversion'.[35] Chapter 2, for instance, argued that democracy is always autoimmune; its suicide is a threat that is necessarily contained in the promise of democracy. Thus, the promise of the 'to come' must be 'a promise that risks and must always risk being perverted into a threat'.[36]

Talking of democracy to come then is a matter of obeying the dual injunction of a deconstruction: to gesture in opposite directions at the same time.[37] On the one hand, perfection can only be treated as a *potential* that cannot be achieved and that could be dangerous, but on the other, it must be positively affirmed through its perfectibility *and* pervertibility. Derrida reveals how the two are tied together in the struggle to bring democracy to presence, to make it come, by playing on the Spanish and Italian double meaning of *si* – both positive as a 'yes', and potential as an 'if'.

> If [*si*] democracy does not exist and if [*si*] it is true that, amorphous or polymorphous, it never will exist, is it not necessary to continue, and with all one's heart, to force oneself to achieve it? Well, *yes* [*si*], it is necessary; one must, one ought, one cannot not strive towards it with all one's force.[38]

The apparently tentative nature of this quasi-positive, quasi-affirmative, *if/ yes* is the indispensable structure of the promise and, thus, of any concept which is to come. It gestures at once towards democracy to come's requisite potential nature, its lack of messianism, but also to the affirmative perfectibility of its messianic promise. And it is this perfectibility which institutes continual dissatisfaction and incessant critique of today's 'democracy'.

Ethical foreign policy to come?

The suggestion of an ethical foreign policy to come is made precisely as a *si,* both an *if* and a *yes*. It encapsulates the *yes*, the desire, the affirmation and perfectibility/pervertibility, the striving *for* an ethical foreign policy; it also captures the *if*, its necessary potentiality, its undecidability and never ultimately achievable possibility. Indeed, because this undecidable potentiality is the necessary condition of their being politics and ethics,[39] the *if* is an inseparable condition of the *yes*. In Chapter 1, I noted the co-constitution of the apparently separate issues of ethics and foreign policy; both concern the construction of, and relation to, otherness. If ethical foreign policy, as it has been understood in the British and European Union (EU) foreign policy texts, has a 'to come', a promise and perfectibility, then it is in this im-possibly responsible relation to otherness.

However, the affirmation of 'ethics' and the 'ethical' is not only controversial in international relations (IR) and foreign policy analysis (FPA),[40] it is also problematic in relation to Derridean scholarship. Geoffrey Bennington argues, quite correctly, that '[d]econstruction cannot propose an ethics' because ethics is 'metaphysical through and through and can therefore never simply be assumed or affirmed in deconstruction. The demand or desire for a "deconstructive ethics" is in this sense doomed to disappointment.'[41] John Caputo, in more provocative terms, uses deconstructive thinking to declare himself *against* ethics because this position best acknowledges 'the lack of safety by which judging is everywhere beset'.[42] He argues that Derrida's declining the idea of an ethics of deconstruction[43] is aimed at 'appreciating' the 'tenuous delicacy' of undecidability.[44]

Bennington and Caputo are right to warn against any easy use of ethics. Derrida himself observes that he has 'too much reticence to use the word [ethics] easily'.[45] However, this should not prevent us from an uneasy, unsafe use of the word. Far from simply assuming or affirming an ethics, I have appealed to ethics as an 'ongoing historical practice',[46] stressing its *ongoingness*, its openness, its to come. There is only disappointment if a closed, decidable ethics is sought – this would reduce ethics to something it necessarily exceeds. The deconstruction and negotiation of a responsible relation to otherness undertaken here is, in contrast, a self-consciously risky affirmation of the undecidability of ethics, an affirmation of its perfectibility *and* pervertibility.

In Derrida's later work, there is a suggestion that he was rethinking what ethics might mean and gesturing towards its perfectibility.

> I tried to argue in my seminar this year that pure ethics, if there is any,
> begins with the respectable dignity of the other as the absolute *unlike,*

recognized as nonrecognizable, indeed as unrecognizable, beyond all knowledge, all cognition and all recognition: far from being the beginning of pure ethics, the neighbour as like or as resembling, as looking like, spells the end or the ruin of such an ethics, if there is any.[47]

Negotiating ethics, this pure relation to the absolute unlike, is what Derrida explicitly calls for in a 'thinking of responsibility which does not stop' at the 'dominant schema' of 'determin[ing] the neighbour' as like our selves.[48] This would be a pure ethics as a purely ethical foreign policy – an absolutely ethical and responsible relation to otherness, to the unlike, the 'foreign'. The thinking of this 'unthought' relation 'is still to come',[49] but the careful negotiation of the possibility and impossibility of this association, one of taking 'in without being able to lodge the other *chez soi* [at home in the self]', motivates much of Derrida's most provocative thought.[50]

This ethical relation to the other and otherness that Derrida seeks to provoke was also sought in Chapter 5 through illustrating a potential negotiation of British and EU foreign policy: a responsible and hospitable saving and welcoming of the other *while retaining its otherness* and without making it the same. The promise, the *if/yes* of such an im-possible ethical foreign policy is what Chapter 5 aimed to *institute* through negotiation while acknowledging its necessary potentiality, which resists final *constitution*. This is why negotiation remains the place of the ethico-political, rather than the ethical itself.

As with the concept of democracy to come, invoking a 'to come' of ethical foreign policy calls for incessant critique of the current claims to its enaction, as well as a consideration of all foreign policy text *as* ethics. This consists of an endless challenging, such as that in Chapters 2–4, of the *closure* towards the future that these texts enact, the future of an ethical, responsible relation to otherness *opened* up by claims to an ethical dimension of foreign policy. Campbell suggests that a potential openness is also demonstrated by FPA literature, especially in Rosenau's description of FPA as a discipline.[51] Those who study foreign policy, says Rosenau,

> … must concern themselves with politics at every level… It is in some profound sense a discipline with limitless boundaries… [Students of FPA must] expand their horizons, enlarge their kit of analytical tools, and probe for meaning in heretofore unexplored areas of social, economic and political life… With the passage of time, in short, foreign policy has come to encompass nothing less than the full range of individual and collective processes whereby people seek to give meaning and hope to their lives.[52]

Campbell suggests that this signals 'the existence of a potential if undeveloped open-endedness' in FPA that could suggest an 'alternative theorization' of foreign policy.[53] However, any potential openness has not been developed, and paths to a possible rethinking of foreign policy connected to otherness, politics and ethics are continually closed. Current thinking in FPA has drastically diversified its techniques and focuses but still seems closed to questions of ethics.[54] This volume has been, in part, a contribution to a more open, ethico-political retheorisation of foreign policy as *text*. This has meant a thinking of ethics and foreign policy together – one as a function and constitutive element of the other in the way they relate to otherness. It also gestures toward a possibility for future research in FPA, research that examines the *politics* of foreign policy and develops upon the potential open-endedness which Campbell identifies.

There is a much clearer openness to the promise and perfectibility of an ethical relation to otherness in the 'ethical dimension' instantiated by both British and EU foreign policy. Mervyn Frost declared himself 'delighted' at the announcement of an ethical dimension in the British case 'because by stressing ethics he [Cook] was merely making explicit what is implicit in all foreign policies'.[55] Although I have made a similar case for the co-constitution of ethics and foreign policy, my reasons for valuing explicitness are very different.

For Frost, the appeal of an overt position-taking regarding ethics is that it allows others to 'judge foreign policy by the standards which the government has set for itself'.[56] In a reply to Frost, Eric Herring assails British foreign policy for its 'vigorous and systematic violat[ion] of the ethics professed in its Mission Statement'.[57] Herring does not share Frost's delight at the explicit statement of an ethical dimension, accusing Cook and Blair of 'dishonesty and hypocrisy'.[58] Ironically, however, Frost and Herring appear to agree upon the reason for Frost's delight: the possibility of judging the ethics of British foreign policy based on the standards it has set for itself. Hence, Herring's critique is precisely a *damning* ethical judgement of British foreign policy. However, to value the affirmation of an ethical dimension only in terms of allowing judgement is severely restricted and restricting. It ignores the *openness* such a statement institutes, an openness to the promise and perfectibility of ethics as foreign policy, an openness to its deconstruction and negotiation, an openness to its *to come*.

The importance of Herring's critique, and others like him who question the ethics of Britain's foreign policy,[59] should not be underestimated. After all, the potentiality of the 'to come' calls for *interminable* critique. But this is not all it calls for. The promise of an ethical foreign policy to come lies in its perfectibility, the perfectibility of an undecidably im-possible relation of responsibility to otherness through negotiation and critique. However, to initiate this perfectibility requires a more fundamental criticism and an unlimited questioning of the possibility of ethical foreign policy. Too often, arguments such as Herring's are made regarding how states *ought* to conduct their foreign policies without questioning what makes both ethics and/ as foreign policy possible in the first place. This volume has provided a sustained deconstructive analysis of the ultimately unfounded foundations upon which this possibility is built.

The undecidable possibility of a responsible relation to otherness depends, first and foremost, upon there being a subject of ethical foreign policy that can relate to otherness. There must be some understanding of what 'we' – and others *like* ourselves – *are* which makes 'us' capable of acting ethically in international affairs. British and EU foreign policy constructs this subject as that which is capable of taking responsibility for the lives and suffering of others. However, the deconstruction in Chapter 2 revealed that such a notion of subjectivity cannot be achieved but always remains undecidable as to its possibility. Its reliance on the im-possible ability to accept responsibility comes undone through the internally inconsistent logic of state failure and a constant shifting in the discourse between different signifiers of subjectivity ('Britain', the 'International Community', the 'International Coalition' and so on).

A potential negotiation of subjectivity, illustrated in Chapter 5, reveals the possibility of an ethico-political decision to affirm a subject in response to a call from the other. This negotiation strives for an openness to a future to come of ethical foreign policy, while closing to its 'worst' calculation, its perversion. The perpetual challenging and critique of any claim to a 'we' who can act responsibly opens up new possibilities, potentially ending the dominant narrative of a 'state' subject in foreign policy. Equally, the ceaseless questioning of the EU as it defines itself leads to a potential openness and hospitality to the other as *truly* other, as *not* European. In this way, Chapters 2 and 5 supplement what Vivienne Jabri calls the 'restyling' of the subject of responsibility in IR.[60] There is certainly a need for Jabri's restyling of the individual subject, taking it beyond a stale debate between cosmopolitans and communitarians, but I have offered different possibilities for affirming *collective* subjects in response to a call from the other.

Despite the undecidability of the subjectivity inscribed in the British and EU texts, it is also important to examine how both represent the possibility of enacting ethical foreign policy. In British foreign policy (1997–2007), this possibility was described as a responsibility for both 'protecting' and 'saving' others. However, like subjectivity, Chapter 3 demonstrated this enactment of responsibility to be undecidably im-possible. Britain's apparently responsible interventions in other countries to 'protect' human life were also, by their own logic, an unethical and irresponsible 'attack' upon other human lives. Equally, the responsibility to 'save' undermined the logic of its own ethicality: the responsible compassion of 'saving' those suffering from poverty and disease, as well as for 'saving' the failing states in Africa who produce such suffering, was also an irresponsible contempt for the other *as other*.

Nonetheless, the unachievable desire for a responsible relation to protect and save the other as an other, which cannot be lodged *chez soi*,[61] must not be renounced. My Sisyphean optimism lies in the promise of such a relation, its perfectibility and the possibility that it could be negotiated through individual ethico-political decisions. An indicative sketch illustrating the potential for such a negotiation was given in Chapter 5. It was noted that a greater responsibility for others as other could perhaps have been enacted by seeking a more open, inclusive 'self' which would have to be created in each individual case. This would involve, in each instance, searching for the least violent, most inclusive, least contemptuous invention of collective identity that protected and saved without the need to convert otherness into the same. Such a negotiation is irreducibly dangerous and cannot rule out the worst calculation of closure, such as a Rwandan genocide, or the shooting of Jean Charles de Menezes. Yet, it also enables the chance of a better relation to otherness. This must remain a *perhaps*, a may be, to come, but negotiation and invention allows that there could be *more* responsibility rather than less.

A deconstruction of the EU's discourse finds that the hospitality granted through the EU's policy of enlargement, its policies towards the Balkans, and the ENP, is also an unethical, irresponsible *hostility* because of the conditions it places on those who seek entry. An unconditional hospitality also includes a hostility by endangering the home which makes hospitality possible. Yet, this undecidable *hostipitality* is the condition of hospitality having a 'to come'. As Deutscher observes, 'there is no model hospitality, only processes always in the course of perverting and improving, this improvement itself containing the risks of perversion'.[62] The indicative negotiation of the promise of hospitality in Chapter 5 produced precisely such a dangerous rethinking of its im-possible undecidability. By thinking inventions of the im-possible hospitality (welcoming of otherness that remained impossible for the EU as it understood itself), it opened a space for a negotiation that could, perhaps, involve the EU welcoming the Turkish other as other, as *unlike*. This, however, must always be a future-oriented negotiation that aims at a rethinking of how the EU conceives itself, both as a geographically and ethically defined 'home'.

To return to Lord Howe's evocative analogy, the deconstruction and negotiation of the undecidable im-possibility of an ethical foreign policy offers a way of, perhaps, leaving the stone slightly higher up the mountain. The focus of Chapter 5 was *how* this can be done, not *where* the stone will necessarily end up. In fact, it will not 'end up' anywhere as the movement of Sisyphus and negotiation is perpetual. However, outside the singular context, it is impossible to judge precisely what height can be gained. Nonetheless, an ethico-political foreign policy of negotiating individual decisions always retains the hope of rolling the stone higher, *improving* the ethicality of foreign policy and realising *more* responsibility in the relation to otherness. This is only possible through retaining a reference in negotiation to the perfectibility and promise of an ethical foreign policy *to come*.

The fulfilment of this promise must remain something beyond our expectation, a messianic without messianism. But the messianic promise remains. The appeal of a deconstruction and negotiation of ethics as foreign policy is that it suggests a *way* of rolling the Sisyphean stone. Conceived as a movement *through*, or a *living with* undecidability, negotiation does not, and cannot, *produce* an ethical foreign policy and reach the top of the mountain. In addition, negotiation always risks the stone rolling further down the mountain, producing the worst, most damaging policy that closes toward otherness. But because ethics and foreign policy are co-constituted as attempts to differentiate the self from the other and relate to this otherness (ethics precisely *as* foreign policy), any foreign policy has little option but to roll the stone.

Why does Sisyphus return time and again to pushing the stone? Why does he go on? Because he has no choice, his task defines him; for Camus he is 'the absurd hero'.[63] Equally, ethics is inherent to foreign policy, and there is no choice as to its inclusion or exclusion. But there can be more or less ethical ethics. Like moving a stone up a mountain, the ethicality of ethics is inherently risky. Negotiation, nevertheless, provides the possibility of a movement that can be taken as a chance *as well* as a risk. It allows an optimism that the stone can be moved higher up the mountain than where it was found. One must imagine Sisyphus optimistic.

Notes

1 Introduction

1. R. Cook, 'Mission Statement', 12 May 1997. Online. Available: http://www.guardian.co.uk/indonesia/Story/0,2763,190889,00.html (accessed 11 July 2003).
2. N. J. Wheeler and T. Dunne, 'Good international citizenship: A third way for British foreign policy', *International Affairs*, 1998, Vol. 74, p. 848.
3. L. H. Gelb and J. A. Rosenthal, 'The rise of ethics in foreign policy: Reaching a values consensus', *Foreign Affairs*, 2003, Vol. 82, p. 5.
4. B. Simms, *Unfinest Hour: Britain and the Destruction of Bosnia*, London: Penguin, 2002.
5. For example, David Chandler claims that ethical foreign policy enables states to avoid domestic accountability for foreign policy. See 'Rhetoric and responsibility: The attraction of "ethical" foreign policy', *British Journal of Politics and International Relations*, 2003, Vol. 5, pp. 295–316. Mark Wickham-Jones argued that the announcement had more to do with electoral strategy and internal Labour party politics. See, 'Labour's trajectory in foreign affairs: The moral crusade of a pivotal power?' in R. Little and M. Wickham-Jones (eds.), *New Labour's Foreign Policy: A New Moral Crusade?* Manchester: Manchester University Press, 2000, pp. 3–32.
6. Simon Jenkins, writing in *The Times*, claimed that '[w]hen foreign ministers turn to philosophy, decent citizens should run for cover'. Quoted in M. Frost, 'The ethics of humanitarian intervention: Protecting civilians to make democratic citizenship possible', in K. E. Smith and M. Light (eds.), *Ethics and Foreign Policy*, Cambridge: Cambridge University Press, 2001, p. 34.
7. D. Miliband, 'The Democratic Imperative', Aung San Suu Kyi Lecture, Oxford, 13 February 2008. Unless otherwise stated, all speeches, interviews and press conferences by Foreign Office Ministers are online. Available : http://www.fco.gov.uk (accessed between 11 October 2004 and 1 May 2008).
8. P. Williams, *British Foreign Policy Under New Labour, 1997–2005*, Basingstoke: Palgrave MacMillan, 2005, p. 210.
9. R. Prodi, 'Report to the European Parliament on the Spring European Council', 26 March 2003. All speeches, interviews and press conferences by R. Prodi, President of the EU Commission, are online. Available: http://europa.eu.int/comm/archives/commission_1999_2004/prodi/speeches/index_en.htm (accessed 16 August 2005).
10. See S. Lucarelli and I. Manners (eds.), *Values and Principles in EU Foreign Policy*, London: Routledge, 2006.
11. See I. Manners, 'The normative ethics of the European Union', *International Affairs*, 2008, Vol. 84, pp. 45–60.

12. P. Singer, *The President of Good and Evil: Taking George W. Bush Seriously*, London: Granta, 2004, p. 5.
13. T. J. Farer, 'Humanitarian intervention before and after 9/11: legality and legitimacy', in J. L. Holzgrefe and R. O. Keohane (eds.), *Humanitarian Intervention: Ethical, Legal, and Political Dilemmas*, Cambridge: Cambridge University Press, 2001, pp. 53–89.
14. F. Tesón, 'Ending tyranny in Iraq', *Ethics & International Affairs*, 2005, Vol. 19, p. 20.
15. M. Frost, 'The ethics of humanitarian intervention', p. 35.
16. The terms 'ethical' and 'moral' are used as synonyms throughout this book, following Hutchings' argument that the distinction drawn between the two by scholars such as Jurgen Habermas is untenable. See K. Hutchings, *Kant, Critique and Politics*, London: Routledge, 1996.
17. D. Campbell, *Writing Security: United States Foreign Policy and the Politics of Identity*, revised edn., Manchester: Manchester University Press, 1998, pp. 68–9.
18. Ibid., pp. 68–9.
19. From now on 'IR' will be used to refer to the discipline and 'international relations' to the empirical matter which the discipline studies.
20. See R. K. Beasley, J. Kaarbo, J. S. Lantis and M. T. Snarr (eds.), *Foreign Policy in Comparative Perspective: Domestic and International Influences on State Behaviour*, Washington, DC: CQ Press, 2002.
21. D. Campbell, *Writing Security*, p. 69.
22. J. N. Rosenau, 'Moral fervor, systematic analysis, and scientific consciousness in foreign policy research', in J. N. Rosenau (ed.), *The Scientific Study of Foreign Policy*, New York: The Free Press, 1971, p. 24.
23. Ibid.
24. Peter Singer makes issues of 'ought' central to ethics in the 'Introduction' to his ethics reader. See, P. Singer (ed.), *Ethics*, Oxford: Oxford University Press, 1994, p. 1.
25. Indeed, this is how ethical foreign policies have been generally discussed in the literature with the two fields joined by an 'and' or an 'of'. For instance, see P. Keal (ed.), *Ethics and Foreign Policy*, Canberra, ACT: Allen and Unwin, 1992; R. W. McElroy, *Morality and American Foreign Policy*, Princeton, NJ: Princeton University Press, 1993; K. Smith and M. Light (eds.), *Ethics and Foreign Policy*, Cambridge: Cambridge University Press, 2001; D. K. Chaterjee and D. E. Scheidt (eds.), *Ethics and Foreign Intervention*, Cambridge: Cambridge University Press, 2003; D. Chandler and V. Heins, 'Ethics and foreign policy: New perspectives on an old problem', in D. Chandler and V. Heins (eds.), *Rethinking Ethical Foreign Policy: Pitfalls, Possibilities and Paradoxes*, London: Routledge, 2007, pp. 3–21; D. B. MacDonald, R. G. Patman and B. Mason-Parker (eds.), *The Ethics of Foreign Policy*, Aldershot: Ashgate, 2007.
26. Originally published in 1966, reprinted as J. N. Rosenau, 'Pre-theories and theories of foreign policy', in Rosenau, *The Scientific Study of Foreign Policy*. Steve Smith observes that, while many developments were later made on Rosenau's general framework, his pre-theory 'lies at the base of them all' – S. Smith, 'Foreign policy analysis: British and American orientations and methodologies', *Political Studies*, 1983, Vol. 31, p. 558.
27. J. Rosenau, 'Pre-theories and theories of foreign policy', p. 117.
28. Ibid., p. 127 – emphasis in original.
29. Ibid., p. 130.
30. Ibid., p. 132.
31. Ibid., pp. 128–9.
32. Ibid., p. 131.

33. J. Derrida, in M. Payne and J. Schad (eds.), *life. after. theory*, London: Continuum, 2003, p. 8.
34. R. K. Beasley et al., *Foreign Policy in Comparative Perspective*.
35. See 'Decision making as an approach to the study of international politics', later reprinted in R.C. Snyder, H. W. Bruck and B. Sapin (eds.), *Foreign Policy Decision Making*, New York: Free Press of Glencoe, 1962, pp. 14–185.
36. See V. M. Hudson, 'Foreign policy analysis: Actor-specific theory and the ground of international relations', *Foreign Policy Analysis*, 2005, Vol. 1, pp. 1–30.
37. See B. White, 'Analysing foreign policy: Problems and approaches', in M. Clarke and B. White (eds.), *Understanding Foreign Policy: The Foreign Policy Systems Approach*, Aldershot: Edward Elgar, 1989, pp. 1–26.
38. See G. Allison and P. Zelikow's 'Governmental Politics' model, *Essence of Decision: Explaining the Cuban Missile Crisis*, 2nd edn., New York: Longman, 1999, pp. 255–324.
39. See W. Carlsnaes, *Ideology and Foreign Policy: Problems of Comparative Conceptualization*, Oxford: Basil Blackwell, 1986.
40. See N. Onuf, 'Speaking policy', in V. Kubalkova (ed.), *Foreign Policy in a Constructed World*, New York: M.E. Sharpe, 2001, pp. 77–95.
41. C. Hill, *The Changing Politics of Foreign Policy*, Basingstoke: Palgrave MacMillan, 2003.
42. J. Derrida, *Margins of Philosophy*, translated by A. Bass, Brighton: Harvester Press, 1982, p. 9.
43. J. Derrida, *Positions*, translated by A. Bass, Chicago: The University of Chicago Press, 1982, p. 26.
44. W. Connolly, *Identity\Difference: Democratic Negotiations of Political Paradox*, Ithaca: Cornell University Press, 1991, p. 54.
45. J. Derrida, *Of Grammatology*, translated by G. Chakravorty Spivak, Baltimore: The Johns Hopkins University Press, 1976, p. 158.
46. Ibid., p. 159.
47. J. Derrida, *Limited Inc*, translated by S. Weber, Evanston, IL: Northwestern University Press, 1988, p. 136.
48. Ibid., p. 137.
49. J. Derrida, *Positions*, p. 60.
50. J. Derrida, *Limited Inc*, p. 136.
51. J. Der Derian, *Antidiplomacy: Spies, Terror, Speed and War*, Oxford: Blackwell, 1992, p. 27.
52. Campbell, *Writing Security*, pp. 68–9.
53. Prime Minister Tony Blair (1997–2007), foreign secretaries Robin Cook (1997–2001) and Jack Straw (2001–2006) and Foreign Office ministers, Peter Hain, Kim Howells, Denis MacShane, Mike O'Brien, Bill Rammell, Ian Pearson and Lord Triesman.
54. J. Derrida, *Positions*, pp. 19–20.
55. Put very forcefully by M. Curtis, *Web of Deceit: Britain's Real Role in the World*, London: Vintage, 2003.
56. D. Chandler, 'Rhetoric without responsibility: The attraction of "ethical" foreign policy', *British Journal of Politics and International Relations*, 2003, Vol. 5, pp. 295–316.
57. R. W. McElroy, *Morality and American Foreign Policy: The Role of Ethics in International Affairs*, Princeton, NJ: Princeton University Press, 1992, especially p. 30; see also W. Thomas, *The Ethics of Destruction: Norms and Force in International Relations*, Ithaca: Cornell University Press, 2001.
58. J. Derrida, 'Letter to a Japanese friend', in D. Wood and R. Bernasconi (eds.), *Derrida and Différance*, Evanston, Il: Northwestern University Press, 1988, p. 3.

59. J. Derrida, *Negotiations: Interventions and Interviews 1971–2001*, translated by E. Rottenberg, Stanford: Stanford University Press, 2002, p. 193.
60. Derrida, *Limited Inc*, p. 141.
61. J. Derrida, *Points … Interviews, 1974–1994*, translated by P. Kamuf, Stanford: Stanford University Press, 1995, p. 200.
62. J. Derrida, 'Signature Event Context', in *Limited Inc*, translated by S. Weber, Evanston, Il: Northwestern University Press, 1988, p. 21.
63. J. Culler, *On Deconstruction: Theory and Criticism after Structuralism*, London: Routledge, 1983, p. 93.
64. For an analysis of these dichotomies, see, amongst others, R. Ashley, 'The geopolitics of geopolitical space: Towards a critical social theory of international politics', *Alternatives*, 1987, Vol. 12, pp. 403–32; J. Edkins and M. Zehfuss, 'Generalising the International', *Review of International Studies*, 2005, Vol. 31, pp. 451–72; and R. B. J. Walker, *Inside/Outside: International Relations as Political Theory*, Cambridge: Cambridge University Press, 1993.
65. J. Derrida, 'Signature Event Context', p. 21.
66. J. Derrida, *Points … Interviews, 1974–1994*, p. 100.
67. See especially J. Derrida, *Of Grammatology*, pp. 52–5, but also J. Derrida, *Positions*; and J. Derrida, *Writing and Difference*, translated by A. Bass, London: Routledge, 2002.
68. Derrida, *Positions*, pp. 41–2.
69. Ibid., p. 42.
70. Ibid., pp. 42–3.
71. Ibid., p. 43.
72. M. J. Shapiro, 'Textualizing global politics', in J. Der Derian and M. Shapiro (eds.), *International/Intertextual Relations: Postmodern Readings of World Politics*, New York: Lexington Books, p. 13.
73. By 'British foreign policy' I mean foreign policy conducted by the government of the United Kingdom, following the example of M. Smith, S. Smith and B. White (eds.), *British Foreign Policy: Tradition, Change and Transformation*, London: Unwin Hyman, 1988.
74. See P. Singer, *The President of Good and Evil: Taking George W. Bush Seriously*, London: Granta, 2004.
75. See C. O'Driscoll, *The Renegotiation of the Just War Tradition and the Right to War in the Twenty-First Century*, New York: Palgrave MacMillan, 2008; T. Kochi, *The Other's War: Recognition and the Violence of Ethics*, London: Birkbeck Law Press, 2009.
76. R. Cook, 'Mission Statement'.
77. R. Cook, 'Beyond good intentions – Government, business and the environment', Speech to the Business and Environment Dinner, 17 November 1998.
78. P. D. Williams, 'The rise and fall of the "ethical dimension": Presentation and practice in New Labour's Foreign Policy', *Cambridge Review of International Affairs*, 2002, Vol. 15, p. 54; M. Curtis, *Web of Deceit: Britain's Real Role in the World*, Vintage: London, 2003, p. 364.
79. J. Kampfner, *Blair's Wars*, London: Free Press, 2003, p. 124.
80. N. J. Wheeler and T. Dunne, 'Moral Britannia? Evaluating the ethical dimension in Labour's Foreign Policy', Foreign Policy Centre, 2004. Online. Available: http://fpc.org.uk/fsblob/233.pdf (accessed 2 June 2004), p. 14.
81. Such questions have been prominently raised especially by Christopher Hill – see 'The capability-expectations gap, or conceptualizing Europe's international role', *Journal of Common Market Studies*, 1993, Vol. 31, pp. 305–28. See also, R. H. Ginsberg, 'Conceptualizing the EU as an international actor: Narrowing the theoretical capability-expectations gap', *Journal of Common Market Studies*, 1999, Vol. 37, pp. 429–54. For a more general introduction to this question,

see K. E. Smith, *European Union Foreign Policy in a Changing World,* Cambridge: Polity, 2003.

82. F. Bicchi, '"Our size fits all": Normative power Europe and the Mediterranean', *Journal of European Public Policy,* 2006, Vol. 13, p. 286.
83. C. Hill, 'The capability-expectations gap', p. 316.
84. F. Bicchi, ' "Our size fits all" ', p. 286.
85. I. Manners, 'Normative power Europe: A contradiction in terms?', *Journal of Common Market Studies,* 2002, Vol. 40, p. 239.
86. See for example, A. Hyde-Price, '"Normative" power Europe: A realist critique', *Journal of European Public Policy,* 2006, Vol. 13, pp. 217–34.
87. H. Sjursen, 'The EU as a "normative" power: How can this be?' *Journal of European Public Policy,* 2006, Vol. 13, pp. 235–51.
88. I. Manners, 'Normative power Europe reconsidered: Beyond the crossroads', *Journal of European Public Policy,* 2006, Vol. 13, pp. 182–99.
89. Manners, 'Normative power Europe', p. 252.
90. I. Manners, 'European Union, normative power and ethical foreign policy', in Chandler and Heins (eds.), *Rethinking Ethical Foreign Policy,* p. 118.
91. Ibid., pp. 117–18.
92. See S. Lucarelli and I. Manners (eds.), *Values and Principles in EU Foreign Policy,* London: Routledge, 2006.
93. H. Smith, *European Union Foreign Policy: What it is and What it Does,* London: Pluto Press, 2002, p. 271.
94. R. Prodi, 'The European project in the world: Between values and politics', Speech to Fondazione Don Tonino Bello Alessano, Lecce, 13 June 2003.
95. J. Solana, Speech at the inaugural conference of the course, 'Towards a New International Morality: The Humanitarian Interventions', University of Alcala de Henares, Madrid, 7 July 2000. Unless otherwise stated, all speeches, interviews, articles and press conferences by J. Solana, High Representative for the Common Foreign and Security Policy, are online. Available: http://ue.eu.int/ cms3_applications/applications/solana/index.asp?lang=EN&cmsid=256 (accessed between 11 July 2005 and 8 August 2005).
96. Ibid.
97. R. Prodi, Report to the European Parliament on the Spring European Council, Brussels, 26 March 2003. See also, R. Prodi, 'Europe and Ethics', Speech to the Conference on Politics and Morality, Vienna, 7 December 2002.
98. R. B. J. Walker, *Inside/Outside,* p. 51.

2 The Subject of Ethical Foreign Policy

1. M. Zehfuss, 'Subjectivity and Vulnerability: On the War with Iraq', *International Politics,* 2007, Vol. 44, pp. 58–71.
2. D. Campbell, *Writing Security: United States Foreign Policy and the Politics of Identity,* revised edn., Manchester: Manchester University Press, 1998, p. 39.
3. L. Odysseos, *The Subject of Coexistence: Otherness in International Relations,* Minneapolis and London: University of Minnesota Press, 2007, p. xii.
4. For useful and brief introductions to the history of the subject and its various displacements by social theorists, see J. Edkins and V. Pin-Fat, 'The Subject of the Political' in J. Edkins, N. Persram, and V. Pin-Fat (eds.), *Sovereignty and Subjectivity,* Boulder, Co: Lynne Rienner, 1999, pp. 1-18, and S. Hall, 'The Question of Cultural Identity', in S. Hall, D. Held and T. McGrew (eds.), *Modernity and Its Futures,* Oxford: Polity Press, 2003, pp. 273-325. For a more in depth examination, see C. Williams, *Contemporary French Philosophy: Modernity and the Persistence of the Subject,* London: Athlone Press, 2001.

5. J. Derrida, '"Eating Well," or the Calculation of the Subject: An Interview with Jacques Derrida', in E. Cadava, P. Connor and J-L. Nancy (eds.), *Who Comes After the Subject?*, New York: Routledge, 1991, p. 98.
6. Williams, *Contemporary French Philosophy*, p. 149.
7. R. Cook, 'Mission Statement', 12 May 1997. Online. Available HTTP: http://www.guardian.co.uk/indonesia/Story/0,2763,190889,00.html (accessed 11 July 2003) emphases added.
8. J. Solana, Speech to the Fernandez Ordonez Seminar, 14 January 2000 – emphasis added.
9. Cook, 'Mission Statement'.
10. R. Cook, 'Human Rights Into a New Century', 17 July 1997.
11. T. Blair, 'Facing the Modern Challenge: The Third Way in Britain and South Africa', 8 January 1999. Unless otherwise stated, all speeches, interviews, articles and press conferences by Prime Minister Tony Blair are online. Available HTTP: http://www.10downingstreet.gov.uk (accessed between 27 August 2004 and 1 May 2007).
12. T. Blair, Speech to Global Ethics Foundation, Tubingen University, Germany, 30 June 2000.
13. See T. Blair, 'Speech on the threat of global terrorism', Sedgefield, 13 July 2004.
14. J. Straw, 'Principles of a Modern Global Community', 10 April 2002.
15. Ibid.
16. Blair, 'Facing the Modern Challenge'.
17. R. Cook, 'Bosnia: a new hope', 4 March 1998.
18. T. Blair, 'The New Challenges for Europe', 20 May 1999.
19. Blair, 'Facing the Modern Challenge'.
20. T. Blair, 'Doctrine of the International Community Speech', Economic Club, Chicago, 24 April 1999.
21. M. Wickham-Jones, 'Labour's trajectory in foreign affairs: the moral crusade of a pivotal power?', in R. Little and M. Wickham-Jones (eds.), *New Labour's Foreign Policy: A New Moral Crusade?*, Manchester: Manchester University Press, 2000, p. 17.
22. Blair, 'Speech on the threat of global terrorism'.
23. Ibid.
24. D. MacShane, 'Diplo-Military Politics: The Future Strategic Context of Conflict Prevention and Conflict Resolution', 25 April 2002.
25. Cook, 'Human Rights into a New Century'.
26. B. Rammell, 'Why Human Rights Matter', 25 November 2003.
27. Blair, 'Doctrine of International Community Speech'.
28. Blair, 'Facing the Modern Challenge'.
29. For example, in relation to Syria and Iran: T. Blair, Press Conference, 15 January 2004.
30. For example, in relation to North Korea: T. Blair, Doorstep press conference in Beijing, 21 July 2003.
31. Blair, 'Facing the Modern Challenge'.
32. J. Straw, 'Shaping a stronger United Nations', 2 September 2004.
33. Blair, 'Facing the Modern Challenge'.
34. Ibid.
35. T. Blair, Party Conference Speech 2001, *The Guardian*, 2 October 2001. Online. Available HTTP: http://politics.guardian.co.uk/labour2001/story/0,1212,562006,00.html (accessed 3 March 2005).
36. T. Blair, Doorstep interview at G8 summit, 28 June 2002.
37. Ibid.

38. Cook, 'Mission Statement'.
39. Specifically Nigeria, see R. Cook, 'Human Rights: Making the Difference', 16 October 1998.
40. T. Blair, Speech to WSSD in South Africa, 2 September 2002.
41. T. Blair, 'Partnership for African Development', 7 February 2002.
42. Rammell, 'Why Human Rights Matter'.
43. T. Blair, Mansion House Speech, 13 November 2000.
44. T. Blair, Statement to Parliament on NATO Summit, 25 November 2002.
45. C. Patten, 'The Role of the European Union on the World Stage', Speech at the India Habitat Centre, Jawarharlal Nehru University, New Delhi, 25 January 2001. Unless otherwise stated, all speeches, interviews, articles and press conferences by Chris Patten, Commissioner for External Relations, are online. Available: http://europa.eu.int/comm/archives/commission_1999_2004/patten/index.htm (accessed 7 July 2005).
46. Ibid.
47. R.H. Ginsberg, 'Conceptualizing the EU as an International Actor: Narrowing the Theoretical Capability-Expectations Gap', *Journal of Common Market Studies*, 1999, Vol. 37, p. 432.
48. J. Solana, 'The voice of Europe on security matters', Address to the Royal Institute for International Relations (IRR-KIIB), Brussels, 16 November 2003.
49. Ibid.
50. R. Rummell, 'From Weakness to Power with the ESDP?', *European Foreign Affairs Review*, 2002, Vol. 7, pp. 453–471.
51. A. Missiroli, 'The European Union: Just a Regional Peacekeeper?', *European Foreign Affairs Review*, 2003, Vol. 8, p. 502.
52. Ibid., pp. 497–500.
53. J. Solana, 'The Development of a Common European Security and Defence Policy – the Integration Project of the Next Decade', Speech to EU-Commission Institut fur Europäische Politik Conference, Berlin, 17 December 1999.
54. Solana, Speech to the Fernandez Ordonez Seminar.
55. J. Solana, Speech on the occasion of the Award of the 'Honoris Causa' Doctorate in Social Science, University of Wroclaw, 2 October 2003.
56. R. Prodi, 'Nation, Federalism and Democracy – The EU, Italy and the American Federal experience', Speech at 'The Nation, Federalism and Democracy' Conference, Trento, 5 October 2001.
57. A. Deighton, 'The European Security and Defence Policy', *Journal of Common Market Studies*, 2002, Vol. 4, p. 728.
58. Prodi, 'Nation, Federalism and Democracy'.
59. J. Solana, Speech – Wehrkunde, Berlin, 5 February 2000.
60. C. Patten, 'The Western Balkans: The Road to Europe', Speech to German Bundestag, European Affairs Committee, Berlin, 28 April 2004.
61. R. Prodi, 'The reality of enlargement', Speech to the European Parliament, Brussels, 6 November 2002.
62. C. Patten, Speech to the Peace Implementation Council, Brussels, 23 May 2000.
63. J. Solana, Interview with *Dnevi Avaz* (BiH newspaper), 24 September 2003.
64. C. Patten, Speech to the Assembly of Kosovo, Pristina, 11 September 2003.
65. R.L. Doty, *Imperial Encounters: The Politics of Representation in North-South Relations*, Minneapolis: University of Minnesota Press, 1996, p. 10.
66. J. Solana, Speech at 'The Fire and the Crystal' Conference, Rimni, 21 October 2001.
67. C. Patten, 'Coherence and co-operation: the EU as promoter of peace and development', Speech to the Swedish Institute of International Affairs, Stockholm, 4 December 2001 – emphasis in the original.

68. C. Patten, 'Europe in the World: CFSP and its relation to Development', Speech to the Overseas Development Institute, 7 November 2003.
69. P. Hain, 'Africa: Backing Success', 13 September 1999.
70. Ibid.
71. J. Straw, 'Failed and Failing States', 6 September 2002.
72. Ibid.
73. T. Blair, Statement to Parliament on the NATO Summit in Washington, 26 April 1999.
74. T. Blair, Speech to the Welsh Assembly, 30 October 2001.
75. T. Blair, Speech to the TUC Conference in Blackpool, 10 September 2002.
76. J. Straw, 'Reintegrating Iraq into the International Community – A cause with compelling moral force', 21 February 2003.
77. T. Blair, Answering questions at MTV forum, 6 March 2003.
78. T. Blair, Press Conference with President George Bush at Camp David, 27 March 2003.
79. Straw, 'Principles of a Modern Global Community'.
80. Blair, Party Conference Speech 2001.
81. T. Blair, Statement to the House of Commons, 8 October 2001 – emphasis added.
82. Straw, 'Failed and Failing States'.
83. Ibid.
84. Ibid.
85. Ibid.
86. J. Straw, 'Human Rights Ensure International Security and Prosperity', 18 April 2002.
87. Ibid., repeated in J. Straw, 'Re-ordering the World', 25 March 2002.
88. Straw, 'Failed and Failing States'.
89. Ibid.
90. J. Derrida, *Rogues: Two Essays on Reason*, translated by P-A. Brault and M. Naas, Stanford: Stanford University Press, 2005, p. 123.
91. J. Derrida, 'Autoimmunity: Real and Symbolic Suicides – A Dialogue with Jacques Derrida', in G. Borradori, *Philosophy in a Time of Terror: Dialogues with Jurgen Habermas and Jacques Derrida*, Chicago: University of Chicago Press, 2003, p. 94.
92. Derrida, *Rogues*, p. 22.
93. Ibid., p. 33.
94. Ibid.
95. Straw, 'Failed and Failing States'.
96. R. Bennett, 'Inside the mind of a terrorist' *The Observer*, 22 August 2004.
97. P. Hamilos, 'Mass murders jailed for 40 years as judge delivers verdict on Spain's 9/11', *The Guardian*, 1 November 2007.
98. For a fuller account, see D. Bulley, '"Foreign" Terror? London Bombings, Resistance and the Failing State', *British Journal of Politics and International Relations*, 2008, Vol. 10, pp. 379–94.
99. House of Commons, *Report of the Official Account of the Bombings in London on 7th July 2005*, London: The Stationery Office, 2006.
100. T. Blair, Monthly Downing Street press conference, 7 November 2005.
101. A. Gillan and H. Muir, 'Lawyer condemns "wild west" police raid', *The Guardian*, 5 June 2006.
102. N. Vaughan-Williams, 'The Shooting of Jean Charles de Menezes: New border politics?', *Alternatives*, 2007, Vol. 32.
103. J. Straw, Media Interviews, Gleneagles, 7 July 2005 – emphasis added.
104. Rammell, 'Why Human Rights Matter' – emphasis added.
105. Straw, 'Failed and Failing States' – emphasis added.

106. Derrida, *Rogues*, p. 45.
107. Ibid.
108. See T. Blair, 'Clash about Civilisations', 21 March 2006 and T. Blair, Third Foreign Policy Speech, Georgetown, USA, 26 May 2006. For an extended treatment of this, see Bulley, '"Foreign" Terror?'
109. Derrida, 'Autoimmunity', fn. 7, p. 188.
110. T. Blair, Speech to the General Assembly at the 2005 UN World Summit, 15 September 2005.
111. Blair, 'Clash about Civilisations'; Blair, Third Foreign Policy Speech.
112. T. Blair, Interview with Channel 4 in Istanbul, 28 June 2004.
113. J. Solana, Interview with *Tasspiegel,* 26 March 2003.
114. J. Straw, Interview BBC Radio 4 on the Draft Iraqi Constitution, 30 August 2005.
115. J. Solana, Interview with BBC Breakfast with Frost, 13 July 2003.
116. T. Blair, Statement in response to terrorist attacks in the United States, 11 September 2001.
117. T. Blair, Statement to the House of Commons following the September 11 attacks, 14 September 2001.
118. Ibid. – emphasis added.
119. Ibid. – emphasis added.
120. T. Blair, 'A New Era of International Partnership', 21 September 1998.
121. Blair, 'Facing the Modern Challenge'.
122. R. Cook, 'Guiding Humanitarian Intervention', 19 July 2000.
123. Sir M. Campbell, Prime Minister's Question Time, 25 January 2006. Online. Available: http://www.theyworkforyou.com/debates/?id=2006-01-25a.1421.7 (accessed 16 June 2006).
124. T. Blair, Prime Minister's Question Time, 25 January 2006.
125. Blair, Speech to the Welsh Assembly.
126. T. Blair, Doorstep interview with the Prime Minister in Riyadh, Saudi Arabia, 1 November 2001.
127. T. Blair, Doorstep interview with the Prime Minister and Chancellor Wolfgang Schuessel of Austria, 16 November 2001.
128. J. Straw, 'The Role of Free Press in Foreign Policy', 16 November 2002.
129. T. Blair, 'Let the United Nations mean what it says and do what it means: Speech to Labour Party Spring Conference', 15 February 2003. Online. Available: http://www.labour.org.uk/news/tbglasgow (accessed 3 March 2006).
130. Ibid.
131. T. Blair, Press conference with PM and Spanish PM Jose Maria Aznar, 31 January 2003; and T. Blair, Press conference with PM and President Bush at the White House, 31 January 2003.
132. J. Derrida, *Of Grammatology*, translated by G. Chakravorty Spivak, Baltimore: The Johns Hopkins University Press, 1976, p. 144.
133. Ibid., p. 142.
134. Ibid., p. 145.
135. J. Culler, *On Deconstruction: Theory and Criticism after Structuralism,* London: Routledge, 1983, p. 102.
136. Derrida, *Of Grammatology*, p. 145.
137. Blair, Doorstep interview with the Prime Minister and Chancellor Wolfgang Schuessel of Austria.
138. Blair, 'Let the United Nations mean what it says and do what it means'.
139. Blair, Prime Minister's Question Time, 25 January 2006.
140. Derrida, *Of Grammatology*, p. 157.
141. Ibid., p. 167.

142. J. Derrida, *Margins of Philosophy*, translated by A. Bass, Brighton: Harvester Press, 1982, p. 8.
143. J. Derrida, *Positions*, translated by A. Bass, Chicago: The University of Chicago Press, 1982, p. 9.
144. Williams, *Contemporary French Philosophy*, p. 17.
145. C. Howells, *Derrida: Deconstruction from Phenomenology to Ethics*, Oxford: Polity Press, 1998, p. 135.
146. Williams, *Contemporary French Philosophy*, p. 133.
147. *Ibid.*, p. 134.
148. J. Derrida, 'Deconstruction and the other: Interview with Richard Kearney', in R. Kearney (ed.), *Dialogues with Contemporary Continental Thinkers: The Phenomenological Heritage*, Manchester: Manchester University Press, 1984, p. 125.

3 Responsibility

1. See, *The Responsibility To Protect: Report of the International Commission on Intervention and State Sovereignty*, Ottawa: International Development Research Centre, 2001.
2. For example, see A. J. Bellamy, 'Responsibility to protect or Trojan horse? The crisis in Darfur and humanitarian intervention after Iraq', *Ethics & International Affairs*, 2005, Vol. 19, pp. 31–54; P. D. Williams and A. J. Bellamy, 'The Responsibility to protect and the crisis in Darfur', *Security Dialogue*, 2005, Vol. 36, pp. 27–47; T. G. Weiss, 'The sunset of humanitarian intervention? The responsibility to protect in a unipolar era', *Security Dialogue*, 2004, Vol. 35, pp. 135–53; A. J. Bellamy, 'Humanitarian responsibilities and interventionist claims in international society', *Review of International Studies*, 2003, Vol. 29, pp. 321–40; I. Williams, 'Writing the wrongs of past interventions: A review of the International Commission on Intervention and State Sovereignty', *International Journal of Human Rights*, 2002, Vol. 6, pp. 103–13.
3. Bellamy, 'Responsibility to protect or Trojan horse?'
4. T. Blair, PM Press Conference, 6 January 2005.
5. R. Cook, 'Mission Statement', 12 May 1997. Online. Available: http://www.guardian.co.uk/indonesia/Story/0,2763,190889,00.html (accessed 11 July 2003).
6. M. White, quoted in A. Seldon, *Blair*, London: Free Press, 1990, p. 499.
7. T. Blair, Party Conference Speech 2001, *The Guardian*, 2 October 2001. Online. Available: http://politics.guardian.co.uk/labour2001/story/0,1212,562006,00.html (accessed 3 March 2005).
8. J. Straw, 'Commitment to the Liberation and Future Prosperity of Iraq', 1 April 2003.
9. T. Blair, Meeting with the Africa Commission in Rome, 27 May 2005.
10. K. Howells, 'Why the UN Millennium Review Summit Matters to the UK', Speech to the IPPR, London, 7 September 2005.
11. T. Blair, Speech to Global Ethics Foundation, Tubingen University, Germany, 30 June 2000.
12. Although the justifications for the Kosovo intervention in 1999 are mixed up temporally with a discourse on territory and proximity – see Chapter 4.
13. Blair, Party Conference Speech 2001.
14. R. Cook, 'Guiding Humanitarian Intervention', 19 July 2000.
15. J. Straw, 'Shaping a stronger United Nations', 2 September 2004.
16. In this way perhaps N. J. Wheeler's book could have more appropriately, though less alliteratively, been called *Protecting* rather than *Saving Strangers*, Oxford: Oxford University Press, 2002.

17. Or, at least, they refuse to take responsibility in the way British foreign policy defines as 'good' and 'right'.
18. A point also made by N. J. Wheeler and T. Dunne, 'Good international citizenship: A third way for British foreign policy', *International Affairs*, 1998, Vol. 74, p. 848.
19. R. Little and M.Wickham-Jones (eds.), *New Labour's Foreign Policy: A New Moral Crusade?* Manchester: Manchester University Press, 2000.
20. P. D. Williams, *British Foreign Policy Under New Labour, 1997–2005*, Basingstoke: Palgrave MacMillan, 2005, p. 7.
21. T. Blair, 'Doctrine of the International Community Speech', Economic Club, Chicago, 24 April 1999.
22. Ibid.
23. T. Blair, 'Facing the Modern Challenge: The Third Way in Britain and South Africa', 8 January 1999.
24. Ibid.
25. Ibid.
26. Cook, 'Guiding Humanitarian Intervention'.
27. R. Cook, 'Human Rights – A Priority of Britain's Foreign Policy', 28 March 2001.
28. *The Responsibility To Protect*, p. VII.
29. Ibid., p.11.
30. Ibid., pp. 74–5.
31. Williams, *British Foreign Policy Under New Labour*, p. 173.
32. B. Rammell, 'Towards the Summit: The Path to Larger Freedom', UKMis, New York, 22 March 2005.
33. J. Straw, 'Our Changed and Changing World', Speech at the 2005 World Summit, New York, 17 September 2005.
34. J. Straw, 'Active Diplomacy for a Changing World', Launch FCO White Paper on International Strategic Priorities, FCO Leadership Conference 2006, 28 March 2006.
35. Blair, 'Doctrine of the International Community Speech'.
36. Blair, 'Facing the Modern Challenge'.
37. J. Kampfner, *Blair's Wars*, London: Free Press, 2003, p. 385. Williams adds to these Britain's more marginal participation in East Timor (1999) and the DRC (2003), see *Foreign Policy Under New Labour*, p. 26 and p. 164.
38. For example: Kampfner, *Blair's Wars*, pp. 48–53; A. Rawnsley, *Servants of the People: The Inside Story of New Labour*, revised edn., London: Penguin, 2001, pp. 270–72; P. Riddell, *Hug Them Close: Blair, Clinton, Bush and the 'Special Relationship'*, London: Politico's, 2004, pp. 101–3; Seldon, *Blair*, pp. 396–8.
39. Blair, 'Doctrine of the International Community Speech'.
40. Ibid.
41. T. Blair, 'Speech to the Muslim Council of Britain', 5 May 1999.
42. Ibid.
43. R. Cook, 'Kosovo and the Modern Europe', 14 April 1999.
44. Blair, 'Doctrine of the International Community Speech'.
45. Cook, 'Kosovo and the Modern Europe'.
46. T. Blair, Statement to Parliament on the NATO Summit in Washington, 26 April 1999.
47. M. O'Brien, 'Morality in Asymmetric War and Intervention Operations', 19 September 2002.
48. T. Blair, quoted in Kampfner, *Blair's Wars*, p. 69.
49. T. Blair, Mansion House Speech, 13 November 2000.

50. T. Blair, Statement at 10 Downing Street, 25 September 2001. Note the subtle difference here between Blair's rhetoric and US President, George W. Bush's, when he said 'Either you are with us, or you are with the terrorists'. G. W. Bush, Address to a Joint Session of Congress and the American People, United States Capitol, Washington, DC, 20 September 2001. Online. Available: http://www.whitehouse.gov/news/releases/2001/09/20010920-8.html (accessed 12 June 2008).
51. Blair, Statement at 10 Downing Street.
52. Ibid.
53. T. Blair, Statement to the House of Commons, 8 October 2001.
54. Ibid.
55. T. Blair, Press Conference on Iraq, 25 March 2003.
56. J. Straw, Iraq Statement, 12 October 2004.
57. T. Blair, 'Speech on the threat of global terrorism', Sedgefield, 13 July 2004.
58. Speeches such as the 'Doctrine of International Community' in Chicago in 1999 and that given at the 2001 Party Conference.
59. Blair, Speech on the threat of global terrorism – emphasis added. When Blair says that he does not consider that Iraq fitted in to 'this' philosophy, 'this' could be understood to mean the traditional Westphalian philosophy referred to immediately before. However, the attention in the section of the speech preceding this extract is focused on his 'new' philosophy (the doctrine of international community), making it his natural referent for 'this philosophy'. In addition, he qualifies what he says by noting the horrible injustice done to his people by Saddam. If by 'this,' he was referring to the traditional Westphalian philosophy, the horrible injustice would be irrelevant as intervention would already be ruled out – the injustice only becomes relevant because his 'new' philosophy *does* allow for intervention.
60. Ibid.
61. T. Blair, Interview with Channel 4 in Istanbul, 28 June 2004.
62. Blair, Speech on the threat of global terrorism.
63. For example, R. Cook, 'Human Rights Into a New Century', 17 July 1997, and B. Rammell, 'Why Human Rights Matter', 25 November 2003.
64. Blair, Speech on the threat of global terrorism.
65. J. Straw, 'Iraq: A Challenge We Must Confront', 11 February 2003.
66. Ibid.
67. Ibid.
68. Straw, 'Commitment to the Liberation and Future Prosperity of Iraq'.
69. T. Blair, Interview with NBC, 4 April 2002.
70. T. Blair, Speech to the TUC Conference in Blackpool, 10 September 2002.
71. J. Straw, 'Reintegrating Iraq into the International Community – A cause with compelling moral force', 21 February 2003.
72. T. Blair, Answering questions at MTV forum, 6 March 2003.
73. T. Blair, Press Conference with President George Bush at Camp David, 27 March 2003.
74. J. Culler, *On Deconstruction: Theory and Criticism After Structuralism*, London: Routledge, 1983, p. 140 – emphasis added.
75. J. Derrida, 'Signature Event Context', in *Limited Inc*, translated by S. Weber, Evanston, Il: Northwestern University Press, 1988, pp.15–6.
76. Ibid., p. 17.
77. Ibid., p. 18.
78. O'Brien, 'Morality in Asymmetric War and Intervention Operations'.

79. T. Blair, 'Let the United Nations mean what it says and do what it means: Speech to Labour Party Spring Conference', 15 February 2003. Online. Available: http://www.labour.org.uk/news/tbglasgow (accessed 3 March 2006).
80. Ibid.
81. T. Blair, Statement to House of Commons opening Iraq debate, 18 March 2003.
82. Straw, 'Iraq: A Challenge We Must Confront'.
83. Ibid.
84. J. Derrida, *The Gift of Death*, translated by D. Willis, Chicago: University of Chicago Press, 1996, p. 2.
85. Genesis 22: 2–12, *The Bible*, New International Version.
86. Derrida, *The Gift of Death*, pp. 67–8.
87. Straw, 'Iraq: A Challenge We Must Confront'.
88. Blair, 'Let the United Nations mean what it says and do what it means'.
89. Ibid.
90. Derrida, *The Gift of Death*, p. 68.
91. Ibid., p. 68.
92. Ibid., p. 67.
93. Williams, *Foreign Policy Under New Labour*, p. 8.
94. R. Cook, 'Prosperity, Conflict Prevention and Democracy in Africa', 24 September 1998.
95. P. Hain, 'Angola Needs Our Help', 20 November 1999.
96. Blair, Mansion House Speech.
97. Riddell, *Hug Them Close*, p. 165.
98. M. White, quoted in Seldon, *Blair*, p. 499.
99. Blair, Party Conference Speech, 2001.
100. Ibid.
101. T. Blair, Speech to WSSD in South Africa, 2 September 2002.
102. T. Blair, BBC Radio Interview to mark World Aids Day, 1 December 2004.
103. T. Blair, PM's article for *The Economist* on G8, 1 January 2005.
104. T. Blair, PM Press Conference, 6 January 2005.
105. T. Blair, Meeting with the Africa Commission in Rome, 27 May 2005.
106. See J. Aglionby, 'UN warning on tsunami threat', *The Guardian*, 31 July 2006.
107. J. Straw, 'A Partnership for Wider Freedom', Centre for Strategic and International Studies, Washington, DC, 18 May 2005.
108. Lord Triesman, 'Africa's Instability is our Instability', Tanzanian Parliament, 15 June 2005.
109. T. Blair, PM's interview with Downing Street website, 30 June 2005.
110. T. Blair, *Carte Blanche* Interview, South Africa, 11 February 2006.
111. Ibid.
112. T. Blair, Speech to Ghana's Parliament, 2 February 2002.
113. T. Blair, 'Partnership for African Development', 7 February 2002.
114. T. Blair, PM's Speech at the World Economic Forum in Davos, Switzerland, 26 January 2005.
115. Ibid.
116. T. Blair, Q&A session given by PM Tony Blair and President Jacques Chirac with French and British students in Paris, 9 May 2004.
117. T. Blair, Speech on Africa, 7 October 2004.
118. Ibid.
119. T. Blair, Press conference with the Italian Prime Minister in Rome, 1 June 2005.
120. Straw, 'Shaping a stronger United Nations'.
121. Ibid.

122. T. Blair, Doorstep Interview at G8 Summit, 28 June 2002.
123. Ibid.
124. T. Blair, Tony Blair and George Bush joint press conference at the White House, 7 June 2005.
125. Blair, 'Partnership for African Development'.
126. J. N. Rosenau, 'Pre-Theories and Theories of Foreign Policy', in J. N. Rosenau, *The Scientific Study of Foreign Policy*, New York: The Free Press, 1971.
127. Blair, Mansion House Speech.
128. R. L. Doty, *Imperial Encounters: The Politics of Representation in North-South Relations*, Minneapolis: University of Minnesota Press, 1996, pp. 127–8. For more of this literature on how representational practices produce a form of neo-colonialism, see R. L. Doty, 'Foreign policy as social construction: A Post-Postivist analysis of US counterinsurgency policy in the Philippines', *International Studies Quarterly*, 1993, Vol. 37, and J. Edkins, *Whose Hunger? Concepts of Famine, Practices of Aid*, Minneapolis: University of Minnesota Press, 2000.
129. Interviewer to Blair, *Carte Blanche* Interview.
130. Ibid.
131. Blair, *Carte Blanche* Interview.
132. I. Pearson, 'G8 2005: A Year For Africa', Tokyo, 6 June 2005.
133. Ibid.
134. Ibid.
135. Lord Triesman, 'Africa's Instability is our Instability'.
136. J. Derrida, *Of Grammatology*, translated by G. Chakravorty Spivak, Baltimore: The Johns Hopkins University Press, 1976, p. 144.
137. T. Blair, Speech to Ghana's Parliament, 2 February 2002.
138. Derrida, *Of Grammatology*, p. 145.
139. Straw, 'A Partnership for Wider Freedom'.
140. Blair, PM's article for *The Economist* on G8 – emphasis added.
141. Blair, BBC Radio Interview to mark World Aids Day.
142. Lord Triesman, 'Africa's Instability is our Instability'.
143. Derrida, *Of Grammatology*, p. 229.
144. Williams, *British Foreign Policy Under New Labour*, p. 95.
145. Thanks to Jenny Edkins for pointing this out to me.
146. Williams, *Foreign Policy under New Labour*, p. 79.
147. For example, T. Blair, PM Press Conference, 6 January 2005, and T. Blair, Press conference with the Italian Prime Minister in Rome.
148. Blair, Speech on Africa.
149. Ibid.
150. Blair, Party Conference Speech 2001.
151. Cook, 'Mission Statement'.
152. J. Persall (ed.), *The Concise Oxford Dictionary*, 10th edn., Oxford: Oxford University Press, 1999, p. 290.
153. Ibid., p. 1090.
154. F. Nietzsche, *Beyond Good and Evil*, translated by W. Kauffman, in W. Kauffman (ed.), *Basic Writings of Nietzsche*, New York: Modern Library, 2000, p. 343
155. F. Nietzsche, *Human, all too Human: A Book for Free Spirits*, translated by R. J. Hollingdale, Cambridge: Cambridge University Press, 1996, p. 322.
156. F. Nietzsche, *Daybreak: Thoughts on the Prejudices of Morality*, translated by R. J. Hollingdale, Cambridge: Cambridge University Press, 1982, p. 86.
157. Nietzsche, *Beyond Good and Evil*, pp. 339–40.
158. Blair, Mansion House Speech.
159. Blair, Speech on Africa.
160. Blair, Speech to WSSD in South Africa.

4 Hospitality

1. I also make this argument in, D. Bulley, 'Negotiating ethics: Campbell, ontopology and hospitality', *Review of International Studies*, 2005, Vol. 32, pp. 645–663.
2. R. B. J. Walker, *Inside/Outside: International Relations as Political Theory*, Cambridge: Cambridge University Press, 1993, p. 117.
3. Ibid., p. 63.
4. Ibid., p. 152.
5. C. Brown, *Sovereignty, Rights and Justice: International Political Theory Today*, Cambridge: Polity, 2002, p. 11.
6. Kant proposed a system of ethical enactment in IR through the cosmopolitan right to 'universal hospitality', while accepting the discourse of inside/outside. In the third Definitive Article for perpetual peace, Kant talks about hospitality as 'the right of a stranger not to be treated with hostility when he arrives on someone else's territory'. A stranger cannot claim the rights of a guest but he or she can claim a *'right of resort'*. I. Kant, *Political Writings*, 2nd edn., translated by H. B. Nisbet, Cambridge: Cambridge University Press, 1991, pp. 105–6.
7. For example, M. Dillon, 'The scandal of the refugee: Some reflections on the "inter" of international relations and continental thought', in D. Campbell and M. J. Shapiro (eds.), *Moral Spaces: Rethinking Ethics and World Politics*, Minneapolis and London: University of Minnesota Press, 1999.
8. See N. Vaughan-Williams, 'Protesting against citizenship', *Citizenship Studies*, 2005, Vol. 9, pp. 167–179; N. Vaughan-Williams, 'Beyond a Cosmopolitan ideal: The politics of singularity', *International Politics*, 2007, Vol. 44, pp. 107–124; M. J. Shapiro, 'The events of discourse and the ethics of global hospitality', *Millennium*, 1998, Vol. 27, pp. 695–713; R. L. Doty, 'Fronteras Compasivas and the ethics of unconditional hospitality', *Millennium*, 2006, Vol. 35, pp. 53–74.
9. For example, see J. Bohmann and M. Lutz-Bachmann (eds.), *Perpetual Peace: Essays on Kant's Cosmopolitan Ideal*, London: MIT Press, 1997.
10. The fact that this can also be seen as a 'domestic' policy is considered later.
11. C. Patten, *Not Quite the Diplomat: Home Truths about World Affairs*, London: Allen Lane, 2005, p. 177.
12. R. Prodi, 'The European project in the world: Between values and politics' Speech to Fondazione Don Tonino Bello Alessano, Lecce, 13 June 2003.
13. J. Solana, Speech at the inaugural conference of the course, 'Towards a new international morality: The humanitarian interventions', University of Alcala de Henares, Madrid, 7 July 2000.
14. Ibid. – emphasis in original.
15. Ibid.
16. The one exception to this rule is in relation to the Kosovo conflict in 1999. Here, we saw a stress placed by Blair especially upon the fact that Kosovo was close to us and, specifically, close to the EU. For example, Blair reminds those who disagree with the intervention, '[w]e are talking here not about some far away place of which we know little. We are talking about the doorstep of the European Union, our own back yard' (T. Blair, 'The new challenge for Europe', 20 May 1999). There are at least two explanations for this aberration. The first is that Kosovo occurred early on in the period under study, when the place of ethics and responsibility were not fully worked out in the discourse. The second is that this is a case of 'intertextuality' – when the EU foreign policy discourse, never wholly separate from the British, significantly influenced the way the intervention was represented. Later in the chapter, I show the way the EU represents its responsibility to the Balkans as precisely because they are on the 'doorstep' of the EU and in our 'backyard'.

17. T. Blair, 'Party conference speech 2001', *The Guardian*, 2 October 2001. Available: http://politics.guardian.co.uk/labour2001/story/0,1212,562006,00.html (accessed 3 March 2005).
18. C. Patten, 'What does Europe's CFSP mean for Asia', Speech to the Japanese Institute for International Affairs, Tokyo, 19 July 2000.
19. J. Solana, 'Reflections on a year in office', Speech to the Swedish Institute of International Affairs and Central Defence and Society Federation, 27 October 2000.
20. See, for example: J. Solana, 'Some reflections about European foreign policy', Address to the Adam Mickiewicz University, Poznan, 12 February 2000; J. Solana, 'The foreign policy of the EU', Speech at the Liberal International, The Hague, 7 November 2000; C. Patten, 'A common foreign policy for Europe: Relations with Latin America', Speech to the Consejo Argentino par alas Relaciones Internacionales (CARI), Buenos Aires, 9 November 2000; C. Patten, 'Developing Europe's external policy in the age of globalisation', Speech at Central Party School, Beijing, 4 April 2002; J. Solana, Address to the national forum on Europe, Dublin Castle, 8 January 2004.
21. R. Prodi, 'The reality of enlargement', Speech to the European Parliament, Brussels, 6 November 2002.
22. R. Prodi, Speech to European Parliament, Strasbourg, 10 February 2004.
23. J. Solana, 'We are not the Africa Corps', Interview by Joachim Fritz-Vannahme and Petra Pinzler, in *Die Zeit*, 12 June 2003.
24. Ibid.
25. Ibid.
26. Patten, 'A common foreign policy for Europe: Relations with Latin America'.
27. Patten, *Not Quite the Diplomat*, p. 174.
28. Ibid.
29. Solana, 'We are not the Africa Corps'.
30. J. Derrida and B. Stiegler, *Echographies of Television: Filmed Interviews*, translated by J. Bajorek, Oxford: Polity, 2002, p. 81.
31. Ibid.
32. J. Derrida and A. Dufourmantelle, *Of Hospitality*, translated by R. Bowlby, Stanford: Stanford University Press, 2000, pp. 47–9.
33. J. Derrida, *Adieu: to Emmanuel Levinas*, translated by P.-A. Brault and M. Naas, Stanford: Stanford University Press, 1999, p. 92.
34. J. Derrida, *On Cosmopolitanism and Forgiveness*, translated by M. Dooley and M. Hughes, London: Routledge, 2001, pp. 16–7.
35. R. Prodi, Speech to the EU-Japan business dialogue roundtable, Brussels, 7 October 1999.
36. C. Patten, 'A voice for Europe? The future of the CFSP', Brian Lenihan Memorial Lecture, Dublin, 7 March 2001.
37. Ibid.
38. R. Prodi, 'The EU, the UK and the world', Speech to Said Business School, Oxford, 29 April 2002.
39. C. Patten, Speech to the Foreign Affairs and Legal Committees of the Albanian Parliament, Tirana, 6 March 2000. It should be noted that, if Albania is *returning* to Europe, the metaphorical road becomes circular – going *from* Europe and returning *to* Europe.
40. C. Patten, Speech to the European Parliament on the Stabilisation and Association Process and the Stability Pact for South Eastern Europe', Strasbourg, 12 April 2000.
41. Ibid.
42. Prodi, 'The EU, the UK and the world'.

43. Prodi, 'The reality of enlargement'.
44. J. Solana, Interview with *Dnevi Avaz* (BiH newspaper), 24 September 2003.
45. J. Solana and F. Frattini, 'Choosing reform', Article in *Politika* (Serbian newspaper), 15 December 2003.
46. R. Prodi, 'A wider Europe – A Proximity Policy as the key to stability', Speech at Sixth ECSA-World Conference, Brussels, 5–6 December 2002.
47. For example, R. Prodi, Speech at the signing of the Treaty of Accession ceremony, Athens, 16 April 2003; R. Prodi, Speech to EU-Balkan Summit, Thessaloniki, 21 June 2003; R. Prodi, 'Looking ahead in transatlantic relations', Dinner speech at Rayburn House with German Marshall Fund of the United States, Washington, DC, 24 June 2003; R. Prodi, 'Sharing stability and prosperity', Speech at Tempus MEDA Regional Conference, Bibliotheca Alexandria, 13 October 2003; R. Prodi, Speech to European Parliament, Strasbourg, 10 February 2004.
48. Derrida, *On Cosmopolitanism and Forgiveness*, pp. 16–7.
49. R. Prodi, 'Europe and global governance', Speech to 2nd COMECE congress, Brussels, 31 March 2000.
50. Ibid.
51. R. Prodi, Inauguration of the European Monitoring Centre on Racism and Xenophobia, Vienna, 7 April 2000.
52. R. Prodi, 'Bringing the family together', Speech to the Academy of Sciences, Budapest, 4 April 2001.
53. Ibid.
54. J. Solana, 'EU foreign policy', Speech at the Hendrik Brugmans Memorial, Bruges, 25 April 2001.
55. R. Prodi, Report to the European parliament on the Spring European Council, 26 March 2003.
56. Patten, *Not Quite the Diplomat*, p. 160.
57. Patten, 'Developing Europe's external policy in the age of globalisation'.
58. Patten, *Not Quite the Diplomat*, p. 152.
59. R. Prodi, 'The EU, dialogue with religions and peace dialogue: "Build Europe, build peace"', Speech at the conference on Christianity and Democracy in the Future of Europe, Camaldoli, 14 July 2002. Just as Patten's metaphorical road appears to be circular (moving *from* Europe and *to* Europe – see reference 39), this language is of *rejoining*. A meta-narrative thus develops in the enlargement discourse of a family home *pre-existing* the EU, one which was perhaps broken up by the Cold War and can now be *reunited*. Enlargement is, therefore, an example of a responsibility exercised towards those closest to the EU, who *were* part of its pre-institutional family home. This is clearly stated by Solana who, soon after taking up his post as HR for the CFSP, claimed that the possibility of enlargement means '[w]e are… confronted with the responsibility for the reunification and reconstruction of Europe' (J. Solana, Speech to the Fernandez Ordonez Seminar, 14 January 2000.)
60. Solana, Speech to the Fernandez Ordonez Seminar. This is repeated many times, see for example, J. Solana, 'Towards a stronger alliance', Article in *European Affairs*, 12 April 2000.
61. J. Solana, Speech to the European Parliament, 1 March 2000.
62. C. Patten, 'Towards a common European foreign policy: How are we doing?', Winston Churchill Memorial Lecture, Luxembourg, 10 October 2000.
63. Patten, 'A common foreign policy for Europe: Relations with Latin America'.
64. R. Prodi, 'Enlargement – the final lap', Speech to European Parliament, Brussels, 9 October 2002.
65. Patten, *Not Quite the Diplomat*, p. 177.

66. C. Patten, 'Europe must solve its own conflicts', Interview with *Die Zeit*, 6 February 2000.
67. R. Prodi, 'Towards a European civil society', Speech commencing second European Social Week, Bad Honnef, 6 April 2000.
68. J. Solana, 'The development of a Common Foreign and Security Policy', Keynote Speech to Diplomatia, Rome, 26 June 2000.
69. C. Patten, 'South East Europe – joining the European mainstream', Speech at the Balkans Conference, FCO, London, 7 July 2000.
70. C. Patten, 'The western Balkans: The road to Europe', Speech to German Bundestag, European Affairs Committee, Berlin, 28 April 2004.
71. R. Prodi, Speech to the European Parliament on Enlargement, Brussels, 13 October 1999.
72. R. Prodi, 'The European Union and the challenge of the 21st Century', Speech to 21st Forum on Financial Policy and Taxation, Karlsruhe, 12 November 1999.
73. Ibid.
74. Prodi, 'The EU, the UK and the world'.
75. Patten, 'A voice for Europe? The future of the CFSP'.
76. This was a constructive ambiguity. While the UK had stated its position that Balkan accession was a moral requirement – see R. Cook, 'Bosnia: A new hope', 4 March 1998; T. Blair, 'The new challenges for Europe', 20 May 1999 – this was by no means a consensus position within the EU as a whole.
77. Patten, Speech to the Foreign Affairs and Legal Committees of the Albanian Parliament.
78. J. Solana, 'The European Union is assisting recovery – but much work remains to be done', Article in *The Wall Street Journal Europe*, 24 March 2000.
79. C. Patten, Speech to the Peace Implementation Council, Brussels, 23 May 2000.
80. Solana, Interview with *Dnevi Avaz* (BiH newspaper). However, as has been suggested (see notes 39 and 59 above), this metaphor does not always work. The 'road' or 'journey' is represented as a circular *return* of the Balkans to the family home. If this is the case, moving back would also take them towards the family home. Given that backwards movement is represented as regressive, the Balkans are not *returning* or *re*joining the same family home, but rather *joining* something very different: the EU.
81. C. Patten, Speech to the OSCE Permanent Council, Vienna, 23 November 2000.
82. C. Patten, Interview with BBC and ITN Television, Zagreb, 24 November 2000.
83. Patten, Speech to the Peace Implementation Council – emphasis in original.
84. J. Solana, Written interview with Solbodanka Jonavoska in *Ultrinski Vesnik* (FYROM Newspaper), 23 February 2004.
85. C. Patten, Speech to the South East Europe Cooperation Process (SEECP) Summit, Skopje, 23 February 2001.
86. Solana, Interview with *Dnevi Avaz* (BiH newspaper).
87. Derrida, *Of Hospitality*, p. 77.
88. Ibid., p. 25.
89. J. Derrida, 'Autoimmunity: Real and symbolic suicides – a dialogue with Jacques Derrida', in G. Borradori, *Philosophy in a Time of Terror: Dialogues with Jurgen Habermas and Jacques Derrida*, Chicago: University of Chicago Press, 2003, p. 129.
90. Derrida, *Of Hospitality*, p. 77.
91. Patten, Interview with BBC and ITN Television.

92. R. Prodi, 'Croatia's journey towards EU membership', Speech to Croatian Parliament, Zagreb, 10 July 2003.
93. R. Prodi, 'On the path to the EU: Challenges and opportunities', FYROM Government Assembly, Skopje, 1 October 2004.
94. Derrida, *Echographies of Television*, p. 17.
95. Derrida, 'Autoimmunity', p. 129.
96. Ibid.
97. S. Butler, quoted in Patten, *Not Quite the Diplomat*, p. 127.
98. Derrida, *Of Hospitality*, p. 27.
99. Derrida, 'Autoimmunity', p. 129.
100. Ibid.
101. See J. Derrida, *Acts of Religion*, translated by G. Anidjar, New York: Routledge, 2002, pp. 356–420.
102. Solana, Speech to the European Parliament.
103. R. Prodi, Speech to the European Parliament on Enlargement, Strasbourg, 13 November 2001.
104. Derrida, *Echographies of Television*, p. 81.
105. R. Prodi, 'My vision of Europe', Lecture to Norman Paterson School of International Affairs, Carleton University, Ottawa, 16 December 1999.
106. R. Prodi, Speech to the European Academy of Sciences and Arts, Bilbao, 28 April 2000.
107. R. Prodi, 'Europe and the Mediterranean: Time for action', Speech at Universite Catholique de Louvain-la-Neuve, 26 November 2002.
108. Prodi, 'Looking ahead in transatlantic relations'.
109. Prodi, 'Sharing stability and prosperity'.
110. R. Prodi, Speech on visit to Bogazici University, Istanbul, 16 January 2004 – emphasis added.
111. Patten, *Not Quite the Diplomat*, p. 142 – emphasis in original.
112. R. Prodi, Meeting with students of Baku State University, Azerbaijan, 17 September, 2004 – essentially the same speech as: R. Prodi, To students and representatives of civil society in Georgia, Tbilisi University, 18 September 2004; R. Prodi, To students and representatives of civil society in Armenia, European Regional Institute of Information and Communication Technologies, Yerevan, 19 September 2004.
113. Prodi, Meeting with students of Baku State University.
114. Ibid.
115. It should be noted that the ENP has been heavily criticised as a realistic offering of any substantial advantages whatsoever. For example, see R. A. Del Sarto and T. Schumacher, 'From EMP to ENP: What's at stake with the European Neighbourhood Policy towards the Southern Mediterranean', *European Foreign Affairs Review*, 2005, Vol. 10, pp. 17–38.
116. R. Prodi, 'Europe in transition: Hopes and fears', Speech at Fifth Europa Forum: 'Europe facing the decision – EU enlargement and global challenges', Brussels, 3 December 2002.
117. Ibid. – emphasis in original.
118. Ibid. – emphasis in original.
119. Ibid. – emphasis in original.
120. Ibid. – emphasis in original.
121. Ibid. – emphasis in original.
122. A few examples include, Prodi, 'A wider Europe – a Proximity Policy as the key to stability'; Prodi, 'Looking ahead in transatlantic relations'; Prodi, 'Sharing stability and prosperity'.
123. Prodi, 'A wider Europe – A Proximity Policy as the key to stability'.
124. Derrida, *Of Hospitality*, pp. 47–9.

125. Derrida, *Adieu*, p. 92.
126. J. Solana, 'The limits of integration – where does the European Union end?', Address to the Europa Forum, Vienna, 19 November 2004.
127. Patten, *Not Quite the Diplomat*, pp. 142–43.
128. Ibid., p. 143.
129. Derrida, *Adieu*, pp. 41–2.
130. However, because the term 'hospitality' in English derives from the Latin *hospitalarius* via the Old French, *hospitalite*, if this dual meaning is constitutive of the subject of French *hospitalite* then it also constitutes the English subject of *hospitality*. J. Persall (ed.), *The Concise Oxford Dictionary*, 10th edn., Oxford: Oxford University Press, 1999, p. 687.
131. Derrida, *Echographies of Television*, p. 17.
132. Derrida, *Of Hospitality*, p. 99.
133. Derrida, *Acts of Religion*, p. 364.
134. Derrida, *Adieu*, p. 56.
135. Derrida, *Of Hospitality*, p. 125.
136. Ibid., p. 55.
137. Patten, *Not Quite the Diplomat*, p. 143.
138. M. J. Shapiro, 'The Ethics of Encounter: Unreading, Unmapping the Imperium', in D. Campbell and M. J. Shapiro (eds.), *Moral Spaces: Rethinking Ethics and World Politics*, Minneapolis and London: University of Minnesota Press, 1999, p. 77.

5 Negotiating Undecidability

1. J. Derrida, *The Gift of Death*, translated by D. Willis, Chicago: University of Chicago Press, 1996, p. 25.
2. Thanks to Debbie Lisle for suggesting this choice of words.
3. J. Derrida, *Negotiations: Interventions and Interviews 1971–2001*, translated by E. Rottenberg, Stanford: Stanford University Press, 2002, p. 25.
4. J. Derrida, *Limited Inc*, translated by S. Weber, Evanston, Il: Northwestern University Press, 1988, p. 116.
5. J. Derrida, *Negotiations*, p. 296.
6. J. Derrida, *On Cosmopolitanism and Forgiveness*, translated by M. Dooley and M. Hughes, London: Routledge, 2001, p. 51.
7. Derrida, *Without Alibi*, translated by P. Kamuf, Stanford: Stanford University Press, 2002, p. 235; see also J. Derrida, *Specters of Marx: The State of the Debt, the Work of Mourning & the New International*, translated by P. Kamuf, New York: Routledge, 1994, p. 35.
8. J. Derrida, *Politics of Friendship*, translated by G. Collins, London: Verso, 1997, p. 263.
9. See, for example, P. Dews, *Logics of Disintegration: Poststructuralism and the Claims of Critical Theory*, London: Verso, 1987; and S. Critchley, *The Ethics of Deconstruction: Derrida and Levinas*, Oxford: Basil Blackwell, 1992.
10. J. Derrida, 'Hospitality, Justice and Responsibility: A Dialogue with Jacques Derrida', in R. Kearney and M. Dooley (eds.), *Questioning Ethics: Contemporary Debates in Philosophy*, London: Routledge, 1999, p. 66.
11. Ibid.
12. J. Derrida, 'Force of Law: The "Mystical Foundation of Authority"', in D. Cornell, M. Rosenfeld and D. Gray Carlson (eds.), *Deconstruction and the Possibility of Justice*, London: Routledge, 1992, p. 28.
13. Ibid.
14. J. Derrida, *The Gift of Death*, p. 77.

15. J. Derrida, *On The Name*, translated by D. Wood, J. P. Leavy, Jr, and I. McLeod, Stanford: Stanford University Press, 1995, p. 64.
16. J. Derrida and B. Stiegler, *Echographies of Television: Filmed Interviews*, translated by J. Bajorek, Oxford: Polity, 2002, p. 11.
17. Ibid., p. 21.
18. J. Derrida, *Of Grammatology*, translated by G. Chakravorty Spivak, Baltimore: The Johns Hopkins University Press, 1976, p. 5.
19. There is a danger in this formulation that the 'worst' is figured only in terms of loss of human life or perhaps in human suffering more broadly. This would make discussion of 'openness', the 'future' and 'the other' merely a way of camouflaging a conventional subscription to the protection of human life. In essence, such a reading would put Derrida in agreement with British and EU foreign policy that the 'ethical' is about the prevention of outrageous human death and suffering – see Chapter 3. However, the 'other' which we keep the future open for is not *just* the human other (other *people*) which contains something of the absolutely other. The other, what Derrida elsewhere calls the future-to-come, is also the coming of justice, responsibility, forgiveness, the gift, hospitality – the *ethical*. These are what remain as unanticipatable and unknowable as absolute otherness; thus, the closure towards their possible coming is also a figure of the 'worst'. Remaining open to such concepts of the 'to come' may well complicate a simple duty to the protection of human life.
20. Derrida, *Negotiations*, p. 12.
21. Derrida, *Limited Inc*, p. 116.
22. Derrida, *Negotiations*, p. 14.
23. J. Derrida and A. Dufourmantelle, *Of Hospitality*, translated by R. Bowlby, Stanford: Stanford University Press, 2000, p. 147.
24. J. Derrida, *Adieu: to Emmanuel Levinas*, translated by P.-A. Brault and M. Naas, Stanford: Stanford University Press, 1999, p. 112–3.
25. Derrida, *Limited Inc*, p. 136.
26. Derrida, *Negotiations*, p. 17.
27. Derrida, *Echographies of Television*, p. 85.
28. For a somewhat less contextualised attempt to draw out the implications of Derrida's concept of 'negotiation', see D. Bulley, 'Negotiating Ethics: Campbell, Ontopology and Hospitality', *Review of International Studies*, 2005, Vol. 32; and D. Bulley, 'Ethical assassination? Negotiating the (ir)responsible decision', in M. Fagan et al. (eds.), *Derrida: Negotiating the Legacy*, Edinburgh: Edinburgh University Press, 2007.
29. See R. K. Beasley, J. Kaarbo, J. S. Lantis and M. T. Snarr (eds.), *Foreign Policy in Comparative Perspective: Domestic and International Influences on State Behaviour*, Washington DC: CQ Press, 2002.
30. C. Patten, 'The Role of the European Union on the World Stage', Speech at the India Habitat Centre, Jawharlal Nehru University, New Delhi, 25 January 2001,
31. T. Blair, 'Facing the Modern Challenge: The Third Way in Britain and South Africa', 8 January 1999.
32. T. Blair, Article in the *FT* on the visit of the Syrian President, 16 December, 2002.
33. T. Blair, Doorstep interview with the Prime Minister in Riyadh, Saudi Arabia, 1 November, 2001.
34. Derrida, *Negotiations*, p. 238. In a sense, everything that results from a negotiation is an unprecedented invention. As observed earlier, each negotiation is a context-bound decision to close and, as such, will differ from one person to the next, and for the same person from one moment to the next. This is not, however, the most radical sense of invention, which would be an invention of the

'im-possible'; here the hyphen joins *and* separates possibility and impossibility, making the 'impossible' far from simply the opposite of the possible (J. Derrida, *Deconstruction Engaged: The Sydney Seminars*, Sydney: Power Publications, 2006, p. 63).

35. P. Hain, *The End of Foreign Policy? Britain's Interests, Global Linkages and Natural Limits* (London: The Fabian Society/Green Alliance/The Royal Institute of International Affairs, 2001).

36. P. Hain, 'The End of Foreign Policy?' Speech at the Launch of *The End of Foreign Policy?* pamphlet, Royal Institute of International Affairs, Chatham House, 22 January 2001.

37. All examples from Hain, *The End of Foreign Policy?* p. 6. Note that terrorism comes lower down the list due to the fact that the pamphlet launched eight months before 11 September 2001.

38. Ibid., p. 7.

39. Ibid., p. 10.

40. Ibid., p. 10.

41. Ibid., p. 12.

42. Ibid., p. 10.

43. R.K. Ashley, 'Foreign policy as political performance', *International Studies Notes*, 1987, Vol. 13, p. 53.

44. Hain, *The End of Foreign Policy?* p. 58.

45. Ibid., pp. 61–2.

46. Hain, 'The End of Foreign Policy?' Speech.

47. See Chapter 2.

48. C. Brown, 'What, exactly, is the problem to which the five-part test is the solution?', *International Relations*, 2005, Vol. 19, pp. 226–7.

49. H. K. Colebatch, *Policy*, 2 edn., Buckingham: Open University Press, 2002, p. 9.

50. Derrida, 'Force of Law', p. 23. This means that even if a negotiation had been successful, Derrida argues that a 'silence is kept concerning the rules or schemas… that produce for us the "better" or less bad mediations' as the temptation will be to attempt a transfer of such rules across contexts (Derrida, *Adieu*, p. 114).

51. D. MacShane, 'The Return of Foreign Policy', 13 February 2002.

52. Ibid.

53. D. Bulley, '"Foreign" terror? London Bomings, resistance and the failing state', *British Journal of Politics and International Relations*, 2008, Vol. 10, pp. 379–94.

54. T. Blair, Third Foreign Policy Speech, Georgetown, USA, 26 May 2006.

55. J. Straw, 'Failed and failing states', 6 September 2002.

56. It could, of course, be argued that the very fact that the subject is already 'known' in such a way means it has already been constituted as an object before it 'actually' fails.

57. See especially, Straw, 'Failed and failing states' and Blair, Third Foreign Policy Speech.

58. J. Edkins, *Whose Hunger? Concepts of Famine, Practices of Aid*, Minneapolis: University of Minnesota Press, 2001, p. 152.

59. M. Duffield, quoted in Edkins, *Whose Hunger?* p. 138.

60. Edkins, *Whose Hunger?* p. 138.

61. For example, T. Blair, PM Press Conference, 6 January 2005, and T. Blair, Press conference with the Italian Prime Minister in Rome, 1 June 2005.

62. T. Blair, Speech on Africa, 7 October 2004, and Blair, Press conference with Italian Prime Minister in Rome.

63. P. D. Williams, *Foreign Policy Under New Labour, 1997–2005*, Basingstoke: Palgrave MacMillan, 2005, p. 93.

64. J. Straw, 'Shaping a Stronger United Nations', 2 September 2004.
65. D. Campbell, 'Violence, Justice, and Identity in the Bosnian Conflict', in J. Edkins, N. Persram, and V. Pin-Fat (eds.), *Sovereignty and Subjectivity*, Boulder, Co: Lynne Rienner, 1999, p. 23.
66. Blair observed that the 'prize' for the success of his Commission 'would be Africa standing proud in its own right in the international community': by implication, either it currently cannot do so, or it can, but neither proudly nor without help (Speech on Africa).
67. T. Blair, Statement to the House of Commons following the September 11 attacks, 14 September 2001.
68. C. Patten, Interview on Sky News, 12 September 2001; see also C. Patten, Interview with Arab News Network, 18 October 2001.
69. J. Straw, 'The Task of Defeating International Terrorism', 11 November 2001.
70. S. Chan, *Out of Evil: New International Politics and Old Doctrines of War*, London and New York: I.B. Tauris, 2005, p. 49.
71. P. Sharp, 'Mullah Zaeef and Taliban diplomacy: An English School approach', *Review of International Studies*, 2003, Vol. 29, pp. 481–98.
72. Ibid., p. 498
73. Ibid., p. 486
74. See Chapter 4.
75. Ibid.
76. It should be noted that M. Zehfuss makes a similar argument from a different angle in, 'Forget September 11' *Third World Quarterly: Journal of Emerging Areas*, 2003, Vol. 24, pp. 513–28.
77. See Bulley, '"Foreign" Terror?'
78. This was successfully increased from 28 to 42 days on 11 June 2008.
79. For a reading of these policies as a 'new border politics', which makes a similar argument about where the state closes toward otherness, see N. Vaughan-Williams, 'The shooting of Jean Charles de Menezes: New border politics?' *Alternatives*, 2007, Vol. 32, pp. 177–195.
80. V. Dodd, 'Police rethink shoot to kill policy' *The Guardian*, 20 August 2005.
81. See Vaughan-Williams, 'The shooting of Jean Charles de Menezes'.
82. Ibid.
83. See V. Dodd, 'Seconds to decide if suspect is suicide threat' *The Guardian*, 23 July 2005.
84. B. Wilding, quoted in P. Taylor, 'The terrorist who wasn't, *The Guardian*, 8 March 2006.
85. Another example being the possibility of political assassination, see Bulley, 'Ethical assassination? Negotiating the (ir)responsible decision'.
86. Derrida, *Negotiations*, p. 195.
87. Derrida, *Negotiations*, p. 296. Similarly, Derrida says in 'Force of Law' (p. 26) that the just decision, 'however unpresentable it may be', is demanded immediately.
88. The context, after all, is boundless and, thus, the decision 'cannot furnish itself with infinite information and the unlimited knowledge of conditions, rules or hypothetical imperatives that would justify it' (Derrida, 'Force of Law', p. 26).
89. Ibid.
90. Derrida, *Negotiations*, p. 298.
91. Ibid.
92. Derrida, *Negotiations*, pp. 178–9.
93. Derrida, *Echographies of Television*, p. 65 – emphasis added.
94. Hain, *The End of Foreign Policy?* p. 62.
95. D. Chandler, 'Rhetoric without responsibility: The attraction of "ethical" foreign policy', *British Journal of Politics and International Relations*, 2003,

Vol. 5, pp. 295–316;   D. Chandler and V. Heins, 'Ethics and foreign policy: New perspectives on an old problem', in D. Chandler and V. Heins (eds.), *Rethinking Ethical Foreign Policy: Pitfalls, Possibilities and Paradoxes*, London: Routledge, 2007, pp. 3–21.

96. Derrida, *Negotiations*, p. 232.
97. M. J. Shapiro, 'The events of discourse and the ethics of global hospitality', *Millennium*, 1998, Vol. 27, p. 713.
98. M. J. Shapiro, 'The Ethics of Encounter: Unreading, Unmapping the Imperium', in D. Campbell and M. J. Shapiro (eds.), *Moral Spaces: Rethinking Ethics and World Politics*, Minneapolis and London: University of Minnesota Press, 1999, p. 77.
99. R. Prodi, 'Europe and Global Governance', Speech to 2 COMECE congress, Brussels, 31 March 2000.
100. C. Patten, 'Islam and the West – at the Crossroads', Speech at the Oxford Centre for Islamic Studies, 24 May 2004.
101. R. Prodi, Inauguration of the European Monitoring Centre on Racism and Xenophobia, Vienna, 7 April 2000.
102. Derrida, *Deconstruction Engaged*, p. 103
103. Ibid.
104. J. Redmond, 'Turkey and the European Union: Troubled European or European trouble', *International Affairs*, 2007, Vol. 83, p. 315.
105. Patten, 'Islam and the West'.
106. Ibid.
107. For an analysis of the importance of the 'Turkish other' in the construction of pre-twentieth century Europe, see I. B. Neumann, *Uses of the Other: 'The East' in European Identity Formation*, Manchester, Manchester University Press: 1999, pp. 39–63.
108. W. Hallstein, quoted in G. Dorronso, 'The EU and Turkey: Between geopolitics and social engineering', in R. Dannreuther (ed.), *European Union Foreign and Security Policy: Towards a Neighbourhood Strategy*, London: Routledge, 2004, p. 49.
109. H. Arikan, *Turkey and the EU: An Awkward Candidate for EU Membership?* Aldershot: Ashgate, 2003, p. 1.
110. J. Casanova, 'The long, difficult, and tortuous journey of Turkey into Europe and the dilemmas of European civilization', *Constellations*, 2006, Vol. 13, p. 239.
111. R. Prodi, Speech to the Turkish Grand National Assembly Ankara, 15 January 2004.
112. R. Prodi, The Commission's Report and Recommendation on Turkey's application, Presentation to the European Parliament, Brussels, 6 October 2004.
113. R. Prodi, Speech on enlargement to the European Parliament, Brussels, 13 October 1999.
114. R. Prodi, Speech during a visit by members of parliament from candidate countries, Strasbourg, 19 November 2002.
115. Prodi, Speech to the Turkish Grand National Assembly Ankara.
116. Prodi, The Commission's Report and Recommendation on Turkey's application.
117. Redmond, 'Turkey and the European Union', p. 310.
118. These issues are noted by B. Rubin, 'Introduction', in A. Carkoglu and B. Rubin (eds.), *Turkey and the European Union: Domestic Politics, Economic Integration and International Dynamics*, London: Frank Cass, 2003, pp. 1–3.
119. S. Benhabib and T. Isiksel, 'Ancient battles, new prejudices, and future perspectives: Turkey and the EU', *Constellations*, 2006, Vol. 13, p. 221.
120. Arikan, *Turkey and the EU*, p. 216.

121. N. Stone, 'Endnote: Turkey and Europe' in M. Lake (ed.), *The EU & Turkey: A Glittering Prize or a Millstone?* Federal Trust: London, 2005, p. 173.
122. Ibid., p. 174.
123. Prodi, Speech to the Grand National Assembly, Ankara; see also, R. Prodi, Speech at Bogazici University, Istanbul, 16 January 2004.
124. R. Prodi, 'Europe and the Mediterranean: time for action', Speech at the Universite Catholique de Louvain-la-Neuve, 26 November 2002.
125. Patten, 'Islam and the West'.
126. Ibid.
127. C. Patten, *Not Quite the Diplomat: Home Truths about World Affairs*, London: Allen Lane, 2005, p. 148.
128. O. Rehn, quoted in Casanova, 'The long, difficult, and tortuous journey of Turkey...', p. 234.
129. Casanova, 'The long, difficult, and tortuous journey of Turkey...', p. 236.
130. Redmond, 'Turkey and the European Union', p. 306.
131. Derrida, *Of Hospitality*, p. 25.
132. R. Prodi, 'Croatia's journey towards EU membership', Speech to Croatian Parliament, Zagreb, 10 July 2003.
133. C. Patten, Speech to the Peace Implementation Council, Brussels, 23 May 2000.
134. Prodi, Speech to the Turkish Grand National Assembly Ankara. See also, Prodi, Speech at Bogazici Univeristy; R. Prodi, 'The European Union's role after enlargement', High-Level Conference on the Future of Transatlantic Relations – ELDR Group, Brussels, 3 March 2004.
135. Arikan, *Turkey and the EU*.
136. It should be noted that, while the overriding understanding of conditionality in this volume is as an imposition of sameness by the EU, it is in fact a more complex picture. Much of this derives from the internal diversity of the Turkish other itself. Some forms of conditionality, such as those regarding minority rights, promote difference and otherness even as they negate it. For example, a Turkish Kurd, a woman or civil liberties campaigner would not necessarily see the EU's conditionality as a violence against otherness. Thanks to Owen Parker for pointing this out to me. However, this interaction is complicated even further when, as I go on to discuss in this chapter, Turkish Islamism has opted to support EU membership partly *because* of the freedoms that result from conditionality, as well as its violence.
137. C. Patten, 'A Common Foreign Policy for Europe: Relations with Latin America', Speech to the Consejo Argentino par alas Relaciones Internacionales (CARI), Buenos Aires, 9 November 2000.
138. Redmond, 'Turkey and the European Union', pp. 316–17.
139. Derrida, *The Gift of Death*, p. 23.
140. Derrida, 'Force of Law', p. 23.
141. C. Patten, Interview with BBC and ITN Television, Zagreb, 24 November 2000.
142. Patten, 'Islam and the West'.
143. J. Solana, Speech – Fernandez Ordonez Seminar, 14 January 2000.
144. Solana, Speech – Fernandez Ordonez Seminar.
145. All factors noted by Prodi in his announcement that the Commission was recommending opening full accession negotiations with Turkey, see Prodi, The Commission's Report and Recommendation on Turkey's application.
146. N. Gole, 'Europe's Encounter with Islam: What Future?', *Constellations*, 2006, Vol. 13, p. 261.
147. Dorronso, 'The EU and Turkey', p. 59.

148. R. Kastoryano, 'Turkey/Europe: Space-Border-Identity', translated by J. Ingram, *Constellations*, 2006, Vol. 13, p. 285.
149. B. Duran, 'Islamist redefinition(s) of European and Islamic identities in Turkey', in M. Ugur and N. Canefe (eds.), *Turkey and European Integration: Accession Prospects and Issues*. London: Routledge, 2004, p. 127.
150. Ibid.
151. Ibid., p. 128.
152. Ibid., p. 133.
153. Leader Article, 'Turkey: A Mandate for Modernisation', *The Guardian*, 24 July 2007.
154. Duran, 'Islamist redefinition(s)...', p. 128.
155. Ibid., p. 142.
156. Ibid., p. 141.
157. J. Derrida, 'Hospitality, Justice and Responsibility: A dialogue with Jacques Derrida', in R. Kearney and M. Dooley (eds.), *Questioning Ethics: Contemporary Debates in Philosophy*, London: Routledge, 1999, p. 71.
158. Benhabib and Isiksel, 'Ancient battles, new prejudices, and future perspectives', p. 221.
159. Ibid.
160. Ibid.
161. C. Black, 'Al-Qaida US has little future in the franchise', *The Guardian*, 17 January 2008.
162. Statistics courtesy of the UN, via BBC Country Profiles, 2007. Online. Available: http://news.bbc.co.uk/1/hi/country_profiles/ (accessed 12 July 2007).
163. At the time of writing, the status of the Lisbon Treaty is unclear following the Irish referendum's rejection of its ratification on 12 June 2008 (result announced 13 June).
164. Prodi, The Commission's Report and Recommendation on Turkey's application.
165. Redmond, 'Turkey and the European Union', p. 307.
166. J. Solana, Speech – Foreign Policy Association, New York, 25 January 2000; Patten, 'Islam and the West'.
167. BBC News, 'EU "should expand beyond Europe"', 12 November 2007. Online. Available: http://news.bbc.co.uk/1/hi/uk_politics/7095657.stm (accessed 18 November 2007).
168. I. Turan, 'Unstable stability: Turkish politics at the crossroads?' *International Affairs*, 2007, Vol. 83, p. 322.
169. A Mango, 'The Modern History of a Solid Country', in Lake (ed.), *The EU & Turkey*, p. 25
170. Turan, 'Unstable stability', p. 321.
171. E. Fokas, 'The Islamist movement and Turkey-EU relations', in Ugur and Canefe, *Turkey and European Integration*, p. 147.
172. Benhabib and Isiksel, 'Ancient battles, new prejudices, and future perspectives', p. 221
173. Duran, 'Islamist redefinition(s)...', p. 134.
174. Derrida, *Echographies of Television*, p. 65 – emphasis added.
175. K. Biedenkopf, B. Geremek and K. Michalski, *The Spiritual and Cultural Dimension of Europe: Concluding Remarks*, Reflection Group initiated by President of the European Commission and coordinated by the Institute for Human Sciences (Vienna/Brussels, 2004), p. 9.
176. R. Prodi, 'Europe in transition: Hopes and fears', 3 December 2002. – emphasis in original.
177. Shapiro, 'The Events of Discourse', p. 697.

6 Conclusion

1. S. Beckett, *The Unnameable*, London: Calder and Boyars, 1975, p. 132.
2. G. Howe (Lord, of Aberavon), Interviewed by D. Bulley, the House of Lords, Westminster, London, 5 April 2005.
3. A Camus, *The Myth of Sisyphus*, translated by J. O'Brien, London: Penguin Books, 2005, p. 115.
4. See, S. Price and E. Kearns, *The Oxford Dictionary of Classical Myth and Religion*, Oxford: Oxford University Press, 2003.
5. Ibid.
6. R. Lattimore, translator, *The Odyssey of Homer*, New York: HarperCollins, 1999, Book XI, ln. 593–600, p. 183.
7. Camus, *The Myth of Sisyphus*, p. 115.
8. Ibid., p. 116.
9. G. Howe, *Conflict of Loyalty*, London and Basingstoke: Pan Books, 1995, pp. 301–598.
10. Camus, *The Myth of Sisyphus*, p. 119.
11. J. Derrida, *Without Alibi*, translated by P. Kamuf, Stanford: Stanford University Press, 2002, p. xxxiii.
12. Ibid., p. 235; see also J. Derrida, *Specters of Marx: The State of the Debt, the Work of Mourning & the New International*, translated by P. Kamuf, New York: Routledge, 1994, p. 35.
13. J. Derrida, 'Force of Law: The "Mystical Foundation of Authority"', in D. Cornell, M. Rosenfeld and D. Gray Carlson (eds.), *Deconstruction and the Possibility of Justice*, London: Routledge, 1992, p. 27.
14. J. Derrida, *Politics of Friendship*, translated by G. Collins, London: Verso, 1997, p. 39.
15. J. Derrida, *Rogues: Two Essays on Reason*, translated by P-A. Brault and M. Naas, Stanford: Stanford University Press, 2005, p. xv.
16. Derrida, *Specters of Marx*, p. 99.
17. J. Derrida and B. Stiegler, *Echographies of Television: Filmed Interviews*, translated by J. Bajorek, Oxford: Polity, 2002, p. 75.
18. J. Derrida, *The Other Heading: Reflections on Today's Europe*, translated by P-A. Brault and M. B. Naas, Bloomington: Indiana University Press, 1992, p. 78.
19. Derrida, *Specters of Marx*, p. 64.
20. J. Derrida, *Negotiations: Interventions and Interviews 1971–2001*, translated by E. Rottenberg, Stanford: Stanford University Press, 2002, p. 180.
21. Derrida, *Specters of Marx*, p. 167–68.
22. Derrida, *Echographies of Television*, p. 13.
23. Derrida, *Specters of Marx*, p. 168.
24. In Beckett's play, the main characters, Vladimir and Estragon, wait on an almost empty stage for an unknown character named 'Godot', who may or may not bring them salvation. They think that an appointment has been made with Godot, but as Vladimir observes, 'nothing is certain'. S. Beckett, *Waiting for Godot*, London: Faber and Faber, 1965, p. 53.
25. Derrida, *Specters of Marx*, p. 75.
26. Derrida, *Rogues*, p. 86.
27. Ibid., p. 91.
28. See, for instance, Derrida, *Specters of Marx*, pp. 83–4.
29. Derrida, *Echographies of Television*, p. 75.
30. J. Derrida, *Deconstruction Engaged: The Sydney Seminars*, Sydney: Power Publications, 2006, p. 100.
31. A. Thomson, *Deconstruction and Democracy: Derrida's Politics of Friendship*, London: Continuum, 2005, p. 29.

32. Derrida, *Echographies of Television*, p. 75.
33. J. Derrida, *Of Grammatology*, translated by G. Chakravorty Spivak, Baltimore: The Johns Hopkins University Press, 1976, p. 5.
34. Ibid.
35. P. Deutscher, in Derrida, *Deconstruction Engaged*, p. 97.
36. J. Derrida, 'Autoimmunity: Real and symbolic suicides – A dialogue with Jacques Derrida', in G. Borradori (ed.), *Philosophy in a Time of Terror: Dialogues with Jurgen Habermas and Jacques Derrida*, Chicago: University of Chicago Press, 2003, p. 120.
37. J. Derrida, 'Deconstruction and the other: Interview with Richard Kearney', in R. Kearney (ed.), *Dialogues with Contemporary Continental Thinkers: The Phenomenological Heritage*, Manchester: Manchester University Press, 1984, p. 120.
38. Derrida, *Rogues*, p. 74.
39. J. Derrida, *Limited Inc*, translated by S. Weber, Evanston, Il: Northwestern University Press, 1988, p. 116.
40. As discussed in the Chapter 1. See, for example, J. N. Rosenau, 'Moral fervor, systematic analysis, and scientific consciousness in foreign policy research', in J. N. Rosenau (ed.), *The Scientific Study of Foreign Policy*, New York: The Free Press, 1971, p. 24.
41. G. Bennington, *Interrupting Derrida*, London: Routledge, 2000, p. 34.
42. J. D. Caputo, *Against Ethics: Contributions to a Poetics of Obligation with Constant Reference to Deconstruction*, Bloomington: Indiana University Press, 1993, p. 4.
43. As he does in J. Derrida, 'Passions: "An Oblique Offering"', in D. Wood (ed.), *Derrida: A Critical* Reader, Oxford: Blackwell, 1992, p. 14.
44. Caputo, *Against Ethics*, p. 3.
45. J. Derrida, *Altérités*, cited in and translated by Thomson, *Deconstruction and Democracy*, p. 127.
46. R. B. J. Walker, *Inside/Outside: International Relations as Political Theory*, Cambridge: Cambridge University Press, 1993, p. 51.
47. Derrida, *Rogues*, p. 60.
48. J. Derrida, '"Eating Well," or the Calculation of the Subject: An Interview with Jacques Derrida', in E. Cadava, P. Connor and J.-L. Nancy (eds.), *Who Comes After the Subject?* New York: Routledge, 1991, p. 116.
49. Ibid.
50. Derrida, *Without Alibi*, p. xxxiii.
51. D. Campbell, *Writing Security: United States Foreign Policy and the Politics of Identity*, revised edn., Manchester: Manchester University Press, 1998, p. 39.
52. J. N. Rosenau, 'Introduction: New directions and recurrent questions in the comparative study of foreign policy', in C. F. Hermann, C. W. Kegley, Jr, and J. N. Rosenau (eds.), *New Directions in the Study of Foreign Policy*, Boston: Allen and Unwin, 1987, pp. 1–3.
53. Campbell, *Writing Security*, p. 39.
54. In a recent survey of the field, ethics is not mentioned at all, see V. M. Hudson, 'Foreign policy analysis: Actor-specific theory and the ground of International Relations', *Foreign Policy Analysis*, 2005, Vol. 1, pp. 1–30; see also V. M. Hudson, *Foreign Policy Analysis: Classic and Contemporary Theory*, Lanham, Md: Rowman & Littlefield, 2007, pp. 3–33.
55. M. Frost, 'Putting the world to rights: Britain's ethical foreign policy', *Cambridge Review of International Affairs*, 1999, Vol. 12, p. 81. For a more in-depth exposition of Frost's position on ethics and foreign policy, see M. Frost, 'The ethics of humanitarian intervention: Protecting civilians to make democratic

citizenship possible', in K. E. Smith and M. Light (eds.), *Ethics and Foreign Policy*, Cambridge: Cambridge University Press, 2001, pp. 33–54.

56. Frost, 'Putting the world to rights', p. 88.

57. E. Herring, 'Response to Mervyn Frost: The systematic violation of ethical norms in British foreign policy', *Cambridge Review of International Affairs*, 1999, Vol. 12, p. 91.

58. Ibid., p. 92.

59. See for example: N. Cooper, who argues that British foreign policy has failed to make the arms agenda more ethical – 'The pariah agenda and New Labour's ethical arms sales policy' in R. Little and M. Wickham-Jones (eds.), *New Labour's Foreign Policy: A New Moral Crusade?* Manchester: Manchester University Press, 2000, p. 163; Davina Millier, who claims that 'ethical considerations, including human rights, have been sacrificed to effect engagement' with countries such as Iran – 'British foreign policy, human rights and Iran' in Little and Wickham-Jones (eds.), *New Labour's Foreign* Policy, p. 189; M. Curtis's suggestion that Britain 'clearly has a generally unethical foreign policy' – *Web of Deceit: Britain's Real Role in the World*, Vintage: London, 2003, p. 362. For more sympathetic critiques, see the articles of Wheeler and Dunne: N. J. Wheeler and T. Dunne, 'Good international citizenship: A third way for British foreign policy', *International Affairs*, 1998, Vol. 74, pp. 847–70; T. Dunne and N. J. Wheeler, 'The Blair doctrine: Advancing the Third Way in the world', in Little and Wickham-Jones (eds.), *New Labour's Foreign Policy*, pp. 61–76 ; and N. J. Wheeler and T. Dunne, 'Moral Britannia? Evaluating the Ethical Dimension in Labour's Foreign Policy', Foreign Policy Centre, 2004. Online. Available: http://fpc.org.uk/fsblob/233.pdf (accessed 2 June 2004). Also, a recent edited volume, D. Held and D. Mepham (eds.), *Progressive Foreign Policy: New Directions for the UK*, Cambridge: Polity Press, 2007, has turned the debate into one of examining the 'progressiveness' of foreign policy under Blair's Labour, a debate that is clearly linked to the issue of ethics (see pp. 1–17).

60. V. Jabri, 'Restyling the Subject of Responsibility in International Relations', *Millennium: Journal of International Relations*, 1998, Vol. 27, pp. 591–611.

61. Derrida, *Without Alibi*, p. xxxiii.

62. Deutscher, in Derrida, *Deconstruction Engaged*, p. 97.

63. Camus, *The Myth of Sisyphus*, p. 116.

Bibliography

Aglionby, J., 'UN warning on tsunami threat', *The Guardian*, 31 July 2006.

Allison, G. and Zelikow, P., *Essence of Decision: Explaining the Cuban Missile Crisis*, 2nd edn., New York: Longman, 1999.

Arikan, H., *Turkey and the EU: An Awkward Candidate for EU Membership?* Aldershot: Ashgate, 2003.

Ashley, R., 'Foreign policy as political performance', *International Studies Notes*, 1987, Vol. 13, pp. 51–4.

Ashley, R., 'The geopolitics of geopolitical space: Towards a critical social theory of international politics', *Alternatives*, 1987, Vol. 12, pp. 403–32.

Beasley, R. K., Kaarbo, J., Lantis, J. S., and Snarr, M. T. (eds.), *Foreign Policy in Comparative Perspective: Domestic and International Influences on State Behavior*, Washington, DC: CQ Press, 2002.

'BBC Country Profiles', 2007. Online. Available: *http://news.bbc.co.uk/1/hi/country_profiles/* (accessed 12 July 2007).

BBC News, 'EU "should expand beyond Europe"', 12 November 2007. Online. Available: *http://news.bbc.co.uk/1/hi/uk_politics/7095657.stm* (accessed 18 November 2007).

Beckett, S., *Waiting for Godot*, London: Faber and Faber, 1965.

——, *The Unnameable,* London: Calder and Boyars, 1975.

Bellamy, A. J., 'Humanitarian responsibilities and interventionist claims in international society', *Review of International Studies*, 2003, Vol. 29, pp. 321–40.

——, 'Responsibility to protect or Trojan horse? The crisis in Darfur and humanitarian intervention after Iraq', *Ethics and International Affairs*, 2005, Vol. 19, pp. 31–54.

Benhabib, S. and Isiksel, T., 'Ancient battles, new prejudices, and future perspectives: Turkey and the EU', *Constellations*, 2006, Vol. 13, pp. 218–33.

Bennett, R., 'Inside the mind of a terrorist', *The Observer*, 22 August 2004.

Bennington G., *Interrupting Derrida*, London: Routledge, 2000.

Bicchi, F., '"Our size fits all": normative power Europe and the Mediterranean', *Journal of European Public Policy*, 2006, Vol. 13, pp. 286–303.

Biedenkopf, K., Beremek, B., and Michalski, K., *The Spiritual and Cultural Dimensions of Europe: Concluding Remarks*, Reflection Group initiated by President of the European Commission and coordinated by the Institute for Human Sciences, Vienna/Brussels, 2004.

Black, C., 'Al-Qaida US has little future in the franchise', *The Guardian*, 17 January 2008.

Blair, T., 'A new era of international partnership', 21 September 1998. Unless otherwise stated, all speeches, interviews, articles and press conferences by Prime Minister T. Blair are online. Available: *http://www.10downingstreet.gov.uk* (accessed between 27 August 2004 and 1 May 2007).

——, 'Facing the Modern Challenge: The Third Way in Britain and South Africa', 8 January 1999.

——, ' "It is simply the right thing to do" Blair appeal: In a nationwide broadcast, the Prime Minister asks 'the whole country to unite behind any troops sent into action', *The Guardian*, 27 March 1999. Online. Available: *http://www.guardian. co.uk/Kosovo/Story/0,,209615,00.html* (accessed 6 October 2005).

——, 'Doctrine of the International Community Speech', Economic Club, Chicago, 24 April 1999.

——, Statement to Parliament on the NATO Summit in Washington, 26 April 1999.

——, Speech to the Muslim Council of Britain, 5 May 1999.

——, 'The New Challenges for Europe', 20 May 1999.

——, Speech to Global Ethics Foundation. Tubingen University, Germany, 30 June 2000.

——, Mansion House Speech, 13 November 2000.

——, Statement in response to terrorist attacks in the United States, 11 September 2001.

——, Statement to the House of Commons following the September 11 attacks, 14 September 2001.

——, Statement at 10 Downing Street, 25 September 2001.

——, Party Conference Speech 2001, *The Guardian*, 2 October 2001. Online. Available: *http://politics.guardian.co.uk/labour2001/story/0,1212,562006,00.html* (accessed 3 March 2005).

——, Statement to the House of Commons, 8 October 2001.

——, Speech to the Welsh Assembly, 30 October 2001.

——, Doorstep interview with the Prime Minister in Riyadh, Saudi Arabia, 1 November 2001.

——, Doorstep interview with the Prime Minister and Chancellor Wolfgang Schuessel of Austria, 16 November 2001.

——, Speech to Ghana's Parliament, 2 February 2002.

——, 'Partnership for African Development', 7 February 2002.

——, Interview with NBC, 4 April 2002.

——, Doorstep interview at G8 summit, 28 June 2002.

——, Speech to WSSD in South Africa, 2 September 2002.

——, Speech to the TUC Conference in Blackpool, 10 September 2002.

——, Iraq Statement to Parliament, 24 September 2002.

——, Statement to Parliament on NATO Summit, 25 November 2002.

——, Article in the *FT* on the visit of the Syrian President, 16 December 2002.

——, Press conference with PM and Spanish PM Jose Maria Aznar, 31 January 2003.

——, Press conference with PM and President Bush at the White House, 31 January 2003.

——, Statement to Parliament following his meeting with President Bush, 3 February 2003.

——, 'Let the United Nations mean what it says and do what it means: Speech to Labour Party Spring Conference', 15 February 2003. Online. Available: *http:// www.labour.org.uk/news/tbglasgow* (accessed 3 March 2006).

———, Answering questions at MTV forum, 6 March 2003.

———, Statement to House of Commons opening Iraq debate, 18 March 2003.

———, Press Conference on Iraq, 25 March 2003.

———, Press Conference with President George Bush at Camp David, 27 March 2003.

———, Doorstep press conference in Beijing, 21 July 2003.

———, Press Conference, 15 January 2004.

———, Q&A session given by PM Tony Blair and President Jacques Chirac with French and British students in Paris, 9 May 2004.

———, Interview with Channel 4 in Istanbul, 28 June 2004.

———, Speech on the threat of global terrorism, Sedgefield, 13 July 2004.

———, Speech on Africa, 7 October 2004.

———, BBC Radio Interview to mark World Aids Day, 1 December 2004.

———, PM's article for *The Economist* on G8, 1 January 2005.

———, PM Press Conference, 6 January 2005.

———, PM's Speech at the World Economic Forum in Davos, Switzerland, 26 January 2005.

———, Meeting with the Africa Commission in Rome, 27 May 2005.

———, Press conference with the Italian Prime Minister in Rome, 1 June 2005.

———, Tony Blair and George Bush joint press conference at the White House, 7 June 2005.

———, PM's interview with Downing Street website, 30 June 2005.

———, Speech to the General Assembly at the 2005 UN World Summit, 15 September 2005.

———, Monthly Downing Street press conference, 7 November 2005.

———, *Carte Blanche* Interview, South Africa, 11 February 2006.

———, 'Clash about Civilisations', 21 March 2006.

———, Third Foreign Policy Speech, Georgetown, USA, 26 May 2006.

Blair, T. and Sir Campbell, M., Prime Minister's Question Time, 25 January 2006. Online. Available: *http://www.theyworkforyou.com/debates/?id=2006-01-25a. 1421.7* (accessed 16 June 2006).

Bohmann, J. and Lutz-Bachmann, M. (eds.), *Perpetual Peace: Essays on Kant's Cosmopolitan Ideal*, London: MIT Press, 1997.

Brown, C., *Sovereignty, Rights and Justice: International Political Theory Today*, Cambridge: Polity Press, 2002.

———,'What, exactly, is the problem to which the five-part test is the solution?', *International Relations*, 2005, Vol. 19, pp. 225–9.

Bulley, D., 'Negotiating Ethics: Campbell, Ontopology and Hospitality', *Review of International Studies*, 2006, Vol. 32, pp. 645–63.

———, 'Ethical assassination? Negotiating the (ir)responsible decision', in M. Fagan et al. (eds.), *Derrida: Negotiating the Legacy*, Edinburgh: Edinburgh University Press, 2007, pp. 128–42.

———, '"Foreign" Terror? London Bombings, Resistance and the Failing State', *British Journal of Politics and International Relations*, 2008, Vol. 10, pp. 379–94.

Bush, G. W., Address to a Joint Session of Congress and the American People, United States Capitol, Washington, DC, 20 September 2001. Online. Available: *http://www.whitehouse.gov/news/releases/2001/09/20010920-8.html* (accessed 12 June 2008).

Campbell, D., *Writing Security: United States Foreign Policy and the Politics of Identity*, revised edn., Manchester: Manchester University Press, 1998.

Campbell, D., 'Violence, Justice, and Identity in the Bosnian Conflict', in J. Edkins, N. Persram and V. Pin-Fat (eds.), *Sovereignty and Subjectivity*, Boulder, Co: Lynne Rienner, 1999, pp. 21–37.

Campbell, D. and Shapiro, M. J. (eds.), *Moral Spaces: Rethinking Ethics and World Politics*, Minneapolis and London: University of Minnesota Press, 1999, pp. vii–xxii.

Campbell, D. and Laville S., 'British suicide bombers carried out London attacks, say police', *The Guardian*, 13 July 2005.

Camus, A., *The Myth of Sisyphus*, translated by Justin O'Brien, London: Penguin Books, 2005.

Caputo, J. D., *Against Ethics: Contributions to a Poetics of Obligation with Constant Reference to Deconstruction*, Bloomington: Indiana University Press, 1993.

Carlsnaes, W., *Ideology and Foreign Policy: Problems of Comparative Conceptualization*, Oxford: Basil Blackwell, 1986.

Casanova, J., 'The long, difficult, and tortuous journey of Turkey into Europe and the dilemmas of European civilization', *Constellations*, 2006, Vol. 13, pp. 234–47.

Chan, S., *Out of Evil: New International Politics and Old Doctrines of War*, London and New York: Tauris I.B., 2005.

Chandler, D., 'Rhetoric without responsibility: The attraction of "ethical" foreign policy', *British Journal of Politics and International Relations*, 2003, Vol. 5, pp. 295–316.

Chandler, D. and Heins, V., 'Ethics and foreign policy: New perspectives on an old problem', in D. Chandler and V. Heins (eds.), *Rethinking Ethical Foreign Policy: Pitfalls, Possibilities and Paradoxes*, London: Routledge, 2007, pp. 3–21.

—— (eds.), *Rethinking Ethical Foreign Policy: Pitfalls, Possibilities and Paradoxes*, London: Routledge, 2007.

Chaterjee, D. K. and Scheidt, D. E. (eds.), *Ethics and Foreign Intervention*, Cambridge: Cambridge University Press, 2003.

Colebatch, H. K., *Policy*, 2nd edn. Buckingham: Open University Press, 2002.

Connolly, W., *Identity\Difference: Democratic Negotiations of Political Paradox*, Ithaca: Cornell University Press, 1991.

Cook, R., 'Mission Statement', *The Guardian*, 12 May 1997. Online. Available: *http://www.guardian.co.uk/indonesia/Story/0,2763,190889,00.html* (accessed 11 July 2003).

——, 'Human Rights Into a New Century', 17 July 1997. Unless otherwise stated, all speeches, interviews and press conferences by Foreign Office Ministers are online. Available: *http://www.fco.gov.uk* (accessed between 11 October 2004 and 1 May 2007).

——, 'Europe and America: The Decisive Partnership', 15 January 1998.

——, 'Bosnia: A new hope', 4 March 1998.

——, 'Prosperity, Conflict Prevention and Democracy in Africa', 24 September 1998.

——, 'Human Rights: Making the Difference', 16 October 1998.

——, 'Beyond good intentions – government, business and the environment', Speech to the Business and Environment Dinner, 17 November 1998.

——, 'Kosovo and the Modern Europe', 14 April 1999.

——, 'Guiding Humanitarian Intervention', 19 July 2000.

——, 'Human Rights – A Priority of Britain's Foreign Policy', 28 March 2001.

Cooper, N., 'The pariah agenda and New Labour's ethical arms sales policy', in R. Little and M. Wickham-Jones (eds.), *New Labour's Foreign Policy: A New Moral Crusade?* Manchester: Manchester University Press, 2000, pp. 147–67.

Critchley, S., *The Ethics of Deconstruction: Derrida and Levinas*, Oxford: Basil Blackwell, 1992.

Culler, J., *On Deconstruction: Theory and Criticism after Structuralism*, London: Routledge, 1983.

Curtis, M., *Web of Deceit: Britain's Real Role in the World*, London: Vintage, 2003.

Deighton, A., 'The European Security and Defence Policy', *Journal of Common Market Studies*, 2002, Vol. 4, pp. 719–41.

Del Sarto, R. and Schumacher, T., 'From EMP to ENP: What's at Stake with the European Neighbourhood Policy towards the Southern Mediterranean', *European Foreign Affairs Review*, 2005, Vol. 10, pp. 17–38.

Der Derian, J., *Antidiplomacy: Spies, Terror, Speed and War*, Oxford: Blackwell, 1992.

Der Derian, J. and Shapiro, M. J. (eds.), *International/Intertextual Relations: Postmodern Readings of World Politics*, New York: Lexington Books, 1989.

Derrida, J., *Of Grammatology*, translated by G. Chakravorty Spivak, Baltimore: The Johns Hopkins University Press, 1976.

———, *Margins of Philosophy*, translated by A. Bass, Brighton: Harvester Press, 1982.

———, *Positions*, translated by A. Bass, Chicago: University of Chicago Press, 1982.

———, 'Deconstruction and the other: Interview with Richard Kearney', in R. Kearney, *Dialogues with Contemporary Continental Thinkers: The Phenomenological Heritage*, Manchester: Manchester University Press, 1984, pp. 105–26.

———, 'Letter to a Japanese Friend', in D. Wood and R. Bernasconi (eds.), *Derrida and Différance*, Evanston, Il: Northwestern University Press, 1988, pp. 1–5.

———, 'Signature Event Context', in J. Derrida, *Limited Inc*, translated by S. Weber, Evanston, Il: Northwestern University Press, 1988, pp. 1–23.

———, *Limited Inc*, translated by S. Weber, Evanston, Il: Northwestern University Press, 1988.

———, ' "Eating Well," or the Calculation of the Subject: An Interview with Jacques Derrida', in E. Cadava, P. Connor, and J-L Nancy (eds.), *Who Comes After the Subject?* New York: Routledge, 1991, pp. 96–119.

———, 'Force of Law: The "Mystical Foundation of Authority"', in D. Cornell, M. Rosenfeld and D. Gray Carlson (eds.), *Deconstruction and the Possibility of Justice*, London: Routledge, 1992, pp. 3–67.

———, 'Passions: "An Oblique Offering"', in D. Wood (ed.), *Derrida: A Critical Reader*, Oxford: Blackwell, 1992, pp. 5–35.

———, *The Other Heading: Reflections on Today's Europe*, translated by P.-A. Brault and M. B. Naas, Bloomington: Indiana University Press, 1992.

———, *Specters of Marx: The State of the Debt, the Work of Mourning & the New International*, translated by P. Kamuf, New York: Routledge, 1994.

———, *On The Name*, translated by D. Wood, J. P. Leavy, Jr. and I. McLeod, Stanford: Stanford University Press, 1995.

———, *Points … Interviews*, 1974–1994, translated by P. Kamuf, Stanford: Stanford University Press, 1995.

———, *The Gift of Death*, translated by Willis D., Chicago: University of Chicago Press, 1996.

———, *Politics of Friendship*, translated by Collins G., London: Verso, 1997.

———, 'Hospitality, Justice and Responsibility: A dialogue with Jacques Derrida', in R. Kearney and M. Dooley (eds.), *Questioning Ethics: Contemporary Debates in Philosophy*, London: Routledge, 1999, pp. 65–83.

———, *Adieu: To Emmanuel Levinas*, translated by P.-A. Brault and M. Naas, Stanford: Stanford University Press, 1999.

———, *On Cosmopolitanism and Forgiveness*, translated by M. Dooley and M. Hughes , London: Routledge, 2001.

———, *Without Alibi*, translated by P. Kamuf, Stanford: Stanford University Press, 2002.

———, *Writing and Difference*, translated by A. Bass, London: Routledge, 2002.

———, *Acts of Religion*, translated by G. Anidjar, New York: Routledge, 2002.

———, *Negotiations: Interventions and Interviews 1971–2001*, translated by E. Rottenberg, Stanford: Stanford University Press, 2002.

———, 'Autoimmunity: Real and Symbolic Suicides – A Dialogue with Jacques Derrida', in G. Borradori, *Philosophy in a Time of Terror: Dialogues with Jurgen Habermas and Jacques Derrida*, Chicago: University of Chicago Press, 2003, pp. 85–136.

———, *Rogues: Two Essays on Reason*, translated by P.-A. Brault and M. Naas, Stanford: Stanford University Press, 2005.

———, *Deconstruction Engaged: The Sydney Seminars*, Sydney: Power Publications, 2006.

Derrida, J. and Dufourmantelle, A. *Of Hospitality*, translated by R. Bowlby, Stanford: Stanford University Press, 2000.

Derrida, J. and Stiegler, B. *Echographies of Television: Filmed Interviews*, translated by Bajorek J., Oxford: Polity, 2002.

Dews, P. *Logics of Disintegration: Poststructuralism and the Claims of Critical Theory*, London: Verso, 1987.

Dillon, M., 'The Scandal of the Refugee: Some Reflections on the "Inter" of International Relations and Continental Thought', in D. Campbell and M. J. Shapiro (eds.), *Moral Spaces: Rethinking Ethics and World Politics*, Minneapolis and London: University of Minnesota Press, 1999, pp. 92–124.

Dodd, V., 'Seconds to decide if suspect is suicide threat', *The Guardian*, 23 July 2005.

———, 'Police rethink shoot to kill policy', *The Guardian*, 20 August 2005.

Dorronso G. , 'The EU and Turkey: Between geopolitics and social engineering', in R. Dannreuther (ed.), *European Union Foreign and Security Policy: Towards a Neighbourhood Strategy*, London: Routledge, 2004, pp. 48–61.

Doty, R. L., 'Foreign policy as social construction: A post-postivist analysis of US counterinsurgency policy in the Philippines" *International Studies Quarterly*, 1993, Vol. 37, No. 3, pp. 297–320.

Doty, R. L., *Imperial Encounters: The Politics of Representation in North-South Relations*, Minneapolis: University of Minnesota Press, 1996.

———, 'Fronteras Compasivas and the Ethics of Unconditional Hospitality', *Millennium: Journal of International Studies*, 2006, Vol. 35, pp. 53–74.

Dunne, T. and Wheeler, N. J., 'The Blair doctrine: Advancing the Third Way in the world', in R. Little and M. Wickham-Jones (eds.), *New Labour's Foreign Policy: A New Moral Crusade?* Manchester: Manchester University Press, 2000, pp. 61–76.

Duran, B., 'Islamist redefinition(s) of European and Islamic identities in Turkey', in M. Ugur and N. Canefe (eds.), *Turkey and European Integration: Accession Prospects and Issues*, London: Routledge, 2004, pp. 125–46.

Edkins, J., *Whose Hunger? Concepts of Famine, Practices of Aid*, Minneapolis: University of Minnesota Press, 2000.

Edkins, J. and Pin-Fat V., 'The Subject of the Political', in J. Edkins, N. Persram and V. Pin-Fat (eds.), *Sovereignty and Subjectivity*, Boulder, Co: Lynne Rienner, 1999, pp. 1–18.

Edkins, J. and Zehfuss M., 'Generalising the international', *Review of International Studies*, 2005, Vol. 31, pp. 451–72.

Farer, T. J., 'Humanitarian intervention before and after 9/11: Legality and legitimacy', in J. L. Holzgrefe and R.O. Keohane (eds), *Humanitarian Intervention: Ethical, Legal, and Political Dilemmas*, Cambridge: Cambridge University Press, 2001, pp. 53–89.

Fokas, E., 'The Islamist movement and Turkey-EU relations', in M. Ugur and N. Canefe (eds.), *Turkey and European Integration: Accession Prospects and Issues*, London: Routledge, 2004, pp. 147–69.

Frost, M., 'Putting the world to rights: Britain's ethical foreign policy', *Cambridge Review of International Affairs*, 1999, Vol. 12, pp. 80–9.

———, 'The ethics of humanitarian intervention: Protecting civilians to make democratic citizenship possible', in K.E. Smith and M. Light (eds.), *Ethics and Foreign Policy*, Cambridge: Cambridge University Press, 2001, pp. 33–54.

Gelb, L. H. and Rosenthal J. A., 'The rise of ethics in foreign policy: Reaching a values consensus', *Foreign Affairs*, 2003, Vol. 82, pp. 2–7.

Gillan, A. and Muir H., 'Lawyer condemns "wild west" police raid', *The Guardian*, 5 June 2006.

Ginsberg, R. H., 'Conceptualizing the EU as an international actor: Narrowing the theoretical capability-expectations gap', *Journal of Common Market Studies*, 1999, Vol. 37, pp. 429–54.

Gole, N., 'Europe's encounter with Islam: What future?' *Constellations*, 2006, Vol. 13, pp. 248–62.

Hain, P., 'Africa: Backing Success', 13 September 1999.

———, 'Angola Needs Our Help', 20 November 1999.

———, 'The End of Foreign Policy?' Speech at the Launch of *The End of Foreign Policy?* Pamphlet, Royal Institute of International Affairs, Chatham House, 22 January 2001.

———, *The End of Foreign Policy? Britain's Interests, Global Linkages and Natural Limits*, London: The Fabian Society/Green Alliance/The Royal Institute of International Affairs, 2001.

Hall, S., 'The Question of Cultural Identity', in S. Hall, D. Held and T. McGrew (eds.), *Modernity and Its Futures*, Oxford: Polity Press, 2003, pp. 273–325.

Hamilos, P., 'Mass murderers jailed for 40 years as judge delivers verdict on Spain's 9/11', *The Guardian*, 1 November 2007.

Held, D. and Mepham D. (eds.), *Progressive Foreign Policy: New Directions for the UK*, Cambridge: Polity Press, 2007.

Herring, E., 'Response to Mervyn Frost: The systematic violation of ethical norms in British foreign policy', *Cambridge Review of International Affairs*, 1999, Vol. 12, pp. 90–2.

Hill, C., 'The capability-expectations gap, or conceptualizing Europe's international role' *Journal of Common Market Studies*, 1993, Vol. 31, pp. 305–28.

———, *The Changing Politics of Foreign Policy*, Basingstoke: Palgrave MacMillan, 2003.

House of Commons, *Report of the Official Account of the Bombings in London on 7th July 2005*, London: The Stationary Office, 2006.

Howe, G., *Conflict of Loyalty*, London and Basingstoke: Pan Books, 1995.

———, (Lord Howe of Aberavon), interviewed by D. Bulley, The House of Lords, Westminster, London, 5 April 2005.

Howells, C., *Derrida: Deconstruction from Phenomenology to Ethics*, Oxford: Polity Press, 1998.

Howells, K., 'Why the UN Millenium Review Summit matters to the UK', Speech to the IPPR, London, 7 September 2005.

Hudson, V. M., 'Foreign policy analysis: Actor-specific theory and the ground of international relations', *Foreign Policy Analysis*, 2005, Vol. 1, pp. 1–30.

———, *Foreign Policy Analysis: Classic and Contemporary Theory*, Lanham, Md: Rowman & Littlefield, 2007.

Hutchings, K., *Kant, Critique and Politics*, London: Routledge, 1996.

Hyde-Price, A., ' "Normative" power Europe: a realist critique', *Journal of European Public Policy*, 2006, Vol. 13, pp. 217–34.

Jabri, V., 'Restyling the subject of responsibility in international relations', *Millennium: Journal of International Studies*, 1998, Vol. 27, pp. 591–611.

Kampfner, J., *Blair's Wars*, London: Free Press, 2003.

Kant, I., *Political Writings*, translated by H.B. Nisbet, 2nd edn., Cambridge: Cambridge University Press, 1991.

Kastoryano, R., 'Turkey/Europe: Space-Border-Identity', translated by J. Ingram, *Constellations*, 2006, Vol. 13, pp. 275–87.

Keal, P. (ed.), *Ethics and Foreign Policy*, Canberra, ACT: Allen and Unwin, 1992.

Kochi, T., *The Other's War: Recognition and the Violence of Ethics*, London: Birkbeck Law Press, 2009.

Kubalkova, V. (ed.), *Foreign Policy in a Constructed World*, New York: M.E. Sharpe, 2001.

Lattimore, R., translated by, *The Odyssey of Homer*, New York: Harper Collins, 1999.

Leader article 'Turkey: A Mandate for Modernisation', *The Guardian*, 24 July 2007.

Light, M., 'Foreign Policy Analysis', in A. J. R. Groom and M. Light (eds.), *Contemporary International Relations: A Guide to Theory*, London: Pinter Publishers, 1994, pp. 93–108.

Little, R. and Wickham-Jones M. (eds.), *New Labour's Foreign Policy: A New Moral Crusade?* Manchester: Manchester University Press, 2000.

Lucarelli, S. and Manners I. (eds.), *Values and Principles in EU Foreign Policy*, London: Routledge, 2006.

MacDonald, D. B., Patman R. G., and Mason-Parker, B. (eds.), *The Ethics of Foreign Policy*, Aldershot: Ashgate, 2007.

McElroy, R. W., *Morality and American Foreign Policy: The Role of Ethics in International Affairs*, Princeton, NJ: Princeton University Press, 1992.

MacShane, D., 'The Return of Foreign Policy', 13 February 2002.

———, 'Diplo-Military Politics: The Future Strategic Context of Conflict Prevention and Conflict Resolution', 25 April 2002.

Manners, I., 'Normative power Europe: A contradiction in terms?' *Journal of Common Market Studies*, 2002, Vol. 40, pp. 235–58.

———, 'Normative power Europe reconsidered: Beyond the crossroads', *Journal of European Public Policy*, 2006, Vol. 13, pp. 182–99.

———, 'European Union, normative power and ethical foreign policy', in D. Chandler and V. Heins (eds.), *Rethinking Ethical Foreign Policy: Pitfalls, Possibilities and Paradoxes*, London: Routledge, 2007, pp. 116–36.

Mango, A., 'The Modern History of a Solid Country', in M. Lake (ed.), *The EU & Turkey: A Glittering Prize or a Millstone?* London: Federal Trust, 2005, pp. 15–28.

Milliband, D., 'The Democratic Imperative', Aung San Suu Kyi Lecture, Oxford, 13 February.

Millier, D., 'British foreign policy, human rights and Iran', in R. Little and M. Wickham-Jones (eds.), *New Labour's Foreign Policy: A New Moral Crusade?* Manchester: Manchester University Press, 2000, pp. 186–200.

Missiroli, A., 'The European Union: Just a Regional Peacekeeper?' *European Foreign Affairs Review*, 2003, Vol. 8, pp. 493–503.

Morgenthau, H. J., *Politics Among Nations: The Struggle for Power and Peace*, 6th edn., New York: Alfred A. Knopf, 1954.

Neumann, I. B., *Uses of the Other: 'The East' in European Identity Formation*, Manchester: Manchester University Press, 1999.

Nietzsche, F., *Daybreak: Thoughts on the Prejudices of Morality*, translated by R. J. Hollingdale, Cambridge: Cambridge University Press, 1982.

———, *Human, all too Human*, translated by R. J. Hollingdale, Cambridge: Cambridge University Press, 1996.

———, *Beyond Good and Evil*, translated by W. Kauffman, in W. Kauffman (ed.), *Basic Writings of Nietzsche*, New York: Modern Library, 2000.

O'Brien, M., 'Morality in Asymmetric Warfare and Intervention Operations', 19 September 2002.

O'Driscoll, C., *The Renegotiation of the Just War Tradition and the Right to War in the Twenty-First Century*, Basingstoke: Palgrave MacMillan, 2008.

Odysseos, L., *The Subject of Coexistence: Otherness in International Relations*, Minneapolis and London: University of Minnesota Press, 2007.

Onuf N., 'Speaking Policy', in Kubalkova V. (ed.), *Foreign Policy in a Constructed World*, New York: Sharpe M.E., 2001, pp. 77–95.

C. Patten, 'Europe must solve its own conflicts', Interview with *Die Zeit*, 6 February 2000. Unless otherwise stated, all speeches, interviews, articles and press conferences by C. Patten, Commissioner for External Relations, are online. Available: *http://europa.eu.int/comm/archives/commission_1999_2004/patten/index.htm* (accessed 7 July 2005).

———, Speech to the Foreign Affairs and Legal Committees of the Albanian Parliament, Tirana, 6 March 2000.

———, Speech to the European Parliament on the Stabilisation and Association Process and the Stability Pact for South Eastern Europe, Strasbourg, 12 April 2000.

———, Speech to the Peace Implementation Council, Brussels, 23 May 2000.

———, 'South East Europe – Joining the European mainstream', Speech at the Balkans Conference, FCO, London, 7 July 2000.

———, 'What does Europe's CFSP mean for Asia', Speech to the Japanese Institute for International Affairs, Tokyo, 19 July 2000.

———, 'Towards a common European foreign policy: How are we doing?' Winston Churchill Memorial Lecture, Luxembourg, 10 October 2000.

———, 'A Common Foreign Policy for Europe: Relations with Latin America', Speech to the Consejo Argentino par alas Relaciones Internacionales (CARI), Buenos Aires, 9 November 2000.

———, Speech to the OSCE Permanent Council, Vienna, 23 November 2000.

———, Interview with BBC and ITN Television, Zagreb, 24 November 2000.

———, 'The Role of the European Union on the World Stage', Speech at the India Habitat Centre, Jawarharlal Nehru University, New Delhi, 25 January 2001.

———, Speech to the South East Europe Cooperation Process (SEECP) Summit, Skopje, 23 February 2001.

———, 'A voice for Europe? The future of the CFSP', Brian Lenihan Memorial Lecture, Dublin, 7 March 2001.

———, Interview on Sky News, 12 September 2001.

———, Interview with Arab News Network, 18 October 2001.

———, 'Coherence and co-operation: the EU as promoter of peace and development', Speech to the Swedish Institute of International Affairs, Stockholm, 4 December 2001.

———, 'Developing Europe's External Policy in the Age of Globalisation', Speech at Central party School, Beijing, 4 April 2002.

———, Speech to the Assembly of Kosovo, Pristina, 11 September 2003.

———, 'Europe in the World: CFSP and its relation to Development', Speech to the Overseas Development Institute, 7 November 2003.

———, 'The Western Balkans: The Road to Europe', Speech to German Bundestag, European Affairs Committee, Berlin, 28 April 2004.

———, 'Islam and the West – At the Crossroads', Speech at the Oxford Centre for Islamic Studies, 24 May 2004.

———, *Not Quite the Diplomat: Home Truths about World Affairs*, London: Allen Lane, 2005.

Payne, M. and Schad, J. (eds.), *life. after. theory*, London: Continuum, 2003.

Pearson, I., 'G8 2005: A Year For Africa', Tokyo, 6 June 2005.

Persall, J. (ed.), *The Concise Oxford Dictionary*, 10th edn., Oxford: Oxford University Press, 1999.

Price, S. and Kearns, E., *The Oxford Dictionary of Classical Myth and Religion*, Oxford: Oxford University Press, 2003.

Prodi, R., Speech to the EU-Japan Business Dialogue Roundtable, Brussels, 7 October 1999. All speeches, interviews and press conferences by R. Prodi, President of the EU Commission, are online. Available: *http://europa.eu.int/comm/archives/commission_1999_2004/prodi/speeches/index_en.htm* (accessed 16 August 2005).

———, Speech to the European Parliament on enlargement, Brussels, 13 October 1999.

———, 'The European Union and the challenge of the 21st Century', Speech to 21st Forum on Financial Policy and Taxation, Karlsruhe, 12 November 1999.

———, 'My Vision of Europe', Lecture to Norman Paterson School of International Affairs, Carleton University, Ottawa, 16 December 1999.

——, 'Europe and Global Governance', Speech to 2nd COMECE congress, Brussels, 31 March 2000.

——, 'Bringing the family together', Speech to the Academy of Sciences, Budapest, 4 April 2001.

——, 'Towards a European civil society', Speech commencing second European Social Week, Bad Honnef, 6 April 2000.

——, Inauguration of the European Monitoring Centre on Racism and Xenophobia, Vienna, 7 April 2000.

——, Speech to the European Academy of Sciences and Arts, Bilbao, 28 April 2000.

——, 'Nation, Federalism and Democracy – The EU, Italy and the American Federal experience', Speech at 'The Nation, Federalism and Democracy' Conference, Trento, 5 October 2001.

——, Speech to the European Parliament on Enlargement, Strasbourg, 13 November 2001.

——, 'The EU, the UK and the world', Speech to Said Business School, Oxford, 29 April 2002.

——, 'The EU, dialogue with religions and peace dialogue: "Build Europe, build peace"', Speech at the conference on Christianity and Democracy in the Future of Europe, Camaldoli, 14 July 2002.

——, 'Enlargement – the final lap', Speech to European Parliament, Brussels, 9 October 2002.

——, 'The reality of enlargement', Speech to the European Parliament, Brussels, 6 November 2002.

——, Speech during a visit by members of parliament from candidate countries, Strasbourg, 19 November 2002.

——, 'Europe and the Mediterranean: Time for action', Speech at Universite Catholique de Louvain-la-Neuve, 26 November 2002.

——, 'Europe in transition: hopes and fears', Speech at Fifth Europa Forum: 'Europe facing the decision – EU Enlargement and Global Challenges', Brussels, 3 December 2002.

——, 'A Wider Europe – A Proximity Policy as the Key to Stability', Speech at Sixth ECSA-World Conference, Brussels, 5–6 December 2002.

——, 'Europe and Ethics', Speech to the Conference on Politics and Morality, Vienna, 7 December 2002.

——, Report to the European Parliament on the Spring European Council, Brussels, 26 March 2003.

——, Speech at the signing of the Treaty of Accession Ceremony, Athens, 16 April 2003.

——, 'The European project in the world: between values and politics', Speech to Fondazione Don Tonino Bello Alessano, Lecce, 13 June 2003.

——, Speech to EU-Balkan Summit, Thessaloniki, 21 June 2003.

——, 'Looking ahead in transatlantic relations', Dinner speech at Rayburn House with German Marshall Fund of the United States, Washington, DC, 24 June 2003.

——, 'Croatia's journey towards EU membership', Speech to Croatian Parliament, Zagreb, 10 July 2003.

——, 'Sharing stability and prosperity', Speech at Tempus MEDA Regional Conference, Bibliotheca Alexandria, 13 October 2003.

———, Speech to the Turkish Grand National Assembly, Ankara, 15 January 2004.

———, Speech on visit to Bogazici University, Istanbul, 16 January 2004.

———, Speech to European Parliament, Strasbourg, 10 February 2004.

———, 'The European Union's role after enlargement', High-Level Conference on the Future of Transatlantic Relations – ELDR Group, Brussels, 3 March 2004.

———, Meeting with students of Baku State University, Azerbaijan, 17 September 2004.

———, To students and representatives of civil society in Georgia, Tbilisi University, 18 September 2004.

———, To students and representatives of civil society in Armenia, European Regional Institute of Information and Communication Technologies, Yerevan, 19 September 2004.

———, 'On the path to the EU: Challenges and opportunities', FYROM Government Assembly, Skopje, 1 October 2004.

———, The Commission's Report and Recommendation on Turkey's application, Presentation to the European Parliament, Brussels, 6 October 2004.

Rammell, B., 'Why Human Rights Matter', 25 November 2003.

———, 'Towards the Summit: The Path to Larger Freedom', UKMis, New York, 22 March 2005.

Rawnsley, A., *Servants of the People: The Inside Story of New Labour*, revised edn., London: Penguin, 2001.

Redmond, J., 'Turkey and the European Union: troubled European or European trouble?' *International Affairs*, 2007, Vol. 83, pp. 305–17.

Riddell, P., *Hug Them Close: Blair, Clinton, Bush and the 'Special Relationship'*, revised edn., London: Politico's, 2004.

Rosenau, J. N., 'Introduction: New Directions and Recurrent Questions in the Comparative Study of Foreign Policy', in C. F. Hermann, C. W. Kegley, Jr. and J. N. Rosenau, (eds.), *New Directions in the Study of Foreign Policy*, Boston: Allen and Unwin, 1987, pp. 1–10.

———, 'Moral Fervour, Systematic Analysis, and Scientific Consciousness in Foreign Policy Research', in J. N. Rosenau, *The Scientific Study of Foreign Policy*, New York: The Free Press, 1971, pp. 23–65.

———, 'Pre-Theories and Theories of Foreign Policy', in J. N. Rosenau, *The Scientific Study of Foreign Policy*, The Free Press: New York, 1971, pp. 95–149.

Rubin, B., 'Introduction', in A. Carkoglu and B. Rubin (eds.), *Turkey and the European Union: Domestic Politics, Economic Integration and International Dynamics*, London: Frank Cass, 2003, pp. 1–3.

Rummell, R., 'From Weakness to Power with the ESDP?' *European Foreign Affairs Review*, 2002, Vol. 7, pp. 453–71.

Seldon, A., *Blair*, London: Free Press, 1990.

Shapiro, M. J., 'Textualizing Global Politics', in J. Der Derian and M. J. Shapiro (eds.), *International/Intertextual Relations: Postmodern Readings of World Politics*, New York: Lexington Books, 1989. pp. 11–22.

———, 'The Ethics of Encounter: Unreading, Unmapping the Imperium', in D. Campbell and M. J. Shapiro (eds.), *Moral Spaces: Rethinking Ethics and World Politics*, Minneapolis and London: University of Minnesota Press, 1999, pp. 57–91.

———, 'The Events of Discourse and the Ethics of Global Hospitality', *Millennium: Journal of International Studies*, 1998, Vol. 27, pp. 695–713.

Sharp, P., 'Mullah Zaeef and Taliban diplomacy: an English School approach', *Review of International Studies*, 2003, Vol. 29, pp. 481–98.

Simms, B., *Unfinest Hour: Britain and the Destruction of Bosnia*, London: Penguin, 2002.

Singer, P. (ed.), *Ethics*, Oxford: Oxford University Press, 1994.

Singer, P., *The President of Good and Evil: Taking George W. Bush Seriously*, London: Granta, 2004.

Sjursen, H., 'The EU as a 'normative' power: How can this be?' *Journal of European Public Policy*, 2006, Vol. 13, pp. 235–51.

Smith, H., *European Union Foreign Policy: What it is and What it Does*, London: Pluto Press, 2002.

Smith, K. E. and M. Light (eds.), *Ethics and Foreign Policy*, Cambridge: Cambridge University Press, 2001.

Smith, K. E., *European Union Foreign Policy in a Changing World*, Cambridge: Polity Press, 2003.

Smith, M., Smith, S., and B. White (eds.), *British Foreign Policy: Tradition, Change and Transformation*, London: Unwin Hyman, 1988.

Smith, S., 'Foreign policy analysis: British and American orientations and methodologies', *Political Studies*, 1983, Vol. 31, pp. 556–65.

Snyder, R. C., Bruck, H. W., and Sapin, B., *Foreign Policy Decision Making*, New York: Free Press of Glencoe, 1962.

Solana, J., Speech to European Parliament, Strasbourg, 17 November 1999. Unless otherwise stated, all speeches, interviews, articles and press conferences by J. Solana, High Representative for the Common Foreign and Security Policy, are online. Available: *http://ue.eu.int/cms3_applications/applications/solana/index.asp?lang=EN&cmsid=256* (accessed between 11 July 2005 and 8 August 2005).

———, 'The Development of a Common European Security and Defence Policy – the Integration Project of the Next Decade', Speech to EU-Commission Institut fur Europäische Politik Conference, Berlin, 17 December 1999.

———, Speech to the Fernandez Ordonez Seminar, 14 January 2000.

———, Speech – Foreign Policy Association, New York, 25 January 2000.

———, Speech – Wehrkunde, Berlin, 5 February 2000.

———, 'Some Reflections About European Foreign Policy', Address to the Adam Mickiewicz University, Poznan, 12 February 2000.

———, Speech to the European Parliament, 1 March 2000.

———, 'The European Union is assisting recovery – but much work remains to be done', Article in *The Wall Street Journal* Europe, 24 March 2000.

———, 'Towards a stronger alliance', Article in *European Affairs*, 12 April 2000.

———, 'The Development of a Common Foreign and Security Policy', Keynote Speech to Diplomatia, Rome, 26 June 2000.

———, Speech at the inaugural conference of the course, 'Towards a new international morality: The humanitarian interventions', University of Alcala de Henares, Madrid, 7 July 2000.

———, 'Reflections on a year in office', Speech to the Swedish Institute of International Affairs and Central Defence and Society Federation, 27 October 2000.

———, 'The Foreign Policy of the EU', Speech at the Liberal International, The Hague, 7 November 2000.

———, 'EU Foreign Policy', Speech at the Hendrik Brugmans Memorial, Bruges, 25 April 2001.

———, Speech at 'The Fire and the Crystal' Conference, Rimni, 21 October 2001.

———, Interview with *Tasspiegel*, 26 March 2003.

———, 'We are not the Africa Corps', Interview by J. Fritz-Vannahme and P. Pinzler, in *Die Zeit*, 12 June 2003.

———, Interview with BBC Breakfast with Frost, 13 July 2003.

———, Interview with *Dnevi Avaz* (BiH newspaper), 24 September 2003.

———, Speech on the occasion of the Award of the 'Honoris Causa' Doctorate in Social Science, University of Wroclaw, 2 October 2003.

———, 'The voice of Europe on security matters', Address to the Royal Institute for International Relations (IRR-KIIB), Brussels, 16 November 2003.

———, Address to the National Forum on Europe, Dublin Castle, 8 January 2004.

———, Written interview with Solbodanka Jonavoska, *Ultrinski Vesnik* (FYROM Newspaper), 23 February 2004.

Solana, J. and Frattini, F., 'Choosing Reform', Article in *Politika* (Serbian newspaper), 15 December 2003.

Solana, J., 'The Limits of Integration – Where Does the European Union End?' Address to the Europa Forum, Vienna, 19 November 2004.

Stone, N., 'Endnote: Turkey and Europe', in M. Lake (ed.), *The EU & Turkey: A Glittering Prize or a Millstone?* London: Federal Trust, 2005, pp. 171–80.

Straw, J., 'The Task of Defeating International Terrorism', 11 November 2001.

———, 'Re-ordering the World', 25 March 2002.

———, 'Principles of a Modern Global Community', 10 April 2002.

———, 'Human Rights Ensure International Security and Prosperity', 18 April 2002.

———, 'Failed and Failing States', 6 September 2002.

———, 'The Role of Free Press in Foreign Policy', 16 November 2002.

———, 'Iraq: A Challenge We Must Confront', 11 February 2003.

———, 'Reintegrating Iraq into the International Community – A cause with compelling moral force', 21 February 2003.

———, 'Commitment to the Liberation and Future Prosperity of Iraq', 1 April 2003.

———, 'Shaping a stronger United Nations', 2 September 2004.

———, Iraq Statement, 12 October 2004.

———, 'A Partnership for Wider Freedom', Centre for Strategic and International Studies, Washington, DC, 18 May 2005.

———, Media Interviews, Gleneagles, 7 July 2005.

———, Interview BBC Radio 4 on the Draft Iraqi Constitution, 30 August 2005.

———, 'Our Changed and Changing World', Speech at the 2005 World Summit, New York, 17 September 2005.

———, 'Active Diplomacy for A Changing World', Launch FCO White Paper on International Strategic Priorities, FCO Leadership Conference 2006, 28 March 2006.

Taylor, P., 'The terrorist who wasn't', *The Guardian*, 8 March 2006.

Tesón, F., 'Ending Tyranny in Iraq', *Ethics & International Affairs*, 2005, Vol. 19, pp. 1–20.

The Bible, New International Version.

The Responsibility to Protect: Report of the International Commission on Intervention and State Sovereignty, Ottawa: International Development Research Centre, 2001.

Thomas, W., *The Ethics of Destruction: Norms and Force in International Relations*, Ithaca and London: Cornell University Press, 2001.

Thomson, A., *Deconstruction and Democracy: Derrida's Politics of Friendship*, London: Continuum, 2005.

Tremlett, G., 'Madrid school used by British on bombers' list'. *The Guardian*, 2 July 2004.

Turan, I., 'Unstable stability: Turkish politics at the crossroads?' *International Affairs*, 2007, Vol. 83, pp. 319–38.

Triesman, D. M. (Baron Triesman of Tottenham), 'Africa's Instability is our Instability', Tanzanian Parliament, 15 June 2005.

Vaughan-Williams, N., 'Protesting against citizenship', *Citizenship Studies*, 2005, Vol. 9, pp. 167–79.

——, 'Beyond a cosmopolitan ideal: The politics of singularity', *International Politics*, 2007, Vol. 44, pp. 107–24.

——, 'The Shooting of Jean Charles de Menezes: New border politics?' *Alternatives*, 2007, Vol. 32, pp. 177–95.

Walker, R. B. J., *Inside/Outside: International Relations as Political Theory*, Cambridge: Cambridge University Press, 1993.

Weiss, T. G., 'The sunset of humanitarian intervention? The responsibility to protect in a unipolar era', *Security Dialogue*, 2004, Vol. 35, pp. 135–53.

Wheeler, N. J. and Dunne, T., 'Good international citizenship: A third way for British foreign policy', *International Affairs*, 1998, Vol. 74, pp. 847–70.

——, 'Moral Britannia? Evaluating the Ethical Dimension in Labour's Foreign Policy', Foreign Policy Centre (2004). Online. Available: *http://fpc.org.uk/fsblob/233.pdf* (accessed 2 June 2004).

Wheeler, N. J., *Saving Strangers: Humanitarian Intervention in International Society*, Oxford: Oxford University Press, 2002.

White, B., 'Analysing Foreign Policy: Problems and Approaches', in M. Clarke and B. White, (eds.), *Understanding Foreign Policy: The Foreign Policy Systems Approach*, Aldershot: Edward Elgar, 1989, pp. 1–26.

Wickham-Jones, M., 'Labour's trajectory in foreign affairs: the moral crusade of a pivotal power?' in R. Little. and M. Wickham-Jones (eds.), *New Labour's Foreign Policy: A New Moral Crusade?* Manchester: Manchester University Press, 2000, pp. 3–32.

Williams, C., *Contemporary French Philosophy: Modernity and the Persistence of the Subject*, London: Athlone Press, 2001.

Williams, I., 'Writing the wrongs of past interventions: A review of the International Commission on Intervention and State Sovereignty', *International Journal of Human Rights*, 2002, Vol. 6, pp. 103–13.

Williams, P. D., 'The rise and fall of the 'ethical dimension': Presentation and practice in New Labour's foreign policy', *Cambridge Review of International Affairs*, 2002, Vol. 15, No. 1, pp. 53–63.

——, *British Foreign Policy under New Labour, 1997–2005*, Basingstoke: Palgrave MacMillan, 2005.

Williams, P. D. and Bellamy, A. J., 'The responsibility to protect and the crisis in Darfur', *Security Dialogue*, 2005, Vol. 36, pp. 27–47.

M. Zehfuss, 'Forget September 11', *Third World Quarterly: Journal of Emerging Areas*, 2003, Vol. 24, pp. 513–28.

——, 'Subjectivity and Vulnerability: On the War with Iraq', *International Politics*, 2007, Vol. 44, pp. 58–71.

Index

For Product Safety Concerns and Information please contact our EU
representative GPSR@taylorandfrancis.com
Taylor & Francis Verlag GmbH, Kaufingerstraße 24, 80331 München, Germany

www.ingramcontent.com/pod-product-compliance
Lightning Source LLC
Chambersburg PA
CBHW050513280326
41932CB00014B/2306